P9-BYJ-533

in her own sweet time

UNEXPECTED ADVENTURES
IN FINDING LOVE, COMMITMENT,
AND MOTHERHOOD

# in her own
# sweet time

## RACHEL LEHMANN-HAUPT

BASIC
BOOKS

A Member of the Perseus Books Group
New York

Published by Basic Books,
A Member of the Perseus Books Group

Designed by Trish Wilkinson
Set in 11 point Goudy

Library of Congress Cataloging-in-Publication Data
Lehmann-Haupt, Rachel.
    In her own sweet time : unexpected adventures in finding love, commitment, and motherhood / Rachel Lehmann-Haupt.
    p.   cm.
    Includes bibliographical references and index.
    ISBN 978-0-465-00919-0 (alk. paper)
    1. Lehmann-Haupt, Rachel. 2. Mothers—United States—Biography.
3. Motherhood—United States. I. Title.
HQ759.L44 2008
306.874'3092—dc22
[B]                                                                      2008055533

10  9  8  7  6  5  4  3  2

*To Clay Felker,*
*who taught me to follow my heart*

*To everything there is a season,*
*a time for every purpose under the sun.*
*A time to be born and a time to die;*
*a time to plant and a time to pluck up that which is planted;*
*a time to kill and a time to heal …*
*a time to weep and a time to laugh;*
*a time to mourn and a time to dance …*
*a time to embrace and a time to refrain from embracing;*
*a time to lose and a time to seek;*
*a time to rend and a time to sew;*
*a time to keep silent and a time to speak;*
*a time to love and a time to hate;*
*a time for war and a time for peace.*

ECCLESIASTES 3:1-8

# Contents

# Author's Note

Facts are very important to me, and I've made sure that all the science and medical information in this book is absolutely correct; however, reproductive science is a fast-moving field and study data change quickly. Dr. Daniel Stein, of St. Luke's–Roosevelt Hospital, was kind enough to read through the manuscript to make sure that it's medically and scientifically correct. I'm eternally grateful for his time.

This book is also a memoir, and while the majority of the scenes are written from extensive notes and tape-recorded interview transcripts, there are also many scenes that I've reconstructed from memory, which means that the quotes may sometimes be more representative of the content and meaning of what I remember being said. Throughout the book, an asterisk indicates that the name, identifying details, and some events related to the individual have been changed in order to protect that individual's privacy. None of the names, as changed, are or are intended to be descriptive of any living individual.

# Introduction:
# Starting Later

We are sitting on the giant root of an oak tree at The Cloisters, a medieval park filled with lush formal gardens on the northern tip of Manhattan. It's late summer. The light bounces off the Hudson River and flickers in the leaves. He looks nervous. I'm shaky too. We've been together almost a year, and I'm wondering whether he might be getting ready to give me a ring.

Instead, he looks away from me. Silence. Then he turns back, and in an awkward tone he says that he doesn't feel the kind of "intangible connection" he needs to get married and start a family with me. Instead of starting our life together, he is ending it.

My stomach lurches. I ask him if we can go sit somewhere else, as though moving might make this feeling go away, push back what was about to happen.

No. He wants to break up. And with those words, everything that I have imagined about our future abruptly blurs: walking on my father's arm down the aisle dressed in a white hourglass dress; living in the downtown loft with the skylight office where I would write; being in my parents' suburban backyard, where our baby would splash in a plastic pool at a Sunday barbecue.

"I'm sorry I wasted your time," he says.

And with that, it's over.

~

Alex* and I met at a rooftop party in Greenwich Village in the summer of 2000. I was thirty-one, and more intensely focused on my career than on my romantic life. I was dating a lot, but I was more interested in meeting up with groups of friends for drinks after work and lingering over dinners at the latest hot spots than I was in nesting at home with one man or starting a family. Getting serious in a relationship that would lead to marriage was in the back of my mind, but I was in no rush.

Alex came to the party on a date with another woman. I was charmed by his shyness; his big, wistful blue eyes; the way he quietly lingered on the sidelines of the gathering. At the bar, a mutual friend introduced us, and after a few minutes of small talk he complimented my social ease and made a self-deprecating comment about his lack of it.

I responded to this subtle flirtation by offering to do the talking for him; then we exchanged cards.

A few weeks later, I decided to take the chance and e-mail him. As an excuse to get together and find out if he was still

---

*Throughout this and all chapters in the book, an asterisk indicates that names, identifying details, and some events have been changed.

with his date from the party, I told him I wanted to write a story about his company. He responded a few days later by inviting me to a party at his apartment, but by then I had gone out of town on assignment. When I got back, I returned his e-mail asking him to get together for drinks. He thought my late response was charming.

We met at a bar with a red glow on Bedford Street. Young business guys swooned at the bar in knock-off Ferragamo ties. Alex pointed to this detail and sardonically mocked the faux romance. I immediately liked his astute observations. A few glasses of wine turned the mood of reserved professionalism into giddy laughter. And then standing on the street corner he kissed me—a kiss so charged that when we parted I walked four blocks before I realized I was heading in the opposite direction of my apartment.

The relationship got serious quickly.

At the time, some of my friends were starting to settle down; a few were even having their first child. These were the friends who started giving me those raised eyebrow looks that said, "When are you going to start?" My grandmother, especially, wanted to know when she was going to be able to give me her diamond ring, the one given to her by my grandfather when she was only twenty-three, the one intended to be my engagement ring.

So I told myself that it was time—time to give myself over to the ineluctable pull of domesticity, time to join my peers in the next phase of life, time to settle on someone and build a life together. But even more than that, it was time to do something about that subtle, timeless urge buried somewhere in the tissue connecting my heart, brain, and my gut. With a start, I

now understood: I wanted to become a mother. I, too, wanted
to rub my cheek along the top of a baby's fuzzy, sweet-smelling
head, to hold a helpless child close, to whisper "I love you."

I told Alex I loved him after only a month. He said he loved
me too. I started getting excited about the future. Almost immediately, I began to romanticize our wedding, our baby, our
life as a family. Everything about him seemed right, like I was
making a responsible—and yes, I'll admit it—socially acceptable choice. He was well educated, ambitious, and tall. His self-
deprecating sense of humor was wonderful: Once he had sent
out a bachelor holiday e-card greeting with a picture of a wanting, dreadlocked Caribbean siren on her knees, covered in
sand, on the beach. But where her face should have been, he
had Photoshopped a picture of his own.

My friends and parents liked him. And I'll go even further:
I liked the attention that I got because I was "in love." One
day at a cocktail party, a family friend put her hand on my
shoulder and said, "If he makes you laugh, then you should
marry him." He did make me laugh, so he became the one
with whom I decided I would begin the next phase. It was the
route my parents had taken, and the one I thought I had to
take as well to become a real adult.

The only problem was that Alex and I weren't really in
love. I didn't realize it at the time, but I was much more in
love with the shiny fantasy of our future than the man himself,
the way he made me feel every day. The more I got to know
him, the more I realized that the differences in the way we in-
teracted with the world were not complimentary. His once-
charming social anxiety began to block us from a certain level
of intimacy that I needed in order to feel really loved and to
be able to commit to our relationship.

In retrospect, I wasn't ready to commit to building a life with anyone because I had not yet discovered the type of intimate connection I needed for such an important and sustaining relationship. I still had more growing to do on my own to understand what this connection might feel like. While I knew that this relationship was not the right one for me, I didn't end it because I was afraid. I thought that if I let go and had to start all over again, I might fall behind. I worried I might never catch up.

Still, that day at The Cloisters, tears streamed down my face because it was he who had made the first move to break up; he who had shattered my fantasy of who people were telling me I should be, and therefore who I believed I should be: a married woman on the path to becoming a mother.

~

After the breakup, I felt like I was caught in a whirlpool at the edge of a rushing social current. I was confused, spinning in circles, and surrounded by new questions: What kind of relationship was right if this one was wrong? If I just invested one year in a nowhere relationship, then how much time would I need to invest in a relationship that actually went somewhere? I had a hunch all my life that I wanted to be a mother, but it wasn't until the breakup with Alex that I felt biology tapping her toes. Her patience was not inexhaustible.

The same year Alex and I broke up, a book burst onto the scene that caused young women all over the country to panic. Sylvia Ann Hewlett, an economist and founder of the liberal Center for Work-Life Policy, published *Creating a Life: What Every Woman Needs to Know About Having a Baby and*

*Career*. In her polemic about the problems women face in balancing career and family, Hewlett, a baby boomer, told scary stories about the pioneering feminist women of her generation who had struggled with conception and infertility because they waited until later in their lives to have children. She wanted to warn the next generation against making the same mistakes. "All of this new status and power has not translated into better choices on the family front," she wrote. "Indeed, when it comes to having children their options seem to be a good deal worse than before. Women can be playwrights, presidential candidates and CEOs, but increasingly they cannot be mothers."

Hewlett argued that women simply had to start earlier. Women should be hunting for husbands in their twenties and having children earlier—long before the age of thirty-five, the dividing line between a regular pregnancy and a "high-risk" pregnancy. Otherwise, they are likely to end up without a family of their own.

*Creating a Life* provoked a media circus. Stories soon appeared in magazines and newspapers about "the new baby panic" that was infecting single women in their mid- to late thirties. Hewlett recited her findings wherever she could—on *60 Minutes*, *The Today Show*, and in a big spread in *Time* magazine—constantly reinforcing the message that women were waiting too long to have babies.

Although it was not Hewlett's intention in writing the book, the publicity that ensued was the beginning of a backlash against the achievements of feminism. Women, of course, were creating this problem all on their own. The *Time* story, for instance, cited an iVillage survey of more than 12,500 women, who answered fifteen questions about fertility. Only 13 percent knew their fertility began to drop at age twenty-seven; 39 percent thought their reproductive capacity was unchanged until forty. The message was clear: women had gotten themselves into this situation through their own ignorance. No mention was made, of course, of the wide array of socio-economic factors that contributed to this trend—including the cost of childcare, or even the decline in the standard of living in America that had made it impossible for a single income to support the majority of households. No, the sisters were doing it to themselves.

The media juggernaut was unstoppable. Those hot independent career women immortalized in *Sex and the City*? They had better trade in their Manolos and get real if they ever wanted to become mothers. A lot of women bought into the panic and blamed themselves for their own irresponsibility. In a May 2002 article in *New York* magazine, journalist Vanessa Grigoriadis wrote: "These days the independence that seems so fabulous—at least to those of us who tend to use that word a lot—doesn't anymore."

"Baby panic" became the new media catch phrase of 2001—not unlike the phrase "marriage crunch," which had taken America by storm in a similar moment of cultural backlash. In 1987, *Newsweek* ran an article claiming that a woman who reached forty without a wedding ring was more likely to be killed by terrorists than she was to get married. We now know that this statistic could not be further from the truth: In September 2007, *Newsweek* retracted the original story, revealing that in fact a forty-year-old woman today has a better than 40 percent chance of marrying. One can't help but wonder how many women suffered from anxiety as a result of that article in the intervening twenty years—or even made bad choices to stave off their putatively inevitable spinsterhood.

In 2001, Hewlett's book hit me like a punch in my unpregnant gut. Her argument hit exactly on the facts of my own situation and intensified my anxiety about my romantic and biological clocks. I was even questioning where I might have gone wrong in my choices. Suddenly I felt bad about all my career ambition and the emotional and financial independence that I had achieved. It was as if I should start listening to another, older cultural message—a learned desperation because I was not in the proper, socially sanctioned place a woman of my age should be.

Sylvia Ann Hewlett did, after all, have some real facts on her side: it is true that as a woman ages, her egg quality declines and pregnancy becomes both riskier and harder to achieve. Older eggs do have a higher chance of contributing to genetic abnormalities and early miscarriages. The American Society for Reproductive Medicine reports that while a thirty-year-old woman has a 1 in 385 chance of having a baby with a chromosomal abnormality, that chance rises to 1 in 192 by the time she is thirty-five. By the time she reaches forty, she has a 1 in 66 chance. It is also true that women have a harder time getting pregnant as they get older. A 2004 study published in the journal *Human Reproduction* finds that 75 percent of women who start trying to conceive naturally at age thirty will succeed in a year. At age thirty-five, about 66 percent will conceive in a year—44 percent at age forty.

But Hewlett also missed some really important facts. Medically speaking, the dangers of a having a child after age thirty-five have become significantly reduced by developments such as noninvasive genetic screening and diagnostic pregnancy tests. And while Hewlett's statistics of the likelihood of getting pregnant at various life stages are correct, they are only statistics. In fact, every woman has her own distinct biology, and the variations among women are massive. In her 2005 book *Every-*

*thing Conceivable: How Assisted Reproduction Is Changing Men, Women, and the World,* journalist Liza Mundy of the *Washington Post* eloquently describes the reality of this blurring line: "After thirty-five, women enter a period of extreme variability. A woman may remain fertile for ten years or she may undergo a precipitous drop in her ability to conceive; her childbearing may be over. As a rough gauge, doctors assume that infertility usually sets in ten years before menopause, which begins, on average, at age fifty-one."

Hewlett left out another important point as well: an increasing amount of evidence shows that aging affects men's biological clocks as well. Today men make up more than half of the cases of infertility. Sperm does not decline in quality as drastically as eggs, but scientific evidence does point to the fact that sperm ages. In a 2006 study of the Israeli military database, researchers studied men to determine whether there was a correlation between paternal age and the incidence of autism and related disorders. They found that children of men who became fathers at forty or older were 5.75 times as likely to have autism disorder than those whose fathers were younger than thirty. So it is quite likely that as the age of marriage and childbearing rises both for men and women across America, poor sperm quality rather than poor egg quality will often be the culprit causing problems for many couples. But where are all the cover stories on that?

Hewlett's book, and the media onslaught that followed it, seem to have reflected a nostalgia for an earlier, simpler age when men were men and women stayed home to take care of their children. And once upon a time, that division of labor made sense. In the agricultural age, women conceived younger and had many more children because children were economic assets as workers on the farm. In the postindustrial age, children are emotional assets but economic liabilities, costing both a middle-class husband and wife or a single parent over $10,000 a year. More often than not, a male head of household cannot support that family on his own. Women need to build their careers in order to become their own economic assets and to support their families. (Many women, of course, have also found that they really like working.) Women have therefore put earning power before procreative power. We are getting married and having children after we get our master's degrees and the corner office.

The age of first-time motherhood and fatherhood is rising all over the developing world, especially in urban centers among the middle and upper middle class. In the United States alone, the number of women becoming pregnant between the ages of thirty-five and forty-four has nearly doubled since 1980. In 2003, the number of women over forty who gave birth in a single year topped 100,000 for the first time.

The nature of human life has changed dramatically in the last hundred years throughout the industrialized world. It's not just that women are waiting longer to have children. People are also living much longer—nearly twice as long. The various stages of our lives—childhood, adolescence, young adulthood, and beyond—are all extending, and sometimes we're shifting the sequence as well. Technology and feminism have made it possible for women to make choices they couldn't have made even a generation ago. Many women are intentionally getting pregnant before they get engaged or walk down the aisle. Some women are even having children as "single mothers by choice" before finding husbands, or freezing their eggs to donate to themselves further down the road. In the midst of the flurry of stories about baby panic, I read an article about a fifty-eight-

year-old British woman who had given birth to twins conceived from donated embryos!

The effect of Hewlett's book, and the baby panic furor that
followed, was to make women feel more constrained by biology
at a time when they should be feeling less constrained than
ever. Women have a range of choices unprecedented in human
history.

Intellectually, I knew this. But emotionally, I was just as
panicked as everyone else.

I am now thirty-nine years old, and I'm still hoping to start
a family of my own. I didn't arrive here by accident. I'm here
because of choices I made along the way—both good and bad.

When I entered college in 1988, my mom said, "Find your
passion. Become yourself." I had always interpreted that statement as an injunction to find and fine-tune my personal interests and career rather than burdening myself too early with the
kinds of compromises necessary to form an enduring relationship and a family. So instead of hunting for stability and convention, I spent my twenties exploring my eclectic interests,
and the more bohemian aspects of my personality: I spent a se-
mester of college in Nepal studying a culture as different from
my own as I could imagine. I climbed peaks in the Himalayas
by myself. After graduation, I traveled and danced into the
sultry night on offbeat islands in Thailand. I moved across
the United States to San Francisco, where I went to graduate
school. And through it all, I surfed through different relationships with men. There were some unforgettable romantic experiences—the sexy, hazel-eyed water polo player who taught me
to play bar shuffleboard and once rode me around the island of
Minorca on the back of a little red scooter; the geeky magazine
editor who was obsessed with retro airplane memorabilia and

with whom I once drove all night to see camels race across the Nevada desert. There was the guy who drank red wine through a straw on our first date because he said he didn't want it to stain his teeth, and the quirky Mormon artist who was hand-drawing the Grand Canal of Venice on a scroll. And there was the one who taught me that even if a man says he is going to call, he might not, and the one who took me out twice before deciding to tell me that he was already living with someone. Each move, each professional adventure, and each relationship revealed a little more of what I wanted out of my life; each choice led to new choices.

I followed my instincts and lived for the moment. Sexual liberation was well-embedded in my social DNA. I took it as a given that birth control gave me freedom, and I believed that this freedom would in turn enable me to further refine my passions and interests and to choose a career that would give me financial control over my life. From there, I could find a partner who would share my interests and ambitions.

At that age I didn't really think about my potential choices for how and when I might become a mother; motherhood was something that I just assumed would happen some time down the road. I wasn't yet searching for my future family; I spent those years studiously trying to avoid getting pregnant.

It was only in the year after my breakup at The Cloisters that I began to make it a top priority to find the father of my imagined children. As I started my new life alone, I began to see all of the new choices and the dilemmas and contradictions created by the newfound freedom to establish a family later. I realized that in this new world there are few social rules and little regulation binding our decisions about who to date, when and if to marry, when to start trying to get pregnant, the new array of choices in advanced reproductive technology, forming alternative families with sperm or egg donors, choosing single motherhood, and adopting.

Because this world is so new, however, there is no road map. Sylvia Ann Hewlett and plenty of others have given advice— often contradictory—based on the experiences of their own generation, but that wasn't what I needed. I wanted advice from someone within my generation who was going through everything I was, and am, going through myself. And since, ultimately, I couldn't find that book anywhere on the shelf, I decided to set to work using the tools of my trade as a journalist to investigate my options as a single woman at the edge of her fertility. I hope that in doing so I can help other women think more clearly about their options as well.

I began my research very simply—by talking to other women and to men, some my age, some younger, some older. I wanted to hear directly from other people about their experiences of becoming mothers and fathers at different life stages and along unconventional routes. I sought out stories, though not the stories of Hollywood celebrities, who became pregnant in their late forties and fifties. The problem with such stories, I've found, is that most of these women did not use their own eggs—a fact that is rarely played up in sycophantic stories in *People* magazine. I wasn't interested in the glossy magazine versions so much as in the stories of regular women who were willing to share with me the most personal details of how they got to motherhood through alternative means.

It's not only single women who struggle with these issues. I've interviewed married women who are uncertain about their careers, even their spouses, but certain their future must include the experience of parenting. They too have wondered how they are going to start a family. They've asked similar questions. How much time do I really have? Can I freeze my eggs? Should I test my fertility? Will motherhood make me happy?

In the course of my investigation, I have explored the most innovative and up-to-date technologies available for women on the edge of their fertility. I've met and interviewed the leading business people, inventors, doctors, and psychological experts in the field of fertility science. I've learned about a wide array of present possibilities, and also gotten a glimpse into a not-so-far-off future. This future may include technologies that allow older women's DNA to be implanted into the working eggs of younger women, and the possibility of restocking a woman's egg supply using bone marrow stem cells.

Advancing reproductive technology is making these new choices possible, but how much should we depend on this technology just because we have it? Of course, there are many women and couples who are facing infertility—not because of their age or because they waited—who don't view the use of this technology as a choice but as their last resort and only chance for a biological child. But it's still important to examine whether the commercialization of reproductive technology is making the act of becoming a parent too much like shopping for a pair of designer shoes. Is it creating a culture of perfectionism in which our ambition to have it all has resulted in an unrealistic desire to create perfect children? How much risk can we take? And how much emotional and physical stress should our bodies go through in order to get pregnant? How old is too old?

At the heart of all these questions lies an even deeper one: when motherhood is no longer a requirement for women, why do we choose to have children? Even when we don't necessarily wait to have children for economic reasons, or because we haven't found the right match, some of us are spending a lot of time actually struggling with the question of whether we want a child to be part of our lives.

During this investigation, I have also continued on my own quest to create the kind of family that's right for me. At times, it is excruciatingly lonely. At other times, downright scary. But sometimes it feels absolutely exhilarating. As I learn about the new possibilities available, instead of feeling like my life has become more limited as I've gotten older, it feels more expansive.

In the course of my research, I've talked to American women in Des Moines, Iowa, and suburban Texas. And I've talked to women farther away, in places like India and South Africa. This broad perspective has allowed me to see the myriad values women bring to bear as they confront the same challenge: planning their futures and their families. Hearing each woman's story has been like looking into a kaleidoscope and seeing fragments of my own life. My perspective changes at each turn of the bezel. The people I met have moved and instructed me, and helped me explore the most difficult terrain I've encountered in the course of writing this book: my own emotions.

I have encountered values radically different from my own and learned from them. At other times, I have experienced intense identification. I have discovered that some women think about family in fundamentally different ways. Some see it through the lens of biology and genetics, and others see it through the lens of socially constructed patterns and taboos.

By connecting all these experiences, I have been able to clarify my own values. As I've worked toward figuring out my own life, I've tried on all sorts of potential scenarios for size— single motherhood, co-parenting with a friend, adoption, and yes, even settling for something less than perfect love. I hope my experiences and my research will provide insight for others into how some of these different choices look and feel. But I can offer no general solutions to the dilemmas women face in this challenging new world of ours, because the answers I've found are specific to me, based on my own values and experiences. Other women will come up with different answers. The only thing I can say definitively is that women who want children—or even are on the fence about it—should take the time to think about these issues early on. As women of a post-boomer generation, we are used to being in control of our lives, professionally and financially. The fact that we do not have control over the duration of our fertility is incredibly frightening, something many of us would like to ignore for as long as possible. But I have learned that no matter how scary some information was at first, it's ultimately liberating to understand my own body's reproductive possibilities—as well as its impossibilities. We have more options than ever; understanding them can empower us and, perhaps most importantly, turn panic into peace.

# 1

### Feathering the Nest

It's a few weeks before my thirty-fifth birthday and I'm staring at a shelf filled with dozens of pale-colored pamphlets with titles like *Donor Insemination: A Guide for Patients, Egg Freezing, Using Donor Eggs, Adoption: A Guide for Patients,* and *Single Mothers by Choice*.

"So you're having trouble having a baby?" asks Dr. Mindy Schiffman, the psychotherapist sitting across the room from me.

"Yes," I say, turning my gaze away from the pamphlets and back toward her. But then I correct myself. "Well, not exactly. I haven't even had sex in four months. I just know that I want to have a baby."

She looks at me quizzically; she's clearly perplexed. I feel a warm flush of embarrassment rising on my cheeks. I wonder if she thinks I'm unhinged, if I'm the only woman who has ever shown up at her office in such a state.

Dr. Schiffman is a petite, angular woman who wears thick black-framed glasses propped at the end of her nose. She has been working in infertility clinics for twenty years, guiding women and couples through the emotionally charged terrain of infertility—and fertility. Every day she talks to women who share a common story: they are in their mid- to late thirties and early forties, later into their fertility cycles, and just starting to seriously consider pregnancy. Her job is to facilitate thoughtful consideration about timing and options. Some of her patients are couples who need to use advanced fertility technology or donor eggs to get pregnant. Others are single women who are thinking about becoming mothers through sperm donors. In today's culture, where so many women delay starting a family in order to develop their careers or find the right mate, concerns about fertility have become so common that the clinic changed its name from Program for IVF, Reproductive Surgery and Infertility to the New York University Fertility Center. The message: fertility is something you should pay attention to long before you actually hit up against infertility.

"I don't want to do it now," I continue. "Maybe next year. Or the year after that. Or even the year after that."

Dr. Schiffman's perplexity evaporates and she breaks into a smile. I realize that she has come across women like me before. I settle back into my chair.

It's been four years since that day at The Cloisters when Alex and I broke up. Recently, I opened the wedding section of the *New York Times* and saw the announcement that he had gotten married.

"I'm still single," I explain to Dr. Schiffman.

I don't want to have a baby right now, but ever since my relationship with Alex ended, the pressure has been growing to find Mr. Right. It hasn't happened yet, and I feel like it's time to consider my options. I had recently had a dream in which I was sitting at a large banquet table with my entire extended family. Even my dead grandmother was there, sitting next to my father. I was apologizing to all of them for taking so long to pass along the family genes.

My life feels stalled out, and everyone else seems to be speeding past me. In the past four years I have seen many of my friends marry and have babies. I have even seen one friend marry, divorce, and fall in love with a new man, all in the time that I've been accepting fix-ups, scanning dating profiles on the Web, and playing barstool roulette—looking into the eyes of strangers, wondering if they could turn into the love of my life.

"I don't worry about the cycle of love ending," I tell her.

Just that morning I had spoken to my father on the phone. He told me about a friend of his, a woman who plays in his monthly poker game. She is seventy, and the only woman in the game. My father told me that she had recently begun dating a man who is almost ninety.

"She has a little trouble with the fact that he is losing his hearing, but love goes on, Rachel," he said.

"I'm just worried about my eggs," I tell Dr. Schiffman.

Of course I haven't just been waiting for fate to step in. I've put my profile on several dating websites, which has given me a lot of choice and control over the men I meet. In recent months, I've thrown my net far and wide, which seems to be the main advantage of using the Internet to meet people. I've dated a gregarious bicoastal television producer who liked to go the farmer's market on Saturday mornings; our short-lived romance among the heirloom tomatoes never became serious though, because after a month he decided to move to Los Angeles permanently. After that, there was the Australian doctor who wore green canvas high tops. One of my friends dubbed him "the hip nerd." He chased me for weeks, but I just wasn't that attracted to him, and then I got an e-mail from a very sexy lawyer with sixties-ish sideburns who lived in a big loft in Brooklyn. I liked his downbeat voice, and the chemistry was much stronger, so I blew off the doctor. But then the lawyer met someone he liked better. I thought about calling the doctor back, but by then it seemed more interesting to totally reboot and start with someone new, which is when I started to realize the main problem with meeting people this way. It has given me too much choice.

The Internet has opened up social networks so far beyond the boundaries of college friends (and their friends), chance encounters, and polite social introductions that it has become an overwhelming maze of possible turns and dead-ends. Dead-ends like the man who posted a flattering picture—twenty pounds lighter—on the site and then showed up looking so different that I wouldn't have come close to recognizing him unless he had approached me. After one wasted evening—during which I suffered through his high-pitched chatter about his love of show tunes, teen vampire novels (he was thirty-eight) and cruise ship comedians—I swore to myself that if this ever happened again, I would feign an emergency after one drink and leave.

I think about these choices one day while standing in the refrigerated section of the supermarket, staring at cartons of orange juice. There are now dozens of different kinds to choose from—no pulp, low pulp, low acid, extra calcium, heart healthy, immunity defense, extra vitamin D, pineapple orange juice, strawberry orange juice. At first I wonder why we've created so many choices.

Having all of these choices generally doesn't make us any happier. In *The Paradox of Choice*, psychologist Barry Schwartz argues that more choice can make our lives better because we have more control over our lives. At the same time, however, if we become too absorbed by all the available choices, they can become overwhelming—leading to stress, bad decision making, dissatisfaction, and even clinical depression.

After spending a few months dating online, I realize that this theory can be applied to the way we date and form families. In 2007, more than 5 million single people signed up to go shopping in the U.S. digital meat market. Match.com, one of the largest online dating services, claims as many as 15 million members worldwide. Between 2002 and 2007, the company saw a 13 percent increase in personal ads from women over the age of thirty-five. While the Internet makes millions of singles available with the click of a mouse, it also sorts potential mates into incredibly specific categories. There's TallPersonals.com ("Size does count!") for the "height-blessed"; DateMyPet.com for the animal-obsessed; The Right Stuff, "The Ivy League of Dating Sites," for those who attended elite colleges; and SingleAnd Active.com, a hookup hub for outdoor adventurers and athletes. On Chemistry.com, you can even choose to be matched according to your biochemical type.

Many sites even use tagging technology to match people according to words that represent their interests and style preferences. For example, if you click on the words "surfing" and "intellectual" in someone's profile, the site will link you with others who also identify themselves with these interests or qualities. It struck me that I could meet my husband—the man with whom I might spend the rest of my life and with whom I could pass my genes down through the generations—just because I wrote that I was "groovy," liked alternative music, and practiced yoga.

I know a lot of women who decide to make it a project to find a husband as if it were their second job. They blitz hundreds of men on the Internet like they are actually sorting through bins at a sample sale, and they go out on two to three dates a week. A scientist friend of mine calls it "increasing the surface area." In chemistry, if you increase the surface area between two substances there is a higher chance of a chemical reaction.

While I suppose it makes practical sense to increase the surface area, it isn't working for me. Over time, I've come to realize that the romantic in me really does believe that you can't force love. I think it's more about elusive timing and fate, which I know I can't control, even when hundreds are spread before me at the click of a mouse.

The anonymity of online dating bothers me too. I rarely share any friends with the people I am meeting, and that raises a lot of trust issues for me. There isn't the accountability that comes with a sense of community—meeting someone through friends, or even a local coffee shop or bar frequented by my neighbors. In the fast-paced world of online dating, there is no onus on anyone to be gracious, kind, or even honest—or to give anyone a second chance. I've found myself just moving on if a date was weird or uncomfortable in any way, and some of my dates treated me the same way. We are all disposable, it seems.

Maybe I just need an attitude adjustment. But after a few months, the electronic meat market no longer appeals to me. It violates my fantasy of meeting Mr. Right in some more meaningful, organic way.

That said, my thirty-fifth birthday is just around the corner, and my clock is ticking.

Thanks to Sylvia Ann Hewlett, the author of *Creating a Life*, my thirty-fifth birthday has become a source of dread for me. "I feel like a wilting lily," I had moaned to a friend a few days earlier. The possibility of a serious relationship seems further away than ever, as does the prospect of motherhood.

I tell Dr. Schiffman about a conversation I'd had with a friend at a dinner party. At thirty-nine, she had just become engaged to a film scout, a scion of a rich and eccentric Chicago family. She told me that she loved him but that she was nervous about getting married. Part of her believed that he might not always be in her life. But she had decided to take the plunge anyway because, she explained, she didn't want to miss out on the opportunity to have a child.

"A child is permanent," she said.

I was taken aback by her comment, and surprised that her craving for more stability made her want to get married not because she believed in the permanence of the institution but because she wanted to commit to having a child with someone. I have always believed that marriage is permanent as well. My parents have been together for better or for worse for over forty years, and my family has always been my rock. But I suppose that in an age when the divorce rate is so high, many people feel that love and commitment are either fleeting, incompatible, or both.

And children can seem like an answer. In a study of single women in their twenties, Kimberly DaCosta, a Harvard sociologist, found that the romantic desire for a baby has replaced the craving for the intimacy of a relationship. Her study concluded that these women imagine the role of mother as a state of permanence and unconditional love. I think back to my friend who had a baby in her mid-twenties. Her own parents were divorced only two years after she was born, and I wonder if, for her, having a baby gave her a sense of security in an age of ephemeral relationships.

I don't know whether this is the reason I'm more focused on motherhood, but in the past few years I too have begun to feel more of a need for permanence. Maybe it has something to do with being an eyewitness that day when two planes crashed into the World Trade Center. I was standing on Greenwich Street when the first tower fell less than a mile from my apartment. The world became more insecure in a heartbeat, leaving me hungry for a sense of safety and the comfort of home.

Or maybe it's just that unlocking so much of myself by moving around, exploring different kinds of relationships, and spending time alone has made me ready to commit to one place and one relationship. What I do know as I stand teetering on the brink of advanced maternal age is that I need to think about how I'm going to get to where I want to be.

"You're feathering the nest," says Dr. Schiffman, explaining that just by asking these questions I'm taking my first step toward preparing to become a mother. "I think all women your age who want to have a child should do this—even if they're not in a relationship."

"I'm a traditionalist," I tell her. "I want to do it the natural way, or at least the way I think is natural, which is to meet a man, fall in love, get married, and have a child."

She smiles in an obtuse way, as if I'm saying something slightly sentimental.

"Have you ever thought about becoming a single mother?" she asks.

"No," I say reflexively.

I really haven't seriously considered this idea, although I keep hearing stories about women my age who are making this choice.

"Most women don't come to see me wanting to be single mothers," she explains. "It's more that they can't find someone and they don't want to wait anymore and risk not ever having a baby with their own genes. Very few women think that they are going to be alone for the rest of their lives. Some feel they might even attract a nicer guy if they have a baby alone."

I contemplate all of this. Maybe she's right, maybe part of starting older is abandoning my romantic fantasy. Maybe this fantasy of the perfect husband, the perfect marriage, is actually holding me back from my vital desire to be a mother. And because my ability to have a biological child is limited by time, while the possibility of falling in love is not, maybe I need to get practical and choose what is in my biological control, first. After all, that choice is part of the privilege that I've earned as a financially independent woman.

Of course the prospect of doing this on my own, being solely responsible for a child, financially and emotionally, seems a bit impractical and utterly terrifying. Honestly, I'm not sure I'm ready for the compromises it would require. I've only just become comfortable taking care of myself in the way I want, and I am prepared to make the compromises to be with the right man. But taking care of a baby all by myself seems pretty radical.

I tell Dr. Schiffman that although separating love and procreation makes sense to me intellectually, it feels very uncomfortable for me emotionally.

"Is that wrong?"

"No," she says. "That's smart. The most important thing that I remind every one of my patients is that this investigation is not for yourself. It's for your child," she says.

It strikes me as funny to think of "my child" when I have no inkling of who the child's father will be. My imagination takes over. I picture a little version of myself, a tiny me like the nasal little child Lily Tomlin used to play, sitting in a huge chair, except this me is sitting in front of a giant computer.

This is a terribly narcissistic image, I tell myself. Do I want to have a child just to clone myself? No.

I then think about the endless march I see on the street these days, babies and small children everywhere, in their Bugaboo strollers, holding mommy's hand, riding on daddy's shoulders.

Was having a baby some kind of status symbol, like owning an iPhone or a pair of Prada shoes? Was I just reacting to peer pressure? Was I trying to keep up with the mommies?

When I think back to my childhood, I can't remember ever fantasizing about motherhood as a primary goal. Even then I had other ambitions. I can remember sitting on my mother's lap at her typewriter, excited to write a play about a princess who is captured by a dragon. I recall that at one point I wanted to be editor-in-chief of a magazine. I can remember giving a dramatic speech about a subject that's lost to time from my tree house during a grown-up party.

I did love babies, though, and I did often think about my favorite neighbor, who had a baby daughter. Almost every day after school I would sit on her doorstep waiting for the baby to wake up so that I might have a chance to hold her.

"You loved babies even when you were a baby," my father has mentioned on many occasions.

I think I didn't fantasize about becoming a mother because I had always assumed that motherhood was something different from a magazine editorship or a writing career—not something I would need to work and strive for. I had always thought of it as something much simpler—a natural inclination to nurture and pass on life, something that would happen along the way. But now, on the cusp of thirty-five, I'm realizing that it's much more complicated than that. I need to think about my options and make plans. I need to manage my fertility like I've managed my career.

As I talk more with Dr. Schiffman, I become increasingly aware of the many choices I have. I can become a single mother through donor insemination before I lose my fertility and before my right love comes along. Or I can wait for my love to come along, gambling that he will appear soon enough that I will still be able to get pregnant naturally. But if I'm not able, there are a number of reproductive technologies—fertility drugs, in vitro fertilization—that might help. And even if I discover I can no longer conceive with my own eggs, I might be able to use a donor egg, or adopt. All of these options are costly, both financially and emotionally; reproductive technology is for the privileged and the strong. Although insurance does cover some procedures, there are a lot of limitations and out-of-pocket expenses.

All of these choices represent a vast departure from my fantasy of perfect romantic love and motherhood. But the older I get, the more I see that I may have to sacrifice some of the romance. I can wait for Mr. Right to come along in a so-called organic way, but then have a baby using man-made technology. Maybe in this era we are actually redefining "the natural way." Or I can continue looking for Mr. Right in a more practical way by increasing the surface area and see if love develops. Like my friend, I can marry someone who is something less than my perfect partner. I know lots of people who marry for reasons other than love; surely the desire to have a baby is better than most. But this option doesn't seem right to me. Sometimes I wish I weren't such a romantic, and I envy people who approach their lives with a more pragmatic attitude. It would certainly make my search much easier, because the romantic ideal creates high expectations; maybe even an ideal that doesn't exist. At this point, I'm just not sure which way to go.

Dr. Schiffman then tells me that I shouldn't feel desperate. I have time. Thirty-five, she reassures me, is actually on the young end of the spectrum to be talking about these issues. Even though at thirty-five a woman's fertility drops by a quarter compared to a woman in her twenties, plenty of women have healthy babies well into their thirties and forties.

As I listen to Dr. Schiffman, I flash back to a memory I have of my own mother. It is 1978. She is eight months pregnant with my younger brother, Noah. We are standing in the unkempt garden of our backyard celebrating her fortieth birthday, surrounded by friends and family. She wears an orange floor-length sundress and holds a woven basket of ladyfingers, passing them out to guests as I follow her around pressing my hands against her enormous belly. Whenever I become sad and worry about starting later, this image calms me.

"I always thought that I had until I was forty," I say.

"You might," says Dr. Schiffman. "Your mother's fertility is often a good marker of your own."

I might. That seems to be the theme of the last ten years of my life—a constant state of might. I might marry him. I might move here. I might meet someone new there. This suspended state of no real commitment is part of the luxury that I've both inherited, as part of my liberated generation, and chosen for myself.

When my mother entered college in 1956, my grandmother told her to find a man. More rigid social rules dictated that she get married in her twenties—or else be condemned to spinster-hood. In 1964, the year my mother and father married, the average age of first marriage for a woman was twenty, twenty-three for a man. Marriage at that time was understood as the dividing line between childhood and adulthood. Being married signaled that you were responsible and employable. But today, "love"—a word that can be defined in many ways—has overtaken marriage as the crucial factor around which people organize their lives and the roles they play with each other. People marry out of love and enter a psychological state of commitment. If both people stay in love, or at least stay committed to getting through everything, then they stay married. But clearly this new definition of marriage doesn't always last, and then people move on to new and different stages of love and relationships.

My mother married my father at twenty-seven. On their wedding day, one older relative patted her tummy with raised eyebrows, wondering if it was a shotgun wedding because she was so old. In fact, my mother had held out for love, but she certainly didn't have as many choices as I do now, nor did she spend as much time searching for the right person with whom to start a family. She met my father, by chance, in the building where they both lived in Greenwich Village. One afternoon in the elevator, his roommate asked her if he could borrow her eggbeater to make whipped cream for strawberry shortcake. She said yes, but she would lend it to him only if she could come over and sample the final product when it was done. When she went to his apartment, she met my father. They married four years later.

As much as I romanticize my parents' chance meeting and their enduring marriage, I know I need to acknowledge that I didn't end up here, in Dr. Schiffman's office in my mid-thirties, solely because of fate or bad luck. At twenty-seven, I too had the choice to get married, and I almost did. But in the end I made a different choice instead.

Andrew* had angelic blond curls. I was living in San Francisco at the time, working for a publishing company, and we met
through a friend. Andrew was like a yellow lab—exceedingly
friendly, loyal, and playful. He was more passionate about living
his life than about professional success; he worked for an insurance company at a job he fell into and didn't really care about in
order to afford the things he loved and that made him happy.
We shared a sense of adventure. He taught me how to drive a
stick shift, snowboard down an icy slope, pitch a tent at the base
of a glacier, and cook a meal on a camping stove smaller than
my hand. I really loved him, but I didn't think of him as The
One, because at that stage of my life I didn't think about The
One. I was living for the moment, and our lives fell together as
part of the flow. After we dated for a little over a year, we moved
in together. I was starting graduate school at Berkeley, and living together seemed right and fun. It also made financial sense
at a time when I was paying to go to school rather than being
paid to work. Pretty soon Andrew and I were buying furniture
together, alternating grocery shopping, and throwing holiday
dinner parties.

But in graduate school, I started to discover a different, more
serious, side to myself. I started to focus on my dream of becoming a writer, and suddenly our adventures together—and our
partnership—didn't feel like the priority. I began questioning
being so settled in this relationship when I still felt so unformed
in other ways, and suddenly I didn't want to make compromises.

At the time, I also started to bond with an older mentor—
a father figure—at graduate school. He saw in my work a pro-

---

*Throughout this and all chapters in the book, an asterisk indicates
that names, identifying details, and some events have been changed.

fessional and artistic potential that I had been uncertain of myself, and he inspired in me a new level of confidence and ambition. Once, I introduced him to Andrew. He asked me what I was doing with someone so professionally unmotivated. And soon I too began to think I was headed in the wrong direction with him.

I recently looked at my journal from that time. I wrote: "This is not real. We're playing house. I know there's another life for me."

As I fell in love with journalism and my new friends at graduate school, my domestic interests waned. I started wanting to return to New York to pursue my career. Andrew wanted to stay in California, doing the things he loved. After I spent a summer interning at a newspaper in New York, Andrew and I decided to part ways. It was sad, but amicable; we just concluded that we were going in different directions and needed to move on. After our breakup, I didn't think for a second about my fertility or the fact that I might be losing the chance to start a family. I was totally confident that I would meet someone else on my new path.

I often think about how if we had married and started a family, I might not have been able to grow to where I am now. Recently, I had dinner with my friend who got married at twenty-four and had her first baby at twenty-five. She admitted to me that she sometimes feels too young to be a mom and have her life so defined when so many of her older friends have yet to become mothers. She even joked that she felt she had to wait until she passed thirty to have her second child. She looked at me, and for an instant I saw ambivalence in her eyes.

"I'm never going to experience the ten years of freedom and searching that you've had," she said.

She's right. I have been free from responsibility to a husband and family. Writing assignments and disposable income have allowed me to travel the world. And I'm a more satisfied, deeper, and better-informed person because of the experiences I've had. But I have also been in this state of "might." And I'll admit it: when I start to question whether I'm just never going to meet the right person, I sometimes regret letting my relationship with Andrew go, not committing to growing up together, compromising, even fighting to make it work for both of us. Sometimes I think that I've become so acculturated to the idea that I should find a perfect-fit situation that I am closing myself off to other opportunities, albeit imperfect ones.

I'm sure my mother didn't think about these things—she didn't have that luxury. Society told her that she had to get married by a certain age, so that's what shaped her decision. She loved my dad, but I don't think she spent any time worrying that he might not be the perfect fit. He was the man she loved at the right time, and that's the life she went with. She assures me that if she had had as many choices as I do she still would have married my dad. But she's not unlike me in her sense of self-exploration, and I often wonder if her choice was more about social convention than she claims.

And so here I am, almost eight years after my breakup with Andrew. I'm on firmer ground in my identity and career, and I'm free to go anywhere I want. But now, just shy of my thirty-fifth birthday, this is where I've chosen to go: a fertility therapist's office, where I'm staring at pamphlets about egg-freezing and single motherhood. Here I am, thinking, *I might. I might become a mother.*

~

A few days later, I sit in a medical lab in the West Village. A friendly nurse sticks a needle into my arm to draw blood as she comments on what good shape I'm in. I laugh—after all, I'm here to find out whether my eggs have begun to atrophy. At the recommendation of Dr. Schiffman, I'm undergoing a simple blood test to measure my follicle stimulating hormone (FSH) level, which will give me some indication of how fertile I am. Since I have no control over when my fertility will begin to decline, I want to learn as much as I can about my body so I can weigh more knowledgably the odds of each possible outcome of the choices before me.

Every month, the pituitary gland in my brain sends out FSH to tell my ovaries to get to work growing the antral follicles that will hold and eventually release an egg. The amount of FSH my body produces will be a clue to my ovarian reserve and the quality of my eggs. By placing me on a scale of 1 to 12, the test can help to predict my chances of conception each month.

"Anything under a 12 is pretty good," says Dr. Nicole Noyes, an ob-gyn and endocrinologist at NYU who specializes in fertility science, when I call her for a medical opinion on the test. "When you're in the prime of your fertility, it should be below a 7. At thirty-five, if you're a 10, you might want to start to worry about your fertility. If your levels are a 6 or 7 then you can probably buy a year and be checked again."

The test is not fail-safe, however. Some doctors argue that because FSH levels can change quickly, and in fact can fluctuate within a range of 20 to 40 percent in a month, the test may give women a false sense of security. "The real predictive value of FSH—and other fertility indication tests that are now being offered—isn't totally known," says Dr. Daniel Stein, an ob-gyn and endocrinologist at St. Luke's-Roosevelt Hospital in New York. "I wouldn't recommend that people decide when they're going to conceive based on their FSH."

Dr. John Zhang, an ob-gyn who runs the New Hope Fertility Center in New York, is more confident about fertility assessment and uses what he thinks is a more sure-fire method. At his clinic, he offers an ultrasound test that measures ovarian reserve. By placing a magic wand–like device inside the vagina, he can look at a woman's ovaries on a screen and actually count the number of antral follicles that contain the eggs and respond to FSH. As we age, the number of antral follicles that release eggs declines along with the quality of the eggs. The number depends on age and individual biology, but Zhang says seven follicles are considered a good reserve regardless of a woman's age.

"Planning means you have to prioritize what's most important," he says. "If you discover that your reserve is high, you might say 'let me postpone another six months, get my job under control, and get the house ready.' If you find that your reserve is low, you might want to freeze your eggs."

Still, there are a lot of uncertainties, Dr. Zhang explains. Even if a woman's antral follicle reserve is high, it doesn't necessarily predict the future of how many follicles she will have in two years or five years. It also doesn't answer the question of how many eggs are still viable.

Dr. Zhang advises that women should start thinking about fertility much sooner than I have. Like most women, I have waited until I'm pressed up against the wall of infertility to start thinking about my options. He thinks this is a huge mistake. Once a woman reaches age twenty-one or twenty-two, she should have a thorough check-up, including an antral follicle count, blood work, and an ultrasound to check her uterus, which will give her a baseline to work with for the future. He tells me a scary story about a twenty-eight-year-old woman who came to him unable to get pregnant after trying for a year. He discovered she had no antral follicles and was experiencing premature ovarian failure, which occurs in 1 to 4 percent of women under the age of forty.

"The earlier a woman discovers that she might run into problems, the better the chance it can be remedied," he says.

The tests are not exceedingly expensive, but they do involve time-consuming trips to the doctor's office. An FSH test costs between $100 and $200 and can be done through any ob-gyn's office or a medical clinic that can do a blood test. Dr. Zhang's antral follicle ultrasound costs a bit more, close to $300, and this technology is not standard or even available in many ob-gyn offices.

The lack of convenience is why Dr. Bill Ledger, a professor of obstetrics and gynecology at the University of Sheffield in England, is trying to make it easier for women to assess their own fertility in the privacy of their homes. He has invented a home fertility test called Plan Ahead that is sold through mail order for around $200 and will eventually be available through pharmacies. In addition to FSH, it tests anti-Müllerian hormone (AMH), which strongly correlates with the size of a woman's ovarian follicle pool, and inhibin B, another hormone produced by growing follicles. The test calculates what he calls an ovarian reserve index. Using a computer model, the test compares the results to levels expected for women of the same age.

Ledger explains that testing the level of all three hormones simultaneously leads to a much more accurate assessment of a woman's fertility. "The problem with measuring just FSH is

that it goes up pretty late in the process of losing ovarian reserve, so it may be too late to do anything," he says. "Inhibin B
and AMH are high when you're young and go down as you get
older. So you can get an early warning if your AMH and your
inhibin B are dropping."

The results of my FSH test will take a few weeks. In the
meantime, I decide to talk to Dr. Stein, who leaned toward
skepticism about relying on an FSH test alone, about other
steps to take in terms of my fertility. Dr. Stein is a jolly, warm
man and a straight shooter. Sitting in his midtown office, he
explains that whether or not a woman is actually trying to get
pregnant, it's always a good time to get her body ready.

"There are certain environmental factors that have been associated with increased egg aging or potential egg damage," he
says. He says that women who smoke more than a half a pack
of cigarettes a day will go into menopause at least two or three
years earlier than those who don't. Excessive alcohol has also
been associated with egg damage. In addition, women who are
twenty pounds above or below their ideal body weight have a
much lower chance of conceiving in a period of six months.

Talking to these doctors and starting to gather information
about my options definitely makes me feel more empowered.
I've learned that there are no guarantees. Even the data that I
can obtain scientifically about my fertility is imperfect and
could lead to false hopes. And that data could tell me something really scary—that I'm infertile. I understand perfectly why
women are tempted to ignore the issue altogether and just hope
for the best. That's certainly what I did for a very long time.

But talking to so many fertility specialists has instilled in
me a sense of optimism. Even if I don't meet Mr. Right right
away, I am becoming more open to the idea of alternative
ways to form a family. Just thinking and talking about these

options begins to normalize them as brave new procreative paths in this new culture.

~

I still have time, I remind myself. Dr. Schiffman gave me confidence that despite the media hype, I shouldn't feel desperate. Thirty-five is still young. But our conversation does get me thinking in a more focused and a bit more practical way about dating. That means choosing only men who are serious about committing to making a family.

I decide to follow the advice that a close friend once gave me. She told me to write a paragraph about the man I wanted to meet. The idea is that if I understand what I'm looking for, I will become more confident, waste less time treading water in less-than-ideal relationships, and focus on what I want, rather than on whether men want me.

I write: Someone who balances me. Someone who supports my weaknesses and strengthens my strengths. Someone who is socially at ease, smart, and in touch with his emotions. Someone who is ambitious and knows where he is going but is willing to occasionally step off that path to go surfing or sailing or escape down a hidden alley in a foreign city. Someone who has a realistic attitude toward money. A mellow and flexible soul who believes in change, questions romantic illusion, loves great food, wants to work hard at growing up together along with life's challenges, and mostly, mostly, knows when to trim the sails to keep the love moving forward.

Although I believe in traditional family, I have never imagined myself as a traditional wife. I don't want a 1950s contract arrangement where husband and wife live in separate spheres of influence and responsibility—meaning, in practice, that the woman stays home with the children while the man earns the money and consequently holds more power in the relationship. I want to be in a relationship of equals, something akin to best friendships, in which my partner and I make decisions as a team, give and take, support and respect each other's passions and careers, and share the duties of child rearing in a flexible and evolved style. Of course this companionate, egalitarian ideal raises the bar significantly in my search for the perfect mate, and it may be one of the reasons why I'm taking longer to get there.

Once I'm done with the paragraph about my ideal man, I decide to go a step further. I start to interview my closest friends about the kind of man they picture for me. I figure that compared to taking a personality test on the Internet or going on a hundred waste-of-my-time dates, I might get a better idea of the right match for me through the people who know and understand me the best.

I make drinks-dates with friends, e-mail old friends I haven't spoken to in years, and even ask neighbors I run into. I ask them all what they imagine when they think of my ideal partner. They say things like: "Gentle, not too quiet." "Outdoorsy." "An entrepreneur." "Someone who is good at calming you down." One friend says: "I picture you with a guy who wears turtlenecks." Another looks at me like I'm crazy and says: "You just need someone who adores you!"

Two weeks before my thirty-fifth birthday, I get a call from my gynecologist telling me that my FSH level is a 2. That means that my eggs are hanging in there and that I'm in good shape as far as my fertility is concerned—though I now know this can change quickly.

"Are you trying to get pregnant?" she asks.

I'm embarrassed to tell her that I'm not, that I'm still looking for a man who might wear turtlenecks, that I'm just a fertility gambler assessing the odds for the best payoff.

"I'm still looking for my right love," I mumble.

"Well, if you don't meet the right one in two years and don't want to give up the chance to have a child, then you might want to consider going to a sperm bank," she tells me point blank.

*"Phew, I can still roll the dice,"* I think.

"How long do I have?" I ask instead.

"I don't really know how long you have," she responds. "You can't predict fertility," she adds. "I have patients who get pregnant naturally at forty-three, and those who are having trouble at thirty-two."

She pauses, and then advises that I should probably get my levels checked again in six months or a year and judge the difference between the two test scores. That should give me a good idea of how quickly my fertility is changing.

"Other than that, just live your life," she finishes.

As I hang up the phone, two more voices come into my head.

"I'm sorry I wasted your time," Alex said.

"Love goes on, Rachel," my father said.

I am in a strange place, but a much more secure one than before I started researching my fertility. I'm alone, but feel that I've taken an important step toward becoming a mother. I am planning my future—or, should I say, an array of possible futures—and the first step, I've learned, is taking care of myself. The irony is not lost. At the moment that I accept that my eggs will soon start to decline, I also realize that I'm the furthest thing from a wilting lily. I'm beginning to blossom.

# 2

⁂

# Buying Time

My cell phone is ringing, but I can't reach it because my feet are in stirrups and my ob-gyn's hand is pressing down on my lower abdomen. I know the phone call is from Nick*, a persistent literature professor I met at a book party three weeks earlier. I had bragged to him that I was training for a triathlon and then, instead of giving him my number, I challenged him to find me. He did (it's not that difficult in the age of Google), and we've been casually dating since. I like him because he saunters around on summer afternoons in flip flops and ripped jean shorts as if he were a surf bum, but in reality he spends most of his time worrying about his life and analyzing the literature of war-torn countries.

We're meeting up tonight at a hip, celebrity-strewn bar in the West Village. He says he likes to go there to be "glamorous" because the only thing he enjoys as much as depressing literature is fashion—and fashion models. He studies the latest edgy labels as closely as Coetzee or Conrad. This paradox amuses me, but I'm not in love.

"How's your romantic life?" asks my OB, looking up from between my legs.

I half smile, and tell her that I'm dating a lot these days.

"Is everything ok?" I ask.

"Yes, you're healthy," she says. "But you're not getting any younger."

I tell her that I'm thinking about freezing my eggs.

~

Oocyte cryopreservation, a technology by which a woman's eggs are harvested from her ovaries and frozen until she is ready to use them, is just entering the reproductive zeitgeist. Some doctors claim that it could be as revolutionary as the birth control pill; others warn that its fast-paced commercialization is dangerous, that companies are trying to cash in on women's anxiety by selling the reproductive equivalent of Botox and by turning well-heeled single women into well-heeled guinea pigs. Either way, the technology now exists, and it's raising a lot of new issues for me, and for other women in my situation, about the possibilities—and impossibilities—of modern motherhood.

I first became aware of oocyte cryopreservation a few months back, just after I turned thirty-five. I received a promotional card in the mail from a new company called Extend Fertility. The front of the card presented a picture of a career woman with a sensible haircut bathing a smiling blue-eyed baby in a tub. Next to the photo, big bold letters screamed, "Fertility. Freedom. Finally." And below it, there was a personal message from the company's founders: "As women, we lead rich and demanding lives. As a result of our abundant opportunities, many of us choose to start our families later in life. Extend Fertility's breakthrough egg-freezing service offers women the opportunity to preserve their fertility and take control of their reproductive health."

*This is exactly what I need*, I thought. It was eerie, almost as if the company knew that I was single and had recently turned thirty-five. (I later learned from the CEO that the timing of the postcard was no accident; the company had hired a marketing company to target affluent single women between the ages of thirty-two and thirty-nine.) I logged on to Extend's website to read a little more about the procedure. It begins with a standard in vitro fertilization stimulation cycle in which artificial hormones stimulate the growth and release of eggs. In a typical IVF cycle, after surgical retrieval, the eggs are fertilized and reimplanted in the uterus. But in egg freezing, the doctors skip the fertilization. They retrieve the eggs and then place them in liquid nitrogen so they can be stored for future use.

I clicked on a tab that said "Why Freeze Eggs?" The answer: "Our opportunities are endless, but our egg supply and quality is not." Then I clicked to some client testimonials. Megan, a pretty thirty-six-year-old acupuncturist, had this to say: "I was starting to feel that my desire to have children was putting pressure on my current relationship. . . . Deciding to freeze my eggs helped me to separate the issues—yes, I want to have children, yes, I am in a relationship, but my desire to have children shouldn't cloud whether we should be having children together."

Freezing her eggs, she wrote, "removed some of the judgment of myself and self-criticism of wishing I had done this or that differently, or some blame I've placed on myself for not having children yet. I feel far less anxious about the future, no matter what the outcome—whether I get pregnant naturally at some point, whether I use these eggs, whether I adopt. Now it's just more about becoming a mother eventually than judging my body for not being the 'perfect' age biologically."

Could this be the answer? Could egg freezing buy me some time to find the right relationship? I thought about my conversation with Dr. Schiffman about separating the search for love from my desire to have a child. Since I still wasn't ready to have a child on my own, this new technology sounded like the perfect choice to calm my anxiety. Suddenly, new images began to form in my mind that looked very different from my romantic visions of a wedding or of a baby playing in a plastic pool. Instead, I saw a giant warehouse filled with tiny drawers of frozen eggs, each with a different woman's name on it. I thought, *if I freeze my eggs now, it might increase my chances to have a baby— and maybe even a second—as late as forty-two, forty-three, forty-four. That would allow me to find love in my own sweet time.*

I clicked on "Educational Events" and discovered that there would be one in New York a few weeks later.

On a winter evening, I headed to the Upper West Side to attend my first Extend Fertility event. It was co-sponsored by *Tango*, a new magazine about love and relationships, and held at the home of the publisher.

I walked into a living room filled with thirty-something women. Some were dressed in low-rider jeans and wedge heels, others in well-tailored business suits. A few were sitting on the floor cross-legged, like little children in a classroom; others were huddled in small groups, whispering, sipping chardonnay, and nibbling on cheddar cheese cubes.

Julie Hammerman, Extend's vice president of marketing, stepped in front of the group. She explained that when Christy

Jones, the thirty-five-year-old CEO of the company, and her all-female project team laid out plans for the company in 2004, they were in their last year at Harvard Business School. This high-powered group was talking about how they could better balance their careers and motherhood, and inevitably the issue of timing came up. Many of them worried that getting pregnant too early would hurt their careers and have long-term effects on their earning power, but of course, waiting too long meant taking the risk of having no children at all.

"There were no options for women who wanted to have a biological child, except to have a child right away," she said.

The group quickly realized that there was a market in need of a product: options for highly educated career women like themselves who either personally or professionally weren't yet in a position to have a child. They wrote a business plan that won a school competition to get some funding. And so Extend Fertility was born. The team started to work with nonprofit organizations, corporations, and numerous women's networking and alumni groups to market the newest choice among women's options: you *can* wait. It's a message of empowerment, they believe, rather than fear.

Hammerman then introduced Dr. Alan D. Copperman, a reproductive endocrinologist with the Division of Reproductive Endocrinology at Mount Sinai Medical Center and medical director of Reproductive Medicine Associates of New York. He stood up, cleared his throat, and pointed to a chart leaning against a posterboard. He zeroed in on a sharp black line that illustrated the decline of a woman's fertility after the age of thirty.

"Eggs are programmed to disintegrate," he explained bluntly. "You don't really have control over it."

We all shifted a bit, listening attentively. I watched as the game faces of the career women around me morphed into furrowed brows. All of us were thinking the same thing: we're able to conquer almost anything in our paths, but fertility is something over which we have no control. And we were all hoping that this new company might be able to offer us some magic bullet that would put an end to our worries.

In our troubled faces, however, Hammerman and Dr. Copperman saw immense potential profit. Egg freezing costs upwards of $15,000. Feminism and capitalism form an uneasy alliance in the world of reproductive technology. On the one hand, Extend Fertility seems sincere in trying to offer women a real option that would help resolve the very serious contradictions between career advancement and family planning. On the other hand, reproductive technology is a fast-growing market, so the profit motive for this new technology was also very real. I wasn't sure if I'd walked into a new kind of consciousness-raising group in which frank talk about fertility has replaced frank talk about sexual self-actualization, or if this was a money-hungry company's subversive marketing campaign to sell the latest reproductive snake oil packaged in the language of feminist empowerment. It seemed a little bit of both.

Dr. Copperman didn't work for Extend Fertility, but the clinic he directed, RMA of New York, was one of five in the Extend Fertility network that offered this emerging technology to its patients. For a cut of the freezing fee, Extend Fertility would handle all the details, including step-by-step counseling services.

"The ideal candidate is under forty, ideally under thirty-five," Dr. Copperman told us. He stressed, however, that the technology was still in the experimental stages. He explained that as of January 2004, experts estimated that approximately one-hundred and fifty babies had been born worldwide from previously frozen eggs. The technology, he emphasized, was not approved by the FDA, nor has the American Society for Reproductive Medicine stamped it with its seal of approval.

Nor is there any guarantee that the technology will actually work. Although Dr. Copperman didn't mention any statistics, Extend's marketing team had recently sent a press release to its mailing list of potential clients announcing that Reproductive Medicine Associates of New York had completed a research study in which 68 out of a total of 79 eggs from four different donors survived the freezing and thawing process. Of those remaining eggs, 61 were successfully fertilized. The team claimed that "one of every four embryos implanted," so they achieved "three out of four pregnancies using frozen eggs from fertile donors," which represents a 75 percent pregnancy rate and a 26 percent implantation rate. Most researchers would say that these results are exaggerated. A 2006 study by Dr. Eleanora Porcu, the inventor of egg freezing, and Dr. Stefano Venturoli— both of the Department of Obstetrics and Gynecology at the University of Bologna—reported a thaw survival rate of 70 percent and an "extremely variable" fertilization rate that ranges from 13 to 71 percent. "Taking together the clinical results published in the past ten years," they wrote, "it is possible to calculate an overall mean survival rate of about 67 percent, and a birth rate per thawed oocyte of around 4 percent."

"Maybe it will work," Dr. Copperman said. "Maybe we'll discover that it will damage your eggs. But if the question is now or later, the answer is now."

After his presentation, almost every hand in the room shot up.

"Can I move my eggs if I move?" someone asked.

"Yes."

"Does health insurance cover it?" asked another.

"No. It's elective. Like plastic surgery."

"What's the return on capital?" asked another.

"I don't want to make any guarantees," he answered.

"Do you offer a layaway plan?" I asked, half-joking.

"Actually, yes," he responded.

After Dr. Copperman's presentation, I mingled with the other potential customers. I met Jane O'Reilly*, a thirty-six-year-old MBA with black curly hair and a wide, toothy smile. A native of South Florida, she had moved to New York from London four months earlier.

"I've always been fond of children and I get along with them, but I've never held having children as a beacon in front of me," she told me. "If I meet the right person and if I'm financially stable, it's a route that I might take. Egg freezing strikes me as a call option."

"A call option on becoming a mother?" I asked.

"Yes," she said. "In finance, you buy an option to buy long on a stock. So you pay three dollars for the option and it gives you the choice to buy the stock at a lower price for a period of time even if the stock goes higher. This is like a call option when your eggs are still good, like when the stock is well priced."

When I asked her why she thinks she hasn't had children yet, she told me a familiar story. She spent most of her twenties bouncing from city to city, trying to find her place and build her career. After business school in Chicago, she moved to Paris and then to London to work for different finance companies. She had boyfriends along the way, but none with whom she wanted to settle down.

"I came close a couple of times," she admitted. "I just haven't found the person I love enough to commit to for my life. When I look at the long term and think about my parents not being around, I'd like to have a companion, but as far as my life is now, I'm fine without one. I don't have to answer a lot of questions and I don't have to compromise."

As we talked, a woman in a gray suit approached us and introduced herself as Sam Montgomery*. A petite African American woman, Sam was just twenty-three years old and starting her career as an administrative assistant in an investment bank. She knew that it could be years before she got married or had children, but she came to the event because she wanted to plan for the future. In reality, she may be closer to Extend's future target market than any of the women in their late thirties, since most studies show that egg freezing is most successful for women who do it in their twenties. And with the technology improving every year, Sam may find herself with an excellent chance of becoming pregnant at thirty-five or forty with her own frozen eggs.

"I wish this possibility had existed when I was twenty-five," I said to her. "But a baby was the last thing on my mind. I wanted to travel the world and have the freedom to explore my career, find myself, get strong on my own. Maybe if I had frozen my eggs, I wouldn't feel as nervous as I do now."

"Nature's cruel joke is that my biology has not caught up with me," Jane breaks in, ruefully. "Now that I'm finally emotionally and financially ready to make a commitment to a family, there is a chance that my body won't cooperate."

"Yeah, but what happens if you do get married and start trying earlier, and then get divorced?" asked a voice behind me. "That's what's happened to me."

Allison Barney*, a tall blond in a flowing yellow skirt, was joining our cluster. She looked a lot more like she should have been meditating in an ashram in Nepal than running a hedge fund. She told us that it was four days before her thirty-fifth birthday and she was considering freezing her eggs as a present to herself.

Allison explained that when she was thirty-one, she spent nine months in couples counseling with her boyfriend of three years trying to decide whether they should get married or not. They both worked long hours in time-consuming, competitive jobs and found themselves struggling with the issue of whether there was enough room for both of them in the relationship. They finally decided to take the plunge—even though they hadn't worked out a lot of their problems.

"One year and one week after the wedding, he walked out," she continued. "He decided that he didn't want to be married. Now when I look back, four years was too many to be involved without getting a commitment from him. After one or two months of our engagement, I should have cut the cord. But then again, maybe I shouldn't say that I wasted my time because I've learned a lot about what I need."

Allison told us that she had recently spoken to her ob-gyn, who told her that egg-freezing technology was still very experimental.

"She said that because I was thirty-five I should probably wait for the technology to improve and instead focus my energies on dating. I have huge regrets about the time I spent from twenty-eight to thirty-three with the wrong person. I feel like I wasted my prime matching-up years."

"You know," she said more quietly. "I sometimes wonder whether I got into a bad marriage because my clock was ticking. My parents said that maybe I wanted to get married because everyone else was, and maybe I wanted to have babies for the same reason."

*Yes*, I think, remembering that day at The Cloisters.

"My dad makes fun of me for never committing," said Jane. "He says that in the 1960s, the motto was 'if it feels good, do it.' And for my generation the new motto is 'if it doesn't feel good, I'm outta here.'"

That night I went home and dreamt about trees with branches weighed down by big frozen eggs.

~

When I tell my ob-gyn about the Extend Fertility event, she shakes her head vigorously. She tells me that egg freezing is a promising technology but that the science isn't far enough along to justify the expense.

She suggests that if I were considering freezing anything that I might want to freeze embryos that I create with donor sperm. The process would be essentially the same as egg freezing, she explains. I would go through a cycle of IVF, but after my eggs were extracted they would be fertilized with donor sperm before they were frozen. Scientifically speaking, she tells me, the technology is less risky than egg freezing because the process has been around longer and is therefore more refined. Embryos are not as delicate as eggs, so they can better withstand the freezing technique, and therefore the pregnancy rates from frozen embryos are much higher than from frozen eggs.

Although the birth rate for embryos created from thawed eggs hovers around 4 percent for women who both froze their eggs and are trying to get pregnant under the age of thirty-five, the birth rate for embryos created with a woman's own fresh eggs and either her partner's or donor sperm prior to freezing are much higher: 28 percent for women trying to get pregnant between the ages of thirty-five and thirty-seven, 23 percent between thirty-eight and forty, and 15 percent between forty and forty-two. These success rates are only slightly lower than those for women going through IVF using embryos that have never been frozen. It makes sense to me now. (Of course, the women who turn to IVF generally do so because of fertility problems. The success rates may well be higher for otherwise fertile women interested in freezing eggs or embryos as insurance for the future.)

As my doctor tells me more about freezing embryos, I realize that although it may be statistically more promising than freezing eggs, it is also much more complicated. It means either having to use sperm donated by a male friend or buying donor sperm from a sperm bank. It also means limiting the possibilities significantly. If I freeze my eggs, I will be leaving open the possibility of getting pregnant later with that perfect man I hope to meet—an option that goes out the window with frozen embryos. If I have my eggs fertilized with donor sperm before freezing them, I could use them later if I decide to become a single mother. I could also use them if it turns out that Mr. Right and I don't meet until after my natural fertility has expired—in which case Mr. Right would also have to be perfectly willing to have a child that was not biologically his. Or we could use donor eggs with his sperm—but would I be perfectly willing to accept that? The mind boggles.

"Have you ever thought about where you might get the sperm?" asks my doctor.

No. I hadn't thought about *any* of this—egg freezing, embryo freezing, donor sperm—until very recently. And now I feel like I've stepped into a science fiction movie. Except it's my life in New York in 2004. My head is spinning.

When I get home, I check my e-mail.

"Hi, Rachel. I'm a consultant with Extend Fertility, and I'd like to offer you a free consultation."

Two days later: "Hi Rachel, we've launched a new website called Laterbaby.org. Please join."

I type "egg freezing" into Google and hundreds of headline and advertisement links pop up. A 2002 story in the *Wall Street Journal* announces "Fertility Clinic Set to Open First Commercial Egg Bank—Controversial Facility Will Target Women Waiting for Mr. Right." The story quotes Dr. Thomas Kim, the director of CHA Fertility in Los Angeles: "We are buying time for them [women in their thirties] by banking their eggs." Another article, entitled "The Big Chill" on the *Forbes* website, explains that "there are 5 million single, childless women in their 30s in the U.S., three times as many as in their mothers' generation," and a piece in *Newsweek* says that even though the technology is still considered experimental "it may not stop single thirtysomethings from lining up with their credit cards and their dreams."

And then there are advertisements: "Find the lowest price for egg freezing and much much more," one site tempts. A site called SaveMyEggs.com leads me to the Florida Institute for Reproductive Medicine, which claims to have "the highest pregnancy rate for frozen eggs in the country." Another link says, "Relax. Take a deep breath. We have the answers you seek" and leads to FertilityTomorrow.com, a clinic that dubs itself "the premier provider of female fertility preservation in the industry."

Why the marketing frenzy? Consider that there are 5 million single women in their thirties in the United States. If each of these women paid for a cycle of IVF at $15,000, plus egg storage fees, a $75 *billion* dollar market would exist for egg freezing. Of course, it's unlikely that every woman in her thirties will freeze her eggs, but even if only 10 percent decided to do so, the potential earnings would be massive.

Investment in reproductive science by private investors and venture capitalists has risen significantly in the past five years. Since 2003 Jorn Lyshoel, an analyst with Pareto Securities in Norway, told me that almost every company that makes the tools for in vitro fertilization—petri dishes, freezing chemicals, and so on—an $80 million global market, is now working on the tools needed for egg freezing.

In this overheated market, it's very hard to separate the real science from the speculative frenzy. So I decide to visit with Dr. Nicole Noyes, the endocrinologist and ob-gyn at NYU Fertility Center with whom I previously spoke about my FSH blood test. Dr. Noyes and her team are just beginning to focus their research efforts on egg freezing. They are not yet aggressively selling egg freezing to the public like Extend Fertility, but she has launched a research study.

I meet her at her apartment on the Upper East Side of Manhattan, and we sit in her sunny kitchen over tea. It's midday, and Dr. Noyes has already sent her three children off to school, finished her surgical schedule, and completed an advanced yoga class. A few days ago, she also achieved her clinic's first pregnancy from frozen eggs.

I explain my situation, and she quickly nods her head. No doubt she's heard this story a thousand times over. In fact, one of the main reasons she decided to embark on a study of egg freezing is that she became frustrated by hearing so many women blame themselves for their panic over their fertility.

She tells me the story of a thirty-eight-year-old patient, an investment banker on Wall Street.

"She's on a busy career track and not in love," she says. "She came to me and asked, 'Should I marry a man who I don't love or should I never have a kid?' Now she is going to freeze her eggs, and she might be able to wait two more years to see if Mr. Right comes along.

"Or if you're studying to be a doctor and you're not going to be done with your residency until you're thirty-three, and you haven't met your husband, is it so crazy to freeze your eggs?" she continues. "This is about intellectualizing your biology."

Dr. Noyes has recently returned from an international course in egg freezing taught by Dr. Eleanora Porcu, the scientist at the University of Bologna who invented the technology. In Italy, Dr. Noyes observed firsthand the dangerous hype surrounding egg freezing. She heard dozens of American doctors talking about offering this new technology and advertising it on their websites immediately.

Companies like Extend Fertility want to get egg-freezing technology to market precisely because of this flood of excitement. While the technology is in an experimental phase, it's essential to recruit "early adopters." Although these women have a fairly low chance of getting pregnant with the technology in its early stages, the knowledge gleaned from these patients will ensure that the technology improves. Extend Fertility—and its competitors—are in one sense aggressively advertising for test subjects who will, at their own great expense, help doctors work the bugs out of this technology.

The very real danger that anxious women will be preyed on by overpromising doctors is exactly why the American Society for Reproductive Medicine has not yet sanctioned the technology as being ready for prime time. Dr. Fred Fritz, the chairman of the board of the society and a professor of obstetrics and gynecology at the University of North Carolina at Chapel Hill told me that "the results we have come from pioneering clinics in the field. It's not a safe assumption that what can be achieved by the leaders can be duplicated in a wider application."

None of the clinics selling egg freezing are evil marketers, but it is important to know who the leaders in the research are, and to keep in mind that there is a profit motive. Barry Behr, an assistant professor of obstetrics and gynecology and director of the IVF lab at Stanford University who was the original consultant to Extend Fertility when Christy Jones was initially launching her company, is currently heading up an independent research study of the technology. He explains that because U.S. clinics live and die by their success rates, the competition to get the egg-freezing technology to market is pushing many American doctors, including ones at clinics in the Extend Fertility network, to publish only their most positive results. This in turn contributes to the false impression of the technology's viability.

"I don't think anyone is lying," he says. "What's occurring is that patients with high probability for success are being recruited into studies. These patients on the whole don't represent the kind of patients who most need this technology." Most of the studies that companies like Extend Fertility rely on are based on success rates using the eggs of fertile women in their twenties. The reality is that most women who seek out egg freezing are in their mid- to late thirties. In fact, to date there have been *no* research studies published on the viability of egg freezing for women over the age of thirty-five—and yet it is exactly that demographic that Christy Jones targeted when she hired a marketing firm to send out her promotional postcards.

Even though Dr. Noyes has recently embarked on just such a study, she believes that without solid research to prove the technology's effectiveness for women over thirty-five, physicians should not be marketing it. She herself will not begin offering the technology until she's completed her first research protocol and achieved a few more pregnancies from frozen eggs. She advises me to wait a year before I embark on freezing eggs or embryos. By then, she hopes, the technology will have improved. And since my FSH numbers are good, she thinks I can afford to wait.

"When is the best time to do it?" I ask.

"Thirty-five, thirty-six, thirty-seven is probably when you should do it," she says. "Even if you freeze them at thirty-five, meet someone at thirty-six, and have a baby, then you may feel rushed to have a second. I see women all the time who had one and then got stuck. If you freeze, you have the option to have one at forty-one."

I decide to listen to Dr. Noyes and wait a year or so for the technology to improve. And for my bank account to grow.

In the meantime, I remain curious about freezing embryos—and particularly about the issue of sperm donors. At this point, my interest is primarily intellectual. I've been dating Nick, the professor, for only a few months, so I'm pretty sure it's a bit early to ask him to lend me some sperm so we can freeze our fashion-forward offspring.

I decide to investigate embryo freezing by following up with a contact I'd learned of a few months earlier. A health writer friend had told me about a young psychiatrist named Nancy Vitali* who, a year earlier, had gone through the process of choosing a sperm donor and freezing embryos.

Nancy and I meet for lunch at a café just off lower Fifth Avenue, around the corner from her office. She is a sporty blond with a cropped, angular haircut that makes her look like she might be as comfortable carting kids around the suburbs in an SUV as she would be hanging out in a downtown club. She is wearing a black knit paperboy hat that she cocks to the side when she sits down at the table. She immediately tells me that she is in the midst of training for her second Iron Man triathlon, and upon spotting my raised eyebrow quickly begins to explain:

"Oh, I run. I once ran a hundred miles along the Great Wall of China. My family is very traditional and male oriented. That's why I play sports and I'm driven to do a lot."

Nancy is forty-two and single. After a few minutes of small talk about her training, life in New York, and her next race—an Iron Man in Hawaii—I plunge in and ask her why she thinks she's still on her own.

"I was never that interested in getting married," she says.

When she was thirty-nine, she ended a four-year engagement to a man ten years younger. Even though they loved each other very much, she told me, they were incompatible when it came to thinking about the way they each wanted to live and raise children. He wanted to live in the suburbs; she wanted to live in the city. They fought a lot over money.

"If we had gotten married and had kids, it would have been a disaster," she says. "Love was not enough."

After the relationship ended, however, she began to worry about her fertility. A doctor friend took her to a medical seminar that laid out the facts. She had never really seriously considered them before, she tells me. A year later, she started to talk to her therapist about having a child on her own. She decided that if a year went by and she still hadn't met someone, she would start looking for a sperm donor.

Nancy took her options seriously; she even went to a meeting of the group Single Mothers by Choice to educate herself. But after hearing stories about how hard it was to date with a baby, about juggling work and childcare, and about the financial sacrifices so many women in the room were making, she says she wanted to run screaming out the door. And she did.

"I didn't have time to walk the dog, let alone have a kid, work like a dog, and manage a nanny," Nancy confesses.

Nancy grew up in 1970s suburban New Jersey, the only daughter of four children. Her father was a doctor, and her mother ran his office. She hints that her mother was an angry housewife, which might be one reason why she has shied away from a traditional marriage and family so far.

Even though Nancy still isn't a hundred percent sure that she wants to become a mother, she likes the idea of keeping her options open. To do this, she chose another kind of physical challenge. She decided to run a race against biological time— by freezing it. It was a procedure that was unheard of among her peers, but it made perfect sense to her.

Nancy began talking to a number of her male friends about donating their sperm to her. Most declined, she says, except for her personal trainer, who agreed to do it—so long as they write a contract establishing that he would have no emotional or financial responsibility for the child if she decided to un-freeze and implant the embryos in the future.

"He had the right stuff to be the biological father," she says. "He was smart and athletic, but we were just friends."

And so they began the process. Very quickly, though, they learned that it wasn't as simple as him going in the bathroom with a sexy magazine, emerging with a vial of sperm, and handing it over to her doctor. The fertility clinic would have to hold the sperm for months and put it through countless genetic tests to make sure it was clear of sexually transmitted or genetic diseases. He also had to sign countless legal documents promising that he wouldn't come back and try to claim custody in the future.

Nancy admits that even her own doctor was puzzled about why she was putting herself through such a complicated set of procedures. "Why don't you just have sex with the guy and get pregnant?" he asked her.

"Why didn't you?" I ask, thinking that it did seem a little less complicated.

But Nancy was offended by her doctor's comment. She didn't want to become a single mother. The whole reason that she was freezing embryos was that she wanted to buy time to meet the person with whom she could raise a family in the context of a loving relationship—even if that meant sacrificing the father's biological relationship to the child. She says that she's an idealist and doesn't want to start her family until the situation is right.

"I have so many friends who are married, living in the suburbs with their families, and miserable," she says.

But Nancy's personal trainer backed out of the deal once he realized how complicated the process was. And indeed, ever since the advent of in vitro fertilization, sperm donation has become a very complicated area of the law. In a 2002 case in Texas, Augusta Roman, a registered nurse, found herself in a custody battle over her unborn child. A day before she was to have embryos implanted in her uterus, her husband, Randy Roman, decided that he didn't want to become a father and that he wanted to end their marriage. His decision set in motion *Roman v. Roman*, one of the first divorce custody battles over a frozen embryo to go to the Texas Supreme Court. (In the end the Texas Supreme Court refused to hear the case because it turned out the couple signed a consent form stating that the embryos would be discarded in the case of divorce.) The case, however, raised new questions that many older parents could face: Whose embryo is it? And whose choice is it to begin a pregnancy?

Once her trainer dropped out, Nancy decided to go to a sperm bank.

"It legally allows you to have embryos that are truly your own," she explains.

Nancy spent months searching through the files of the sperm bank for the right donor.

"It was practically as hard as dating," she explains. "Most of the guys sounded really nerdy; smart, but myopic. It was a total turnoff."

But then it hit her that she was going about the choosing process in the wrong way. It didn't matter whether she liked these candidates; after all, she wasn't dating them. What mattered was whether they had desirable traits to help her to create healthy embryos.

"It's a process totally different from choosing love or letting love choose you," she tells me. "In a way, it's totally objectifying."

She ended up choosing an MIT student who had a good medical history.

"I fell in love with his baby picture," she says.

The little boy who would be her potential baby's father had curly brown hair and a devilish face.

"He reminded me of my ex-fiancé," she confesses, blushing.

She also paid an additional fee for "identity-release" sperm, which means that her potential child will have the legal option to look up his or her father's identity when he or she turns eighteen.

Nancy went through an IVF cycle and produced eight eggs. Her doctor created six embryos, which he then froze. She now pays a yearly storage fee to keep her frozen embryos in a special container until she is ready to use them.

I ask Nancy if she thinks her decision was worth the trouble, if it made her feel better about her options. Less anxious?

"Totally," she says, with no doubt in her voice. "I have six babies. I now feel like I have the option even when I'm fifty, and I don't have to be as anxious about trying to meet someone. It just made me more relaxed," she says.

"How old do you think is too old to become a mother?" I ask her.

"I would do it at fifty-six if I'm in as good shape as I'm in now."

The idea that egg freezing could create a wave of fifty-six-year-old new mothers gives me some pause. In recent years, celebrities like Elizabeth Edwards and Joan Lunden have made the news by having babies in their fifties. And of course there is the story of the sixty-six-year-old woman in Romania. I can't help but think that this is problematic. If an older mother becomes sick, for instance, that's a lot of responsibility to put on a young child. Should teenagers be put in the situation of having to take care of aging parents? A statement that Dr. Schiffman made in our initial meeting has now become a recurring thought. *"This is not about you, it's about your child."*

Even if technology makes it possible to have a child at a more advanced age, shouldn't consideration be given to the quality of life of that child?

I also wanted to know whether freezing embryos has any adverse affects on the development of the fetus. Later, I learned that there is a broad difference of opinion on this issue; some researchers have found a higher occurrence of certain cancers and genetic abnormalities in "frosties"; others think these increases are so microscopic that it's hard to link them to cryopreservation or advanced reproductive technology directly.

Of course, men having been having children into their sixties for years and years, but traditionally with much younger women. Reproductive technology is creating a new "normal," and I honestly don't know what the socially legitimate age is

As my brother, a biological determinist, recently put it, the sole reason humans exist is to create more humans. So if we don't have children, then there is something broken in our nature. The comment made me furious. I thought about the people I know who have consciously decided that parenting is not the right role for them and have therefore chosen to live what we now call "child free." If we are living in an age when we can intellectualize our biology by choosing not to get pregnant, to freeze eggs or embryos, then maybe these conscious choices are part of biological evolution as well.

"Are you sure that you want to be a mother if you've waited this long?" I ask.

"Yes," she says. "I know I have that impulse. I feel like I want to go check in on my embryos all the time."

But then she pauses, staring at the table. After an awkward moment of silence, she looks up and into my eyes.

"To answer your question," she begins. "I really don't know, but I want to keep my options open. Part of me says 'do it now.' Women who make a third of my income do it alone. I just really want a partner."

~

A few weeks after my meeting with Nancy, I come home after a date with the persistent professor with the distinct feeling that it was our last. I could tell by the way he was looking around the restaurant at other women that his heart was not in it; neither was mine. We enjoy each other's company, but it's clear that we aren't falling in love with each other and that we're just biding our time. I plan to call him for a post mortem the next day, but tonight something more pressing is on my mind. I am slightly tipsy, and I decide to call Will*, one of my closest male friends.

for a woman to declare herself too old. After all, two centuries ago women gave birth much younger and died in their forties. They never expected to see their children through college or middle age, so who is to say that experiencing these life stages with your child makes you a better or even a good parent? Is giving a child the foundation for a good life when they are young sufficient?

"I'm a late bloomer," says Nancy, slightly defensively. "It's not right for me now. Right now I'm busy with my patients, working on a paper, doing analytical training, and training for an Iron Man. It's overwhelming. I'm also making changes in my life in relationships with men. I think I could be a great mother and give a kid a lot of love, but there's no partner and I really don't want to do it alone."

I look at Nancy and wonder whether in fact she may just not want to have children. The social pressure on women to become mothers is strong; in some ways it represents the ultimately feminine act. Motherhood is no longer the mandate it was in earlier generations, but it seems to have become a status symbol. Gossip magazines now announce every new celebrity baby bump with the same pomp and circumstance as a high-profile wedding or divorce, and fashion magazines portray models and celebrities side-by-side with immaculately dressed babies as if they were accessories on par with the latest Prada bag or Gucci high heels. Certainly, I feel the social pressure myself; whenever I hear the news that a friend is pregnant, my desire to have a child gets stronger. I have to remind myself that becoming a mother should not be about achieving status or keeping up with my peers. Despite all of the other advances of feminism, it remains very hard for a woman, even in the most socially liberal environments, to proclaim that she doesn't want children—it's considered unnatural.

Will and I met when we were colleagues at a start-up magazine in the late 1990s, and we have remained close confidants in everything from our love lives to our careers ever since. At points in our relationship, we have tried to be lovers. To be more precise: we've had sex a few times when we were both feeling lonely or confused. But the idea of being boyfriend and girlfriend, or more, never seemed right to either of us. I know that a lot of women say this preemptively as a way of protecting themselves from the fact that they really are in love in these kind of relationships. And I'll admit that I've probably thought more seriously about the possibility of becoming a couple than he has, mostly because men seem more capable than women of separating sex and love. Once, when I was very lonely, I even told Will that I thought I might be in love with him. But I think I was confusing the fact that I loved him with the idea of being in love with him—these things can get complicated in relationships with male friends. The fact is that when I began to think about the realities of us living together as a couple day-to-day, it felt totally wrong and strange. One thing that modern love has taught me is that there are many flavors of intimacy, and you often have to try out a bunch of different roles with a man before you settle into the one that works best for your relationship. Will and I have now settled as friends, and we are about as close as I am with many of my girlfriends. Strangely, all our experiences and history add up to more continuity and stability than I've had with many of my actual boyfriends. He feels like family.

These days, Will is taking a break from the New York rat race. A few months ago, he drove across the country to "get off the grid," as he put it. He ended up at a meditation retreat center and organic farm near the ocean in northern California. Now he is living in a trailer and spends hours a day gardening or sitting on a meditation pillow contemplating the questions that most of us just don't have time to think about. Once, when we were chatting on phone, he idly asked, "You know you're going to die, right?"

Sperm had been on my mind ever since my conversation with Nancy, and I figured this was the kind of thing about which a man who spends hours a day on a pillow meditating might have something interesting to say. What I didn't quite anticipate, in my slightly boozy, romantically dissatisfied state, was asking him to be my sperm donor.

"If I don't find the right man in the next few years, would you give me some of your sperm?" I blurt out.

"Are you making a pass at me?" he asks.

"No."

But I can hear the excitement in his voice, like I've just ensured his genetic legacy.

He laughs nervously. "Do you realize what you just asked me?" he responds. "You just asked me if I want to have a child with you."

"No," I say. "I've asked for some of your sperm. I just want to borrow some of your genetic material so I don't miss my chance to become a mother."

What I'm saying feels half real, but the words have come out, so now I'm curious to find out where the conversation goes. One thing I know is that Will is a serious person who will give the question proper thought. And that's what he promises to do. He's flattered that I've asked him to play such an important role in my life, he tells me, but before getting back to me he needs to spend some more time sitting on his pillow.

# 3

## Shopping for Mr. Goodsperm

I'm more relieved than heartbroken after my short-lived relationship with Nick, the fashionista professor, is over—except for the night I go to the engagement party for my good friends Katie* and Leo*. It's a crisp evening in early March, and a small group of us have gathered in their elegant living room in SoHo to raise glasses of champagne. The lights of the financial district glitter through a big picture window in the background. As the toasts wind down, I happily watch Katie lay her head on her fiancé's shoulder with an expression of comfort and relief. It all seems perfect for her, and I feel a tinge of envy—especially because I'm there without a date. While deep down I'm happy to be free of the weight of a relationship that was going nowhere, I feel self-conscious being alone in this cluster of couples.

I'm sitting on the sofa with Katie's aunt, a woman with a quirky glamour, whom I love as much for her eccentricity as I do for her rational advice about love and life. When she gives

me that look that says "What's happening in your love life?" I
tell her that I just ended a short relationship, and am open to
fix-ups. After a pause, I blurt out: "And I'm thinking about
freezing embryos if I don't meet someone soon."

She looks at me like I've just beamed down from Mars and
started talking in a different language. I start laughing, realizing that I've become so steeped in these new ideas about reproduction that I'm beginning to see them as normal, when in
fact, for most people, especially older people, they still seem
totally cutting edge.

"Why don't you set a deadline?" she suggests in a practical
tone. "If you don't meet a man by the time you're thirty-six,
start to pursue pregnancy on your own. That way you'll have
your baby, the pressure will be off, and you can focus on finding true love without the biological imperative."

It sounds like odd advice, but after all of the conversations
I've been having it's beginning to make more sense to me. I explain to her, though, that I'm having trouble giving up my ideal.

"Give it up," she says. "Look around. Almost half these
people will be divorced—or miserable—in ten years."

She's right, of course. The national divorce rate is now
hovering around 43 percent. Giving up the romantic ideal and
setting a deadline would probably help me relax a bit and stop
scrutinizing every man I talk with as a potential father for my
child. I know that feeling sized up in this way makes men quite
uncomfortable. A male friend once told me that he had had a
first date with a woman who was clearly looking for a baby
daddy, and it felt like a job interview. She even asked him if he
would be the kind of dad who changed diapers.

Still, it's really hard for me to imagine raising a child on my
own, even though it's something I want to seriously consider.
There are just so many questions: How would I conceive? If

Will agrees to donate, would we have sex, or would he just hand over a vial? If he doesn't, would I go to a sperm bank and choose an anonymous donor? And how would I manage financially? How would I negotiate single motherhood and my career? How would I date with a baby at home? How would my dates feel about me being a single mother?

I know I have a lot to think through. And I realize that I am very lucky to live at a time when I can seriously consider the option of single motherhood. America has come a long way in its thinking about single mothers. Being a single mother is no longer a source of shame; often, it is an emblem of female empowerment. The cultural stigma of the "illegitimate child" seems to have all but disappeared. Now it seems hard to believe how controversial it was in 1992, when the title character of network television's *Murphy Brown* famously became a single mother. On the show *Friends*, Rachel had a baby on her own with help from Ross, her friend and former lover. In a now-famous scene in *Sex and the City*, Miranda triumphantly decides against an abortion, not because she is "pro-life" but because, single or not, she is a mature adult, and this is her chance to become a mother. And pre–Brad Pitt, Angelina Jolie turned single motherhood into an international political mission.

Single motherhood isn't just a trend on TV and in Hollywood; it is a burgeoning phenomenon across the country. Between 1970 and 2006, the number of households headed by single women grew from 3 million to 10 million. An estimated 50,000 children are born to single mothers every year, and around one third of the mothers are women who have *chosen* to become pregnant on their own.

A whole new industry has emerged to serve the needs of these women. It is a micro-economy of single "mom-trepreneurs," and the online constellation of help is, for the most part, inspiring.

Type "single mothers" into Google and thousands of links pop up for every political, social, and sexual orientation. There are sites for shared babysitting, shared housing, financial advice, self-published guidebooks, single-mom rock bands, even a company started by single moms that sells shirts featuring a picture of a pole dancer and the slogan "I $upport $ingle Moms." (More power to those pole dancers, but I have to say that if I found myself shaking it for dirty old men—or even not-so-dirty and not-so-old men—in order to pay the rent and feed my baby, I would not consider it progress.)

The most vital evidence of the emergence of single motherhood as a socially acceptable option is the growth and visibility of the advocacy and support organization Single Mothers by Choice, which Jane Mattes, a psychoanalyst, founded when she became a single mom in 1980. The women in this social set are turning to friends, gay and straight, to current and former lovers, and to Internet sperm banks to help them conceive because they are ready to have children, Mr. Right is not yet in the picture, and they don't want to lose the chance to have a child.

As soon as I discovered the group's website, I decided to call Jane to find out more.

"Are you pregnant?" she asks within the first minute of our conversation.

No, I tell her, I'm just thinking about and researching the option.

She immediately launches into her story. In 1979, Jane discovered that she had gotten pregnant by a man she describes as a "great guy to date when someone more serious wasn't around." When she told him that she planned to keep her baby, he said she would make a wonderful mother, but that he had no interest in marrying her or participating in the child's life. At the time, she had a successful private practice and financial stability, so the decision to have and raise the child on her own seemed possible.

Even though it was the beginning of the boom-boom eighties, and shoulder-padded women were climbing the ranks of male-dominated professions, becoming a single mother was a radical decision.

"I was doing something really out there. And I'm not that kind of person. I'm a very mild-mannered good girl—I don't like to rock the boat. But I looked at it as a practical decision."

Mattes was thirty-six when she got pregnant. She says that she had wanted to have a child for a number of years and was even considering adopting, so when she became pregnant, she decided this was her chance. Most of her friends were already parents, and she wanted to keep up with the trajectory of their lives. Like them, she was done with her life as a single woman. She was ready for a new phase, ready to focus her energies on raising a child.

"I thought, I have patients, plants, a cat. So I'll have a baby. How hard can it be?"

But after her son was born, she was shocked to realize how naïve she had been. She was constantly exhausted and had little emotional support. But the hardest part, she tells me, was the way other people reacted—all of the odd looks, and the questions.

"People's jaws would drop," she says. "You could see them thinking, 'What's the equation? You're not sixteen. You're not a divorcée. You're a successful thirty-seven-year-old woman. What do you mean there's no father?'"

Jane was insulted—worried because she didn't want her son to feel different from other kids because he didn't have a father. So six months after her son was born, one Sunday afternoon she

decided to throw a coffee and cake gathering for a few other single mothers she had been connected to through friends.

It wasn't meant to be any sort of feminist awareness-raising
session, she explains. She was just looking for other women to
talk with about the experience of raising a child on their own
in their thirties.

"I wanted to know if it was me having such a hard time, or
if it was just really, really hard to be a single mother."

"So what did you learn?" I ask.

"It's just really hard!" she answers, laughing. "But we found
out that in some ways it was easier than being married. I started
to learn that married women complained about their husbands,
who would come home and, instead of offering emotional support, they would expect a clean house and a nice dinner."

But it had to be even harder than the hard part of being
married, I thought. If her son cried in the night, she would
have to get up to comfort him each and every time—no taking
turns. If a meeting ran late at work, she would have to solve the
problem on her own—no husband to pinch hit. She would
have to take her child to school every morning, deal with every
tantrum, every bout of the flu, all on her own, without a partner to turn to for comfort and support. The more I thought
about it, the harder it seemed.

"You're it twenty-four hours a day. It was hard to be on all
the time," she says.

Of course Jane hired babysitters, but she said that she had
bad luck with nannies. Her mother ended up doing a lot of the
caretaking when Jane was at work.

"I'm her only child," Jane explains, "and she was late in becoming a grandmother just like I was late in becoming a
mother. She was over the moon to be a part of it. I had to throw
her out of the house when my son was eleven."

By that time, her coffee-klatch support group had begun to grow and evolve, and she had discovered that having a community of other single-mother families more than normalized her son's life. It provided a lot of the emotional support that she believed other women were getting from their more traditional households.

Twenty-eight years later, Single Mothers by Choice has grown into an international organization with over two thousand active members and over 11,000 who have joined since the group's inception. There are close to thirty chapters, formal and informal, worldwide. In the most liberal cities, such as New York and Los Angeles, the stigma she faced in the mid-1980s is nearly gone. But there is also a growing number of SMCs, as the members call themselves, in more conservative parts of the country, like Dallas, Texas. In Texas, single motherhood is still considered a radical choice, and many doctors won't artificially inseminate or perform in vitro fertilization.

Jane's story and the growing number of SMCs seem revolutionary—a whole new way of raising children—and even though I'm frightened by the prospect of taking on the amount of responsibility single motherhood requires, our conversation is inspiring. Single motherhood no longer feels as foreign to me as when Dr. Schiffman first brought it up in our initial meeting. Jane even tells me that many SMCs end up finding Mr. Right and getting married after they have a child.

"People who really want to get married seem to get married," she says, in a reassuring tone.

I close my eyes and start to imagine a new scene. *I'm in Central Park pushing my adorable baby in a jogger stroller. He or she drops a toy. A cute guy picks it up and starts chasing after me. He is a single divorced dad . . .*

As my mind shifts from panic at the thought of how much work single motherhood would actually entail to bucolic fantasies of locking eyes with the perfect man over a Bugaboo, I realize I have a whole lot more to think about. Apparently Jane realizes that too, because she tells me that a lot of women get involved in Single Mothers by Choice at this stage. She calls them "thinkers," and the organization even runs meetings that focus specifically on the questions that I'm considering. As a psychoanalyst, she also sees individual patients exploring these questions. She tells me that while she loves that women are considering alternative means of forming families, she doesn't want anyone to think it's a magic solution. Before talking about the choice of single motherhood, she says, she encourages her patients to explore first the deeper issues of what's getting in the way of having a relationship.

On a sunny Sunday afternoon, I take the subway to the Upper West Side to attend my first "thinkers" meeting. I walk into the basement of the Goddard Riverside Community Center on Amsterdam Avenue. Dozens of women in their thirties and forties are huddled in small groups. Some are bouncing babies on their laps, some are pregnant. They are laughing and chatting and look like they are having fun.

The first thing that strikes me is how pretty so many of the women are. I know I shouldn't be thinking this, but my immediate reaction is to wonder why they're all single. I'm shocked at myself: this is the kind of logic I hate when I see it in other people, the assumption that single women are single because there's something wrong with them. Of course, it's not just other people who think this—I've caught myself falling into this trap before, wondering if the reason I'm still single is that there's something really wrong with me. As horrified as I am by my own sexism, I find it strangely reassuring that the women are not freaks but rather lovely, normal people.

We sit around the room in a circle of chairs. A mother of twins stands up and asks everyone to introduce themselves. As we go around the room, no one identifies herself by her profession like most people do in New York. Instead, each woman states her age and when and how she got pregnant. Those of us who don't have babies identify ourselves as thinkers.

There's the leader, a forty-seven-year-old who had twins with donor eggs and donor sperm, and the forty-six-year-old who got pregnant naturally after the second intrauterine insemination and named her blue-eyed daughter after her father. There's the forty-four-year-old who miscarried three times before she got pregnant with a donor she knew; the thirty-nine-year-old who got pregnant on her fifth IUI; the forty-two-year-old who had four miscarriages and one round of Clomid before getting pregnant with twins on her fourth IVF—and then reducing the pregnancy to one child; and the forty-two-year-old who is seventeen weeks pregnant with twins from donor sperm after one IUI. "I'm feeling really lucky and really queasy," she says, breaking into tears.

After the introductions, we break into smaller groups; the mothers are in one group, the pregnant women in another, and thinkers and tryers in a third. I drag my chair over to the circle of thinkers and tryers. The conversation shoots around from fears of financial instability to practical advice on donor sperm and reproductive technology to frustrations with dating.

"I'm sick of waiting. I'm just ready to be a mom," announces a tanned and trim thirty-four-year-old psychologist.

"You feel totally lost when it's your own life. It's hard to think objectively of all of this," says another thirty-four-year-old half-Jewish and half-Indian doctor who is so beautiful that I can't stop staring at her.

Another woman, a forty-one-year-old Ph.D. student dressed in flowing Indian pants, says she's tried everything: online dating, set-ups, even a professional matchmaker. She's hoping a child will take off the pressure to get married and also launch her into new social circles where she can meet other single parents.

I begin talking to a pretty painter from Brooklyn who is wearing a black, low-cut dress. She's thirty-eight and has been dating someone on and off for the last year. This is her second meeting, and she's thinking about getting artificially inseminated with donor sperm next month.

"I'm still not sure what road to go down—keep dating him and hope he commits soon or just go for this on my own," she says. "Each choice is so different emotionally."

One of the themes that comes up often in these groups is the idea of "giving up the dream"—facing the reality that by starting a family as a single woman, you have to put the cart in front of the horse. This, of course, does not mean Mr. Right will never come galloping in.

The painter tells me that part of her feels like raising a child on her own will actually be easier.

"I'm very strong willed, and I don't like to compromise," she says. "I'm the product of a divorce. My parents were always fighting about their relationship—and it was never about me. If I do this on my own, it can be totally about the child, not the relationship."

At that moment, Sonya*, the forty-six-year-old who got pregnant naturally, walks over to the group and hands me her year-old baby. I ask her if she ever gets scared. She says she was freaked out in the beginning, but now has a great support network of other single girlfriends who come over to babysit when she needs a break. She hasn't started dating again, but wants to as soon as she starts feeling more confident about her postpregnancy body.

I'm most curious about how these women plan to tell their children that a donor created them and they have no father. My father, for better and for worse, is one of the most important figures in my life; he has shaped who I am in so many ways—both my strengths and my weaknesses. I can't imagine what my life would be like if he had been some mysterious figure my mom referred to as "the donor." And it's also hard for me to imagine saying that to my child.

"I'll cross the bridge when I get to it," says Sonya. "I guess I'll say something like, 'There are lots of different kinds of families now. Two mommies. Two daddies. We're a family with one mommy. Look around—there are a lot of us.'"

The painter jumps into the conversation. "My biggest issue is whether it's fair to have a child because I want one—knowing that he or she is going to grow up without a father," she says, thinking aloud. "But I guess there's no guarantee that if I were married that he or she wouldn't end up growing up in a single household anyway."

"I think most of us have waited so long that the child is the focus," says Sonya. "Most of the time people see that you're doing a good job alone and they admire you."

An artsy-looking woman with her hair tied up in a blue scarf walks over to our group and places her toddler on the table to change her diaper. Every few seconds she leans over and says, "Hello, my sweet love," and kisses her stomach.

I ask her if she ever feels stigmatized.

"I don't want anyone to think that my kid is undisciplined because of the single mom thing, so I'm probably too hard on her," she says. "Because I'm a single mother, I'm open game. My parents are always commenting on *my* parenting and never on my siblings', who are in traditional families."

"Oh, I don't feel that way," says Sonya. "My attitude is, my entire extended family is their family. Children need to learn from all adults.

"I think it's easier being single than married," Sonya continues. "I know so many married moms who just bitch about their husbands. There are great husbands and fathers out there, but that is a whole other relationship you have to keep up. People say that you miss the little joys like, 'Oh, did you see that smile?' But I have a nanny to share that with—I feel like *she's* my husband."

In her monthly SMC newsletter, Jane always addresses the "daddy issue." "It is essential in any discussion that you be able to differentiate in your own mind between the concept of a 'daddy,' which is a social role, and a 'father,' which is a biological one," she writes. "Everyone has a father, but not everyone has a dad."

When we talked, Jane told me that she made sure her son had a godfather. He had dinner with them regularly and took her son to the park every week for nine years. She also enrolled him in the Big Brother organization. She told me that her main worry was dealing with separation.

"Separating from one child is harder," she says. "And it's easier for one child to cling to the mother. You have to give your child a really strong foundation to enable them to separate from you. It's harder, I think, because they are obviously leaving you alone if you're not married. At one point my son said, 'It's not healthy for me to be so close to you, Mom,' and I said, 'You're right. Thank you.'"

Given how much time SMCs spend thinking and talking about the issue of how to make up for the absence of a dad in their children's lives, I'm not surprised to find that studies show little evidence that these children are any less well-adjusted than children with dads. In 1998, the Sperm Bank of California published the first study on the children of donors. It concluded, decisively, that children brought up in one-parent homes were just as emotionally healthy as children brought up in two-parent homes. What mattered more to the children's emotional stability than the number of parents, or whether the parents were gay or straight, was whether their parents' relationships were satisfying and whether their parents could manage interpersonal conflict.

I leave the meeting thinking that single motherhood, though hard, is a possibility I should seriously consider if I don't meet the right person in a year or two. I could really relate to the women at the meeting. All of them were very independent-minded and extremely conscientious in their thinking about the right choices for themselves and for the children they had brought into the world. They were very honest about the challenges of single motherhood, but ultimately they all seemed really happy about the decision they had made.

The only thing that is giving me pause as I walk to the subway is what Jane had said to me about exploring more deeply the question of why I was single, what in me might be getting in the way of having a relationship. Becoming a single mother now would just be sidestepping that question, and regardless of what I decide about the timing of motherhood, I know that's an issue I need to resolve in the long term—and not just for myself;

if I have issues with intimacy, that would inevitably affect my relationship with my child, not just with potential partners.

So I decide to see Dr. Schiffman again. It's been six months since our last meeting.

"Still single. Still not pregnant," I say, breaking into nervous laughter as I enter the room.

"Do you still want to have a baby soon?" she asks.

I tell her about the conversation with my friends' mother and about the SMC meeting. She says I should really think in terms of worst-case scenarios, and again reminds me: *This is not about you. It's about your child.*

This comment prompts a new image to pop into my mind: *I'm totally alone. It's 4 a.m. My baby is sick and won't go back to sleep. I have to be at work in three hours. No one is there to help me.*

Dr. Schiffman asks me to think about some other scenarios too: What happens if in three years I meet someone who wants to have kids? How would I integrate my first child into that family? What about the complications of using a known sperm donor? What would happen if the donor met the child and feels a connection and demands custody?

"Even with a written legal document there is no guarantee that can't happen," she warns.

Dr. Schiffman raises her eyebrows and looks at me as if she's about to ask a difficult question. But instead, she begins to tell me the story of a thirty-three-year-old woman who came to her and said that she was thinking about getting pregnant on her own. She counseled the woman to think about taking a little more time to find a relationship or exploring why she is having trouble finding a relationship, rather than just skipping ahead and becoming a mother. I tell her that Jane Mattes has raised the same question about relationships and that I am genuinely confused about the answer. Some days I think I'm single just because of bad timing or luck—that it just happens that the right man for me hasn't come along yet. But on other days I do wonder if it goes deeper than that, if I am unconsciously undermining myself somehow in the way I relate to men or approach my relationships. These questions loom over me all the time, and I know I'm not going to resolve them instantly.

Dr. Schiffman assures me that merely by asking myself the questions and exploring my feelings I am taking an important step. Ultimately, however, the judgment over the timing of when to have a child is mine.

"It's not my role to play God," she says. "If you really want to have a baby on your own, I can't stop you."

~

I had accepted Jane's offer to send an e-mail to the members of Single Mothers by Choice, telling them that I'm doing research for a book and looking for single moms to talk to about their experiences. Pretty soon, my in-box is filled with friendly notes from single moms offering to talk about their experiences and even offering to let me hang out with them to see the everyday realities of raising a child alone.

One of the first women I hear from is Ann Holland*, a thirty-seven-year-old mother of two from Des Moines, Iowa. She writes that she became a single mom at the age of thirty, and in the casual tone of a good friend, signs off with, "Call anytime!" It's another hint of the strength of this new network.

I call the next day, but, oddly, the first thing she says is, "Can I call you back when my husband is home and watching the kids?"

I'm confused.

"I thought you said you were a single mom," I say.

"I was," she says.

It's a story I want to hear, so one weekend I fly to Des Moines to meet Ann and her family. I arrive on a snowy morning in early spring and check into a quaint red brick B&B near Ann's home in the Beaverdale section of the city. Even though she has a bad cold, she offers to pick me up and take me over to her house.

"One thing about having kids is that you're constantly getting their colds," she tells me as she pulls into the driveway of the B&B in her silver minivan. Ann is doll-like, with bright blue eyes, rosy cheeks, and soft, white, freckled skin. I feel comfortable with her immediately and hop into the front seat. Her two-year-old towheaded son, Sam*, is strapped in a car seat in the back, playing with a yellow truck.

We drive over to her house, a slate blue Victorian, where she lives with Sam, her daughter, Susie*, and her husband. In a toy-strewn living room, Ann introduces me to her husband of two years, Tim McGregory*, and her five-year-old daughter, Susie, who is lying upside down on the couch. Ann places her son on the couch and immediately Susie tries to push her little brother off. She is wearing a T-shirt that says "I can't live without my lipstick," and her eyelids are smeared with bright pink eye shadow and glitter.

"Look at me, Daddy! Look at me!" she calls.

"She's clearly not vain," says Ann, slightly embarrassed by her daughter's sassy behavior.

"It's hard to be a fancy girl," Susie says to her mom. "I'm not allowed to wear makeup to school yet," she says to me.

"She gets that attitude from me," says Tim.

Ann laughs, and then whispers to me, "Or the donor."

Tim, originally from Canada, is tall and thin, with short black hair and a quiet manner. After we all settle on the couch over cups of herbal tea, Ann leans back and turns up her palms.

"This is basically it," she says, pointing to her family. "We go to hockey games on Friday nights, sometimes, and Unitarian church services on Sunday. It's not like your glamorous city life."

"I also spend a lot of time alone in my tiny apartment," I tell her.

She laughs.

Ann describes herself as "very liberal," despite living in a state that is traditionally conservative. Iowa is 80 percent white, with a higher-than-average number of married households and one of the lowest divorce rates in the country. Ann herself was raised in a conservative Methodist family, but the route she took to get to the family she has now looks nothing like what she learned in her parents' church—even though an immaculate conception was involved.

Ann explains that when she was twenty-eight, she began dating Brett*, a tall blond lawyer on her volleyball team. Their romance ignited quickly, and within a few months they began talking about a future together. All around her, friends were getting married and having children. In Iowa, she says, many people marry right out of college. The average age of a first marriage in Iowa is around twenty-four, compared to twenty-six or twenty-seven in the rest of the country. She felt she was already off-track.

After Ann and Brett dated for a year, she began to pressure him to get engaged. He consented, but refused to tell his family.

Ann took this as a sign that he wasn't totally committed to the future of their relationship.

"One day we were talking about our wedding plans and he just came out and said 'I can't do this.'" He wasn't ready, he explained, and their commitment felt wrong. A few days later he broke up with her altogether.

Ann was devastated; it seemed like now it could be years before she started a family. Looking back, she admits that the relationship probably broke up for that very reason. They were *her* plans to start a family.

"I pushed him rather than letting him ask me to marry him," she acknowledges. "I knew I had more time, biologically, to have a child. But I thought if I started looking for someone, I could be forty by the time I had a baby, and I didn't want to wait any longer. My parents were desperate for grandchildren."

I ask her if she had made decisions based on her parents' biological clocks rather than her own.

"I don't think so," she answers.

I ask mostly because at times I have felt pressure from my parents to have a baby. Not that either of them has ever looked me in the eye and commanded me to have a baby, of course. But they do make a lot of comments about their friends with grandchildren and how happy they are. I suppose they may just be innocent comments, but at my age I certainly hear them as not-so-subtle hints.

Rather than taking more time to find a lasting relationship, Ann turned to her parents and told them that she still wanted to have a child and was thinking about doing it on her own. A few years earlier, she had worked with a local fertility doctor to donate some of her eggs to help infertile women, so she already felt very comfortable with the idea of separating the biology of conception from a love relationship.

"I wanted to make sure that my parents wouldn't be too freaked out," she says. "I thought if they were super freaked, I wouldn't do it, but they were super supportive."

Even though this decision was socially radical in their community, Ann's parents told her they would support her emotionally and by helping out with childcare.

"When my boyfriend and I were dating, my parents freaked out that we had premarital sex. This way, I didn't have to have sex to have my daughter, so in a way they were okay with it," she jokes.

Ann had a stable job at a large insurance company in Des Moines, and she was confident that she would be able to manage juggling work and motherhood on her own with the help of her family. So she went to see the same fertility doctor who helped her donate her eggs years earlier. He checked to make sure her reproductive system was still in working order. After reassuring her that everything seemed healthy, the doctor pointed her to a number of online catalogs of anonymous sperm donors. She began sorting through hundreds of profiles.

Choosing a sperm donor created a whole new set of choices. As it turns out, sperm shopping is not unlike dating services that offer online searches in order to match desired criteria.

The website of Ann's chosen sperm bank presented her with a menu of options. Depending on how much she wanted to pay, she could view in-depth medical profiles that would tell her everything from whether her donor had a history of heart disease in his family to whether his great aunt suffered from scoliosis. She could read long essays written by the donor himself that would tell her if he enjoyed taxidermy, dreamt of traveling to Inner Mongolia, or aspired to find a cure for cancer. A voice recording would give her an idea of whether his voice was high pitched or low and gruff. A baby picture would even give her a tiny glimpse of the physical features that could be mixed with her own genetic material.

At the California Cryobank, one of the largest sperm banks in the United States, a prospective parent can even spend an extra $75 to buy a Keirsey Temperament Sorter assessment of a potential donor. The donor is given a seventy-question test that places him in one of four temperament categories: rational, guardian, idealist, or artisan. The medical director of the bank likes to joke that anyone who purchases sperm from a donor will know more about the guy than he knows about his wife of forty years.

It used to be that sperm donation was a secretive business. In fact, in 1954 a court in Illinois ruled that even with the husband's consent artificial insemination was considered adultery and the child illegitimate. Later, the case was overturned, but the act was still stigmatized. A man could clandestinely make some extra cash by donating his sperm to an infertile couple or single woman. More typically, the mother's ob-gyn chose the sperm—often of his handsome tennis partner or the husband of a nurse—and the mother hoped for genetic health and good looks. The donor signed a waiver of anonymity, locked himself in a room with a cup and a sexy magazine, and never had to think about the emotional or genetic consequences again.

In his book, *The Genius Factory: The Curious History of the Nobel Prize Sperm Bank*, journalist David Plotz tells the story of Robert Graham, an eccentric scientist who dreamt of creating a smarter population by banking the sperm of Nobel Prize winners and subsequently lifted the veil on artificial insemination. The Repository for Germinal Choice made worldwide headlines and began to take doctors out of the loop of choosing sperm, he explains. Graham's eugenic vision of a society of superkids eventually failed because, as it turned out, most of

the kids born of Nobel sperm were altogether average. More-
over, there was actually very little demand for superbabies. But
the bank did contribute to turning women seeking sperm into
customers, reproductive medicine into shopping, and sperm
banking into big business, he writes. There are now hundreds
of sperm and egg banks across the country, and more than forty
thousand babies are born from donor sperm and eggs a year, according to industry records. The most well-known banks include Fairfax, Zytec, the Sperm Bank of California, and
California Cryobank.

As I listen to Ann's story, I start to think about the last year
of my life. I have spent many hours sorting through potential
date profiles on the Internet. But it's a different story with a
donor sperm. In online dating, it has become easy to reboot if
the perfect match doesn't present himself right away. In online
sperm shopping, there's no turning back once the child is conceived. And it's ultimately much more of a crapshoot than dating. While the process of making all of the choices—eye color,
disposition, intelligence—make it seem like women have a
great deal of control over the outcome, in reality all they can
do is hope for the best. "It's tempting to think that with enough
knowledge, you will get exactly the child you want, as you can
buy exactly the car you want," writes Plotz. "But there is serendipity in DNA. A great donor can pass on a lousy set of genes.
Women shop carefully for sperm in hopes of certainty. But
there is no certainty in a baby."

Ann was nonetheless extremely picky in choosing the right
sperm. Medical history mattered, and so did appearance. Ann
describes herself as "short and on the chubby side," so she
decided that tall, thin genes might balance out her family
traits. She also wanted a blue-eyed, blond-haired donor, like
herself, because she was worried about how it would effect her

and her child if people kept saying that he or she must look more like the father.

Ann narrowed her choice down to ten potential donors and then ordered a longer profile of each. She finally selected a six-foot-tall, 170-pound Swedish, English, and German donor with a good medical history, clear blue eyes, and blond hair. In his profile, he said he was a great athlete, creative, had a good sense of humor and a strong personality, and that his favorite color was green. In twenty years he said he hoped "to have a happy healthy family and get paid obscene amounts of money for doing what I love."

"I liked that," she says. "I also liked that he was creative because I'm not at all. I studied science."

"It's a very different process than when you're dating," she continues. "It's not exactly like you care about someone's blood type or whether their mother had diabetes."

She also listened to voice recordings.

"It was almost too personal," she says. "But then again I was going to have his sperm injected into me!"

After four month of inseminations, and one pregnancy that ended in a miscarriage, she became pregnant with her daughter.

"It was weird to not have sex and then suddenly be pregnant," she comments.

On a freezing day in January, Ann's mother and her best friend, Karen, took her to the hospital. Susie was born by C-section at 7:31 a.m.

Hearing Ann's story, particularly her description of her anguish when her relationship ended at twenty-eight, confirmed for me that however anxious I am about my reproductive future, I am hardly alone. But something about the idea of choosing my baby's father from a list of physical traits really troubles me. Of course, many of the women at the SMC meeting had gotten pregnant this way, and it hadn't bothered me at all then. But now, confronting the reality of it, I realize that even if the children of single mothers turn out perfectly healthy and happy, I believe that a child should be raised by a father as well as a mother. I am aware, of course, that many American children do not grow up in traditional two-parent households. Intellectually, I know I should not insist on this as the normative standard. But my reaction to Ann's story forces me to acknowledge that I am imbued with the social values my parents passed down to me, and I can't escape them just by intellectualizing the issue.

After Susie has left the room, I ask Ann and Tim if she ever asks about her biological father. Ann explains that she and her daughter have had a number of talks about Susie's biological father, and that she has shown her his donor profile. She and Susie have discussed the fact that she may have inherited her creativity from him.

Ann has even met other mothers and some of Susie's siblings through the Donor Sibling Registry, a burgeoning online community that now matches donors and offspring. She clicked on the site a few years ago, before she was married, to see if she might find more information about Susie's biological father. Sure enough, his donor number was listed. Although she couldn't contact him directly, she learned that Susie had some half siblings. She has now exchanged Christmas cards with some of the other donor families. But Susie isn't all that interested in the subject, so Ann hasn't made any effort to get involved with the other families apart from the occasional note or Christmas card. Now that she is married to Tim, she feels like this is Susie's true family.

"It's just a biological connection," she says, referring to Susie's relationship with the other offspring of her sperm donor.

"I know some people view as it one big family, but to me family is a social construct. This is my family now."

Since I myself have had the fantasy of meeting Mr. Right after I've had a child by myself, I'm particularly curious to hear more about how Ann met Tim.

Ann tells me that when Susie was born, she had established—with help from her employer as well as her parents—a very good arrangement that enabled her to survive as a single mother. Ann's parents lived nearby, and her mother had promised to take on the role of daycare provider. Her boss, a recently divorced single mother, was also supportive and allowed her to work flexible hours. (Ann chose to take reduced pay in exchange for cutting back on her hours so that she could spend more time with Susie.)

During her first months as a mother, however, Ann often felt lonely. But when Susie turned six months old, she started asking her parents to babysit at night as well, so she could go out more frequently with her friends. Ann tells me that the freedom this allowed her was an even greater gift than her parents' financial support.

Even when her parents weren't available to babysit, Ann was becoming more proactive about her social life. She would take Susie to dinner parties and put her to bed in the bedroom while she caught up with her friends.

"I was only friends with people who were accepting of my situation," she says.

Ann was not the type to place a personal ad or join an on-line dating service. At work, however, she was becoming close with her new colleague, Tim, an actuarial assistant. He was a recent college graduate, seven years younger than Ann. At first, they would hover around each other's desks talking about their favorite books, but pretty soon they started having lunch together.

After a few months, Ann felt comfortable enough with Tim to accept his invitation to a Friday night hockey game. A few nights after that, he came over to her house to watch a movie after Susie went to bed. Friday night hockey quickly became a weekly event for the two of them until one night when, during a break between periods, Tim turned to Ann and awkwardly asked if they were in fact "dating." They both burst into laughter and then leaned in and began kissing. Neither had expected that their friendship would turn romantic.

"I think I was prepared never to meet anyone," says Ann.

They got engaged after a year, and then two weeks before their wedding, Ann found out that she was pregnant with her second child. She was thirty-six.

Ann didn't tell her parents about the pregnancy until after the wedding for fear that they would be upset that she had had premarital sex. But right after the wedding, Tim and Ann announced to her family that she was pregnant and that Tim would be adopting Susie. Susie now calls Tim "Daddy," and Ann says she barely remembers a time when he wasn't around.

Susie walks back into the room and interrupts us. "What are you talking about?"

"When I was an SMC," says Ann.

"What's an SMC?" asks Susie.

"A single mother by choice," says Ann.

"I don't want you to do that again," says Susie.

"I don't want that either," says Tim to Susie.

"Well, I can't do that again because I'm married now!" Ann points out. She turns to me: "Having Susie by myself was such a defining moment in my life. It's odd that now she barely remembers when it was just her and me."

When Susie has left the room again, I ask Tim how he feels about not having a biological connection to his daughter. He says that the fact that Susie's biological father was a sperm donor rather than Ann's former partner has made it much easier for him to fill the role of daddy.

"It makes it more complicated with another father in the picture," he says. "With Ann, I knew I could actually *become* Susie's dad."

Later that afternoon, Ann and I sneak off for a girls' lunch at an Italian restaurant downtown. Over pasta, Ann confides that she didn't want to say it in front of her husband, but that in many ways being a single mother was easier.

"I was the only one making decisions," she says. "And I had a job and didn't have this sense of boredom," she says.

After Ann and Tim got married and their son, Sam, was born, Ann decided to stay at home with the children. She likes many things about it, such as spending her time doing work that doesn't make money. She currently volunteers for an organization that promotes natural childbirth. But she also says that she has a hard time with the role of stay-at-home mom.

"When I first quit, I missed working. I missed my friends and got very lonely," she admits. "I wasn't made for playing with trains and Barbies all day long. Sometimes I feel like I'm going crazy.

"Now, most people I know don't even know that I was a single mom. I don't think of myself as a traditional person, and I feel strange to have a lot of people view me as someone who is submissive to her husband," she continues.

And then Ann says something to me that I will never forget.

"One thing I've learned is that there is no one right way. I don't want people to think that I was a single mom and I got the fairy-tale ending. It's kind of offensive. It implies that what I had before wasn't enough or wasn't perfect. I was doing great before, and I'm doing great now. This is the fairy-tale ending, part II."

~

My mother has never liked to celebrate Mother's Day. She believes that the holiday was created to make kids feel guilty and spend unnecessary money on stupid cards. So I've never bought her a Mother's Day card, and if we happen to be on the phone that day, I always make sure not to mention the holiday. But this Mother's Day is different. After all my months of research, motherhood is on my mind.

Early in the morning, I call my mom just to say hi. We have a very open relationship, and I rarely hide what's going on in my life from her. I don't tell her about my sex life or anything really intimate, but we're close.

So far, I haven't mentioned my fertility investigation to either of my parents. It feels too personal. The decision is mine. It is my future, not theirs. This child will exist long after they are gone, so I think not telling them is my way of testing whether this is something that I really want to do alone, not just give to them a grandchild.

On the phone I ask if I can come over for dinner that night.

"We're not celebrating Mother's Day," Mom says, firmly.

"No, no. Don't worry," I reply.

I meet my mom that afternoon at Fairway on the Upper West Side to shop for dinner. Then we drive up to the house I grew up in, which is in Riverdale, a small neighborhood in the Bronx. My brother, Noah, who is eight and a half years younger, and I decide to take over the cooking that night. He grills the steaks, and I make a roasted vegetable casserole. We sit around the kitchen table in the exact same places that we've always sat: my father in the corner to my left, my brother to my right, and my mother to his right.

We talk for a few minutes about my brother's new company and my father's upcoming retirement.

"So I'm thinking about having a baby," I say. "It's Mother's Day after all, and this is something that I've been thinking about a lot lately." All three of them look at me with shock.

"Are you even dating someone?" my mother asks.

I laugh. "Don't worry, I'm not pregnant—yet."

I don't know why I suddenly decided to tell them. I guess their approval is an important part of my decision. And like Ann, I might need their help if I decide to go it alone.

"I've been investigating different options," I tell them. "I've decided that if I don't meet the right man by next year—or maybe the year after that—I'm going to seriously consider having a baby on my own with a sperm donor."

I tell them about Ann. "Her parents were happy that she didn't have premarital sex," I say, smiling.

My dad laughs.

Then I tell my family about the things I've learned in the course of my research into single motherhood.

"So if you can choose genetic traits, are you going to pick a Jew?" asks Dad once I've explained the process of choosing a sperm donor.

My mom is Jewish, which makes me Jewish according to Jewish law. My father is a blue-eyed Episcopalian, though his grandfather on his father's side was a Jew.

"Can you pick the sex?" he asks.

"I don't know yet. I'm just starting to think about it. I hope I'm going to find the guy. But if I don't, I like the idea that there is another option."

"What if you have a boy, and he doesn't have a father figure?" my brother asks.

"You could be a father figure," I say.

"I'm too young to be a father," he blurts back childishly.

He thinks for a second. "Well, I guess an uncle is a father figure. But I won't change diapers."

"I've got a lot of male friends, and I hope that at some point I'll meet a man," I add.

My parents say they'd be available for babysitting anytime. They don't ask too many other questions. I sense that they are trying to show respect for the fact that this is my life and my decision. My mother does advise me that they are going to retire soon and live on a fixed income, so I won't be able to lean too heavily on them for financial help.

Life as a single mother isn't exactly my dream, but talking to my family about it and having another option does make me feel less anxious for the moment. Rather than feeling like time is slipping away, I've found an alternative route that my family supports, intellectually and with help if I decide to follow through with it.

We sit in silence for a few minutes, and then my father turns to me.

"Thanks," he says.

"For what?" I ask, thinking he is thanking me for telling them that I might give them a grandchild.

He smiles. "Thanks for cooking."

# 4

Friends and Fatherhood

Over lunch with a girlfriend, I describe my visit with Ann in Iowa. I tell her how it made single motherhood so much more plausible for me, especially since Ann had pulled it off in such a conservative environment. I know it would be easier living in New York, where nontraditional families abound. But I explain that I just can't imagine getting pregnant with an anonymous donor. It seems so sterile. So I tell her about my proposition to Will.

"But you've had sex with him!" she exclaims.

"I know."

"Why don't you do it again and not use birth control?" she suggests.

At first I think she is implying that I trick him. I tell her I would never want him to be the father of my baby if he didn't want to be—whether we were together or not. What would be the point of bringing a child into the world by stealing sperm from my friend? Forcing a man into a role that he doesn't want to play is about the most selfish route to motherhood I can imagine. If I were to get pregnant by accident, or if we had sex purposely to get me pregnant but chose a relationship different from a traditional marriage for raising the child, it might be a different story. But willfully tricking a man is unthinkable.

But then she explains that it would just seem easier for us to have sex if he agreed to my proposal, and so the conversation gets me wondering about Will's decision. When I get home, I call to check in with him. The outgoing message on his cell phone tells me that he is on an eight-day silent meditation retreat and will return calls as soon as he can speak again.

~

Rattled by the idea of getting pregnant with an anonymous sperm donor, I start to seek out single moms who have gotten pregnant with the sperm of a friend, or at least someone they know.

Through Jane Mattes, I meet Maggie Hopkins*, a real estate lawyer living in Washington, D.C. We exchange a series of e-mails, in which Maggie tells me that a few months after her thirty-sixth birthday she was inseminated with the sperm of a gay friend. She's now in her second trimester.

Rather than writing back and forth, I want to talk to Maggie; I want to understand how she reached this decision and how she feels about it on a personal level. I ask her if we could set up a phone call, and she tells me to ring at exactly noon on Sunday. It's clear she is both a very busy and very precise person.

Maggie picks up the phone after one ring. We make small talk for a few minutes about her most recent case. Then she tells me how overworked she is and how exhausted she feels from the pregnancy.

Maggie speaks with a slight Southern drawl, but her tone is disarmingly matter-of-fact. So I just jump right in and ask what made her decide to become a single mom.

She tells me that she had wanted to become a mother since she graduated from law school, when she was twenty-four. She began planning for motherhood financially and emotionally with the idea in her mind that she might end up doing it on her own.

This surprises me. I ask her why she thought about having a child on her own at such a young age.

"I've always been a realist," she says. "Many of my friends don't plan for the distinct possibility that they may not meet Mr. Right. You've got to have Plan A, Plan B, and Plan C."

There is something disquieting about her intense rationality. I recognize that Maggie had done exactly what many of the doctors I've spoken with have advocated: she started thinking about her fertility very early. But I also remember what I was like at twenty-four—unhurried, free, open to a world of possibility. Maybe I'd be in a better place now if I had started calculating my steps toward motherhood back in my early twenties, but it's hard to identify with Maggie's extraordinary—and precocious—pragmatism. It seems not just unromantic, but almost deliberately antiromantic.

"Plan A was to meet Mr. Right and fall in love and have a traditional family in my twenties," she explains. "That didn't happen."

During law school, Maggie lived with her boyfriend, also a law student, for a couple of years. The two talked about a future family, but as they both got specialized in their career interests, they realized that they were no longer compatible.

"In your twenties, you don't think, 'This is my last chance,'" she states.

After graduation, Maggie moved to Los Angeles and threw herself into her career. She had a number of boyfriends over this period, but as she started to work on—and win—important cases, her job became more satisfying and more intellectually gratifying. Soon it was the center of her life, and there wasn't much room left for dating.

"I still wanted Plan A to work out, so I waited," she says.

Maggie decided to set a deadline: if she turned thirty and was still alone, she would have a child on her own.

As I've gotten older I've become more of a planner too, and I know in my own life that my tidy agendas have sometimes blinded me to possibilities that might have been right for me, so I ask her directly, "Do you think you might have missed a chance that you didn't see with someone?"

"No," she says, sternly.

Maggie is fierce and independent, and she clearly loves a challenge. Over the course of the conversation, I learn that she has traveled all over the world by herself: safaris in Africa, backpacking in Southeast Asia, and trekking in Nepal. I like this about her, and hope that our shared passion for travel will allow me a way in with Maggie, a way to get beneath her tough skin. I tell her about hiking to the top of a Himalayan peak when I was twenty-one.

"I got caught in a protest in Nepal," she tells me, loosening up a bit. "We had to scramble to find food and water."

Maggie and I have a lot in common—on paper, at least, we'd look like peas in a pod. No doubt, as women of the same generation, we've received similar messages about women's liberation. My parents taught me that self-sufficiency was more important than finding a man. Being too needy is something I've always feared. Many of the most satisfying things I've done in my life are things I've done on my own. Theoretically, I should like and admire Maggie. And yet I find her completely off-putting. I've often worried that because of my independence, I might come off as too defensive or too tough, sending a potential husband the message "I don't need you," or "I could leave you." If I'm getting this feeling from Maggie after only a few minutes on the phone, surely the men in her life have gotten it too. I wonder if the reason I dislike her is that she represents one of my major fears about myself.

Maggie's independence, though, was not formed by the feminist movement. She tells me that she's self-sufficient for a different reason: she has to be. She has a very distant relationship with her family, particularly her mother, and therefore doesn't feel she has a strong safety net.

She came of age in a suburb of Charlotte in the 1960s. Like most of the families in her neighborhood, her parents had a traditional relationship: her father worked and her mother stayed at home and raised Maggie and her older brother.

Maggie says her mother never really wanted to have children, but she had little choice at the time because that's what married women in North Carolina suburbs were supposed to do. She says her mother received no support at home from her father, who worked around the clock as a lawyer.

"She loved me and my brother," says Maggie. "But she did not love being a mom. She once told me that if she had to do it all over again, she would not have had kids."

When Maggie told her parents that she planned to become a single mother, her dad was disappointed and worried, because he believes that a woman needs a man. But Maggie says that her mom was delighted—even though she knew it was going to be a challenge for her daughter.

"She says that in many ways she always felt like a single mom," Maggie explains.

It dawns on me that Maggie has chosen to replicate both her mother's role and her father's. Like her father, she's become a hard-working lawyer. But she's also on her way to recreating her mother's experience by taking on the task alone, without the help of a more modern partnership, and risking the social and emotional isolation that comes with being a single parent. I wonder if her mother recognized this when Maggie told her of her decision. If she had suffered as a mother, why did she encourage her own daughter to go down this seemingly more difficult path?

"I want a family," Maggie says. "This is clearly a less attractive choice than having children with the perfect husband. I know that." But she has chosen to be alone rather than settling for someone less than perfect. "There are other women who would just like to have a companion, but I would rather be alone than in a relationship with a man that I don't love."

I can certainly relate to that.

In 1998, when she was about to turn thirty, Maggie began to look for a biological father for her child. Unlike Ann Holland, however, she didn't like the idea of an anonymous sperm donor. So she turned to her friends Alix* and Ricky*, a gay couple she had known for years.

"At the time, I was scoping around for sperm from my guy friends," she says. "My girlfriend would say, 'There is sperm all around you; all you have to do is go to a bar.' But I didn't think it was moral to just have sex with a guy and get pregnant. If I were a guy, I wouldn't want someone to take advantage of me in that way."

But Ricky and Alix were shocked by Maggie's request, mostly because they thought Maggie was too young to be considering single motherhood. They turned her down and told her that she needed to focus on dating instead. Since her career was thriving, she decided they were right, so she decided to gamble and change her deadline to thirty-five.

Nearly four years passed, and Maggie dated, but she didn't meet anyone significant. Then, in 2001, right after the World Trade Center attack, she went to her ob-gyn for an annual check-up and discovered that she was in the first stage of cervical cancer. The cancer had developed from the common HPV virus, which she had contracted in her twenties. Her doctor told her that depending on how her condition progressed, she might eventually have to have a hysterectomy. He also told her that the sooner she had a child the better.

Maggie took the news as a sign that it was time to stop waiting for the right relationship and just get pregnant. Her experience is not uncommon: In her book *Single by Chance, Mothers by Choice*, Rosanna Hertz, a women's studies professor at Wellesley College, explains that many women choose single motherhood after a "catalytic" event such as Maggie's. When they "cross [this] threshold, realizing that even if they don't know exactly what is on the other side, moving toward motherhood is better than staying in place."

Around the same time, Alix and Ricky adopted a daughter. Maggie went to their baby shower and approached her friends again about donating sperm.

"Ok, guys," she said. "You've got your baby. Now help me with mine." Alix and Ricky had a change of heart. They had chosen an open adoption and planned to stay in regular contact with their daughter's birth mother. They knew how happy the birth mother had made them by giving them the chance to become parents, and they decided that they wanted to pass that gift along to Maggie. And being part of an open adoption had also given them a better idea of the role they might play in Maggie's child's life.

The question, then, was, which one of them would donate their sperm?

At first, Alix said he thought it shouldn't be him, because he had bad acne as a child and a history of heart disease in his family. Ricky has blond hair, beautiful blue eyes, long black eyelashes, and a better health history. But then the three began talking regularly about how their modern family might look. They decided to model it on an open adoption and began role-playing certain scenarios in order to come to the terms of a contract.

"Let's say I have a son, and when he turns ten I decide I'm going to send him off to military boarding school," Maggie began. "If he called you, crying, saying that he was miserable, I think you could console him, but you couldn't play any role in the decision of whether or not he would stay at school or come home."

"I would say, 'Did you tell your mom? You need to discuss this with her,'" said Alix.

"How could you not let him come home immediately?" responded Ricky, surprised.

Maggie immediately knew that Ricky's strong opinions could be a potential problem.

"I think you and Ricky are going to fight," said Alix, playing referee. "You are too much alike."

So the three decided that Alix would be the donor. Maggie drafted a contract indicating that he would have no parental rights. These types of contracts are nonbinding, meaning that they show only intent. So if Alix were ever to decide to seek custody of his biological child, they could use the contract as a guide even though its terms could still be argued away in a court of law. In Maggie's will, her close girlfriend Eliza is named as the legal guardian. If Maggie were to die, Alix and Ricky would have no parental rights at all.

"They would be considered family in the same way that my close friends are considered aunts and uncles," she says.

As the details of Maggie's path toward motherhood fell into place, she stopped building her own practice in Los Angeles and resettled in Washington, D.C., with a job at a large law firm—not because she wanted to get on a partner track, but in order to get maternity coverage.

"After my first day at my new job, I had an appointment with a fertility doctor," she tells me.

A few weeks earlier, Alix had gone to a fertility clinic in Austin, Texas. He suffered a brief moment of panic when he realized that there was only heterosexual porn in the room where he was sent to make his donation, but then he remembered that Lance Armstrong had once been at the same clinic. Apparently just the thought of Lance did the trick. Alix's sperm was then frozen, packed in a cylinder, and sent by Federal Express to Maggie's doctor's office in Washington. It took four inseminations for her to become pregnant.

She admits that as soon as she got pregnant, she began to mourn the fact that she is not having a child with a man she loves. But then she rationalizes: "It's not like I have this man who loves me and has decided he doesn't want to have kids and it's the choice between me being with the love of my life and having a child."

I decide to press a little harder.

"Jane Mattes told me that she advises women to explore what's getting in the way of having a relationship before they make the choice to have a child on their own."

"Oh, I went to therapy," she shoots back. "I think it's good for people to have self-awareness and figure out their psychic pain and how to be better people. I have a pretty good idea of what my issues are. That doesn't mean I've solved them. I decided to separate the partner thing from parenting."

But then she softens a bit and explains that it's not that she doesn't want an intimate relationship with a man, but that it scares her.

"My way of dealing with it is that I tend to get into casual relationships and date men who are beneath me, not as smart as me," she says. "Although I like hanging out with them and love them, there is part of me that believes they're never really available."

I'm astonished by how resolute Maggie is, even in her self-awareness, and I wonder if I'm being too hard on her. It's taken me a long time to sort myself out as much as I have; there's no standard schedule that suits everyone. Maybe it's true that she is just putting parenting first and will one day be in a position to meet a better kind of man for her.

"I've spent time forcing myself to have intimacy," she says. "But now I'm just really happy, and if it happens it happens."

Maggie's first trimester was so hard on her physically that she asked herself again why it was so important to her to have a biological child.

"I was so nauseated that I just sat staring at my stapler for three months," she says, describing her new job. One day in court, she made a mistake on a filing and apologized to the other litigator, a woman, explaining that she was pregnant and not thinking clearly.

"Unplanned, I see," the litigator said to her, knowing that Maggie wasn't married.

"Actually it was planned," said Maggie.

Embarrassed, the woman apologized. But Maggie tells me that it was one of the very few times she's felt judged for making the choice to become a single mother. Most of her friends and colleagues consider her decision brave and support her completely.

For Maggie, one thing that has emerged out of all of the physical challenges of pregnancy is the realization that she has much less control over her life than she once thought. She has learned the limits of all of her planning and rational decision making.

"I don't think there is a logical explanation for why you want to have children," she acknowledges. "You can add up the numbers over and over, and every time you analyze whether it works, you realize there is no way to measure the rewards or losses. I really can't measure the amount of sleep I'm going to lose, or how much money I'm going to spend on this child. I just have to accept what comes."

"Are you happy with the choice you've made?" I ask her.

She tells me she is. "I feel like I could meet a man every day until I die," she says. "But I can only have a child now, and I know that I don't want to be eighty years old and not have a child."

After I get off the phone with Maggie, I spend some time thinking about why I reacted so strongly and so negatively to her. I had exactly the opposite reaction to Ann—I found her totally inspiring. I wonder if it's because of her second fairy-tale ending. By the time I met her, single motherhood was behind her. She had made a bold feminist decision, but ended up with a life that looked more like a Norman Rockwell painting.

Maggie's decision to become a single mother, however, is playing out in real time—and it's much scarier for me. Ann described her years as a single mother in an idealized past tense. Maggie's story forces me to confront the stark reality of the choice I'm considering.

Maggie's stridency, I think, also obscures the fact that single motherhood raises really complicated questions about the shape of contemporary feminism. In the version of feminism I grew up with, women were supposed to fight for equality in their relationships with men—not abandon the males of the species altogether. We weren't supposed to become a race of Amazons, were we?

I wonder how progressive single motherhood is after all. In some ways, it seems to be a step back for women. Maggie's mother may have been miserable as a stay-at-home mom in North Carolina, but at least she had a means of financial support. Maggie has to play both roles—the single mother and the breadwinner. In the brave new feminist world I grew up imagining, men were supposed to bear more—not less—of the burden of raising children.

The thing that's bothering me most, though, is the guilt I feel about my father. I love him so much, and I'm so grateful for everything he's given me. If I decide to have a child without a father present, would he interpret that to mean that I felt the role he has played in my life isn't all that important? I can imagine that he will probably be proud of me if I decide to become a single mother, and tell me that he thinks I'm strong enough to handle anything. But I worry that he will also wake up in the middle of the night sometimes, wondering what he did wrong to make me take this route.

~

As I think about the importance of my dad's role in my life, I start to wonder about the men who donate their sperm. Instead of focusing on how I feel about it, or how my child would feel about it, I decide to look at the question from the other side. Why do men become sperm donors? Do they forget about it once they have donated their DNA, or do they continue to wonder whether they have sons and daughters somewhere in the world? What happens if their biological children want to find them someday?

It turns out that many single mothers who chose anonymous donors are asking similar questions, and many are striking out to locate these men. This choice is not only changing the role of the biological father to one that falls somewhere between distant biological connection and avuncular step-parenthood, it is also further expanding the circles of single-mother families. The Internet is one of the main catalysts for this change.

In 2000, Wendy Kramer, a divorced mother from Boulder, Colorado, accidentally started a revolution among donor families when she decided that she wanted more information about her son's sperm donor.

In 1989, Wendy and her husband had found themselves facing infertility issues that made them decide to use a sperm donor. The couple picked a donor through the California Cryobank. After Kramer was inseminated, she says, she never really thought about the consequences of her choice. But when her son, Ryan, turned nine, he started asking about where he came from. Wendy couldn't lie to him. The more he asked, the more she needed to find out about his donor. Her sperm bank wouldn't give her any information about the man, but it did tell her that her son had at least three half siblings.

"It's out of control," Kramer tells me over the phone one morning. "Sperm banks don't update medical information. They don't share it with the families. They don't even know who the families are."

So one day Kramer and her son were driving home, and they decided to take matters into their own hands. She launched a small Yahoo Group with a message headed: "Donor 1058?"

She wrote: "I'm the mother of an awesome ten-year-old boy. I know that he has at least three half siblings, and he would like to find out their whereabouts. I hope this board will serve others who are looking for their donor children or siblings."

Ryan's biological father found him through that search, but the Kramers must keep the story private in order for Ryan to maintain a relationship with him. In the meantime, hundreds of other donor offspring began posting the name of their sperm banks and their donor's number as well. Since that time, thousands of matches have been made.

The group is now a website called DonorSiblingRegistry.com, which has become a central hub of modern family bonding. Through DNA testing and Google searches, mothers and donor offspring are seeking out their "bio dads." To date, there are no privacy laws protecting bio dads from being found—though of course every donor has the option of not responding to any correspondence from the mothers or their children. But in fact many biological fathers are willingly stepping forward, which suggests that at least for some donors, a lingering curiosity, if not something more, remains well after the initial donation is made.

Half siblings, donor offspring, and donors are now meeting and bonding on all levels of intimacy. Some e-mail photos and medical information; others actually meet in person. The women of Single Mothers by Choice are even forming subgroups online, using the donor number as the web address. It's an odd sort of cyber-polygamy: some of these big families—whose only bond is biology—are meeting up for family picnics, exchanging holiday cards, and even planning huge family vacations through which half siblings can meet and form relationships.

What began as a pet project to satisfy a child's curiosity has ballooned into a major source for the creation and understanding of the new shape of family. Wendy Kramer has emerged as a national spokeswoman for the rights of donor children, and her main focus is to organize what she calls "the chaotic and altogether unregulated sperm donor industry."

"We haven't done that here in the U.S. because it is big business," she says. "In other countries, they've asked the question publicly: what's in the best interest of the child being born?"

It seems the most vital question to me, and I can't imagine becoming a single mother until I have a satisfying answer. At this point, I know I believe that all children have the right to as much information about themselves and their origins as they want. Even if studies and the people I meet do show that children of single parents are just as well off as those with two parents, I still want to be sure that I would be comfortable telling my own children about their origins. If my mother had told me that my biological father was an anonymous sperm donor, how would I have felt about that? Of course, that's an impossible question to answer—I have a real father, and I can't imagine it being any other way. Ours is the first generation to have these options; we are entering into uncharted terrain.

I have to remind myself, though, that motherhood is uncharted terrain under any circumstances. Every child is different; every relationship is different. Even under the best of circumstances, choosing motherhood will always require a leap of faith.

When Richard Lawson*, a Southern California film sound engineer gave vials of sperm to the California Cryobank in the

1980s, he never expected what his life would look like years later.

"I donated because I was struggling to pay the rent and support my family. That was the reason I did it. Pure and simple," he says. "My wife would joke that I might get a knock on my door in eighteen years."

It turns out that his wife's joke was prescient.

In 2000, he got a call from the California Cryobank telling him that a young woman was looking for her biological father. They wanted his permission to give her his contact information. At first, Richard, was stunned. For a few days, he and his wife talked over the consequences of a meeting.

"The intangible angst of many sperm donors is, 'What if one of my biological kids is in trouble?' or 'What if their parents are cruel to them?'" he says. "I'm not sure I could leave them in an awful situation."

Richard and his wife decided that it was very important for a young person to understand his or her origins, so he decided to give the bank a way for her to contact him.

A few days later, he got a phone call from a bright and bubbly teenager who lived only an hour away. His biological daughter was far from in trouble. She was happy and healthy, had just graduated from high school, and was preparing to go to college in the fall. She was just curious about her biological origins.

Richard agreed to meet her and her mother in a local mall.

"At first it was very emotional," he says. "It was also a little awkward. You're meeting this person that you have no reason to meet except for the fact that you're genetically related to them."

The most shocking aspect of the meeting was that they looked so much alike. Beyond that, it was a normal social encounter in which they talked about their lives and tried to find out if they had common interests.

Richard has now gotten in touch with two other children, whom he refers to as his daughter and son. They have regular contact and visit with each other a few times a year.

While Richard says he doesn't feel like these children's father in the traditional day-to-day sense of the role, he does feel a strong connection—though not the same one he feels with the children he and his wife have raised. "I feel protective of them. I don't want them to get hurt," he says of his bio kids. "But there is a huge gap. I never got to see them when they were kids. I never got to bathe them. There's all this bonding that goes on when you're actually with the kid."

It's that love—the kind of love that is shaped by daily interaction and nurturing—that every child deserves. But of course not every child gets that, regardless of the shape of the family. Parents die, parents get divorced and move out, sometimes parents stay but are just bad parents. Sometimes other people step in and make up for that loss—grandparents, uncles and aunts, family friends, step-parents, godparents. Who am I to proclaim that every child deserves to know his or her biological father from the beginning of their lives?

But I do wonder what happens when the thing that is missing suddenly appears. How does it affect both the life of the child and the life of the mother when a bio dad enters into the picture later in life? If I choose an anonymous donor, or even an open ID donor, the bio dad would never have to know what he was missing—and neither would my child. And we could keep it that way until my child was eighteen, or possibly forever, if that's what I, and eventually my child, choose. But with Will, or any friend, it would be different. What if, after years of absence, he decided to become a presence in our lives? Then everyone would know what they had missed along the way.

These questions led to another Internet search, and pretty soon I found the New York Sperm Bank and called Dr. Albert Anouna, the director. Because so many single woman were calling about sperm donation, he told me, in 2005 he started a new program that takes open ID donors a step closer to the relationship that I might have with Will as my baby's bio daddy. After noticing the increasing number of single women who procreate with male friends who are not romantic partners, Dr. Anouna decided to create a way for potential mothers to meet and interview their donors in person before their offspring are even conceived.

"It allows people to make clear-cut choices from the beginning," he says. "The recipient and the donor can exchange information and be responsible to each other."

One of Dr. Anouna's first recruits was Luc*, a thirty-three-year-old biotechnology researcher who lives in Paris with his wife. He had read an article on the Internet about the growing number of single women who were seeking sperm donors, and Dr. Anouna's new program. The story hit a humanitarian nerve, and he decided to contact Dr. Anouna.

"It wasn't a question of the money," he tells me over the phone from Paris. "I wanted to help."

That doesn't mean, however, that he wants his potential offspring to consider him—or even call him—"daddy."

"To be a dad, first there must be a family with a wife," he says. "The dad is the guy who raises the children. He is the guy who gives guidelines for life. There is a difference between giving your progeny to someone who can't have children so they can have the chance. I'm giving my genetic material to help."

In 2005, Luc was on business in New York and decided to meet with Dr. Anouna to discuss the option of becoming a donor. If accepted into the program, Luc would get paid $500 when a woman received his sperm and an additional $300 if he met her in person. In that meeting, he and the recipient would come up with a contract that would spell out the agreements they made about his relationship with his offspring in the future.

After his meeting with Dr. Anouna, Luc went back to Paris to talk to his wife about becoming a donor. At the time, he and his wife were also trying to have children of their own, as well as adopting a child from Africa. The first thing his wife wanted to know was how he might feel if a child showed up at his door without his mother and asked for help.

"I told her that I hoped this wouldn't happen," he says. "If any of these children came to me, I would have to say that there was a contract and there is no way that I can be their dad."

Before committing wholeheartedly, however, Luc had to be accepted into the program. The process involved a six-month battery of genetic and blood tests. Since 2003, sperm used by sperm banks must meet FDA regulations. It must be screened for HIV and other communicable and genetic diseases, and, depending on the clinic, the donor must meet certain height and weight requirements. Sperm is also tested for proper mobility and survival in freezing.

Luc also had to go through an evaluation with a psychiatrist. His evaluation would be provided to potential parents as part of his psychological profile. "It was good, because I was able to talk about my fears about donating," he tells me. The psychiatrist asked Luc about everything from his sexual orientation to what time he wakes up in the morning to what he eats for breakfast and whether or not he likes to travel.

"He wanted to see if I was well balanced and not some crazy person who wants to give away sperm in order to create a master race or something like that," he says.

The psychiatrist also asked him a lot of questions about his childhood. "It was the first time in my life that I talked to a guy I didn't know about things like that," he reveals. "I told him things that I don't even talk about with my wife."

Luc found himself telling the doctor that before he was born, his parents had a daughter who died.

"He wanted to know whether the loss of this child was connected to my interest in becoming a donor," he says. "I can't say for sure that it's not. Maybe there was something missing in my life because I remember when I was a child asking my parents to give me a sister."

A few months after his evaluation, Luc—and his sperm—got accepted into the program. He donated twenty vials that Dr. Anouna promptly froze. Then one day, Luc got a call from Dr. Anouna saying that Amy*, one of his patients, was interested in his sperm. He didn't tell him much, except that she was a dentist in West Texas living alone with her son and that she wanted to give him a sibling. Dr. Anouna had given her the report compiled by the psychiatrist along with Luc's photograph, physical description, and medical history, and she was keen to speak with him.

"He asked me if he could give her my contact information," he says. "I said she could call or e-mail me."

The two began talking by e-mail. Amy sent Luc an e-mail saying how happy she was that someone was interested in helping her.

"It's such a gift," she wrote, along with a long list of questions about his grandparents, everything from the color of their hair and height to their personality traits.

"We had ten or so e-mails back and forth," Luc tells me.

The whole point of Dr. Anouna's program is for the mother to meet her potential donor in person prior to the insemination. But because of the distance between Paris and Texas, Amy decided that she had enough information up front to move forward without a face-to-face encounter.

When I speak to Amy, she tells me that she likes Dr. Anouna's program because she received seventy pages of information about Luc, which was more than what the other sperm banks provided.

"I could tell you whether he prefers pretzels or corn chips," she explains.

After Luc agreed that he didn't need to meet Amy in person to feel comfortable with the arrangement, the two of them signed a contract through the bank in which Luc agreed to meet his offspring in the future if he or she wanted that.

"I had the choice," says Luc. "I said, 'Go ahead.'"

Luc didn't realize the implications of this green light, however, until he found himself walking through Central Park with the mother of his progeny a few months later. Four months after their phone conversation, Luc and Amy discovered in the course of an e-mail exchange that they would be in New York in the same week. They decided to meet on a Saturday afternoon in Central Park, near the ice skating rink. Luc assumed that because Amy wanted to meet, it meant the insemination was successful. And it was. But from the moment they introduced themselves, Luc was subjected to a series of major surprises.

"Oh, you look beautiful," he said, looking at her belly.

"Oh, it's not me who is pregnant," Amy answered immediately. "It's a gestational surrogate in California."

"It's not you! Why?" Luc asked.

Amy explained that she had a medical problem that made it impossible for her to carry a child, even though her eggs were still viable for conception, so she had decided to hire a surrogate mother. Surrogate pregnancies, Amy had learned, were illegal for single women in Texas. So through the Internet she found a surrogate who lived in California, where it is legal. The two women established a contract stating that the surrogate would carry the baby conceived with Amy's eggs and Luc's sperm.

Luc's sperm was flown from New York to California, where Amy went through a cycle of in vitro fertilization. Two embryos conceived from her eggs and Luc's sperm were then implanted in the surrogate's womb. Amy also had an additional eight embryos frozen and put in storage.

The surrogate was now four months pregnant.

"How are you going to explain that to the children?" Luc asked.

"It's going to be natural," she said. "When they are old enough to understand, I'll explain that they were born in California and have a genetic father in France."

Luc accepted this answer, but the more he thought about further potential consequences, the more he felt like his humanitarian impulse had been slightly naïve.

"Will you meet them in the future?" Amy asked.

"Why not," he said, not sure what he had gotten himself into.

The meeting in the park allowed them to verbalize a moral contract in addition to the nonbinding legal contract they signed through the New York Sperm Bank.

"We decided that if I meet the children, it will be in a park or in a hotel," says Luc. "I'll ask my wife if she wants to come and join us. I would be more comfortable with that."

At the end of the meeting, they shook hands and parted ways. But there was something that Luc wasn't happy about: the additional frozen embryos. During their meeting, Amy had asked Luc if he would mind if she donated them to other women who might need them. Today there are many organizations that provide "embryo adoption" services, even though the American Society for Reproductive Medicine does not support the use of the word "adoption" in their advertisements. (Many of these are in fact religious organizations pushing a pro-life political agenda. They are trying to prevent the embryos from being donated to stem cell research, or from being discarded altogether.)

"Nobody told me that this kind of situation could develop," Luc says. "If I had the chance to decide this in the contract beforehand, I would have said that I didn't want other women having access to those embryos. I would prefer that she give them to science for stem cell research or throw them away."

Luc had sold his sperm to Amy like any other anonymous donor, and legally she can do with it what she wants. But his experience brings up the possibility that this closer kind of arrangement requires a new kind of contract in which the biological father has broader rights in determining what the birth mother can and cannot do with his sperm.

Five months after Luc and Amy met in Central Park, the California surrogate gave birth to fraternal twin girls. When the twins turned two months old, Amy e-mailed Luc photographs. One of the babies had a deep olive complexion. In her note, she asked if he knew where the dark skin came from.

"It probably came from my grandfather from the South of France. He had a permanent tan," Luc wrote back. Amy suggested that she come to France with the twins when they turned one year old so they could meet the man responsible for giving them life.

"She wants the girls to know me, but she doesn't want them to think I'm their father," he says. "It's strange. I guess we'll see when we meet."

While Luc doesn't consider himself the twins' dad in a traditional sense either, he does plan to offer them advice in the future if they ask and give them physical affection.

"I'll let them hug me and sit on my lap," he says.

"I'm going to think about them in the same way that I think about my friends' children. I'll look at them a little differently because they look like me. But if something is not going right and I see the girls treat me like their real father, I will say that we have to stop right now. I will tell their mother that she has to explain to them that they can't call me Dad."

But the goodwill between Luc and Amy evaporated a few months later, after Amy sent Luc an e-mail reporting that she had found a couple to adopt the additional embryos. She asked whether Luc would agree to be in contact with the couple.

"I just closed the e-mail and didn't respond," he says. "I don't want to be in contact with ten other families. I guess I was a little naïve."

Only time will tell what the future will bring for Luc and Amy and their children. Maybe she will contact him again when she plans to go to Paris, and maybe he will feel like he has to make a connection.

It seems to me that each sperm donor and birth mother have to develop the moral code of their relationship in the process of building it. The decision to create a life with another person is always an intense and deeply personal one, even when it begins with a man masturbating into a donation cup. I realize that if I decided to take this route with Will, we would need to spend a lot of time thinking through our contract, and considering as many eventualities as we could imagine. Maggie was smart, I realize, to role-play possible scenarios with her child's bio father. Of course, there is always a limit on how much anyone can plan—whether with a husband, a life-partner, or a bio dad. Just as there are no guarantees about the child who will emerge, there are also no guarantees as to how *any* relationship will turn out in the long run.

~

Will and I are sitting across from each other over breakfast at a café in my neighborhood. It's been around six months since I asked him the fateful question. I'm nervous about his answer. After all I've heard—warnings about complicated relationships, stories about legal battles—I've realized that an anonymous donor is the less messy course, even if it means not knowing the father of my baby in a more personal or intimate way. Still, even though I'm highly skeptical about all that is involved in becoming a single mother with a known donor, I want Will to give me the option to choose.

Because I'm nervous, I keep accidentally kicking Will under the table with the sharp heel of my shoe. We make small talk, but it's obvious why we are sitting here. After ten minutes, I fall silent.

"So," he says. "I can't do it."

My heart sinks, even though I know deep down that he is right. But rather than hearing him out, I jump in and try to head him off, as if we were breaking up and I am turning the tables to be the breaker-upper rather than the broken-up.

"I can't either," I say. "I've been thinking about all the what-ifs. What if I had a baby and we drew up a contract that you would not have any financial or day-to-day obligation, that you would play only an avuncular role in my child's life, and then you changed your mind and decided you wanted to be more involved? What if I fell in love with a man who wanted to adopt our baby? Then, what would your role be?"

I rattle on like this for several minutes, until I notice that Will is visibly annoyed with me.

"This is not only about you," he shoots at me. "You haven't even let me talk."

He's right. I stop talking.

"I want to be able to help you, and I want to be generous," he says. "But I can't bring a child into the world and play the role of distant, or even secret, father. I don't think it would be fair to the child."

He tells me how important his relationship to his father was, and how he can't imagine bringing a child into the world if he couldn't play the active role of father. His parents divorced when he was three, and his mother was his primary caretaker. He and his father lived on different sides of the country. Donating his sperm to me just strikes him as another route to the same bad situation for a child.

"It's not like you decided that you're in love with me, and you're telling me that you want to have my child. You asked me for my sperm."

He continues. "I think by asking me this, you're creating and negotiating a confusing situation rather than facing the challenge of the situation before you, which is that you want to find the right man to father your child. You're afraid that you are running out of time."

At first I feel defensive about his reaction, but then I realize that he's right. I'm anxious about time, and I'm trying to find an alternative to what I really need to do, which is focus on finding the right relationship.

Then he asks another question. "Is all of this your round-about way of telling me that you're in love with me?"

Will has a knack for asking great philosophical questions.

"No, I'm not in love with you," I say honestly. I do love Will, but not in the way I've loved other boyfriends. At times, I've fought against this because Will and I are so close that it often seems like we *should* be madly in love with each other, even though we're not.

"You know," I say, smiling, "I think if you had offered to give me your sperm, it would have been so generous that it might have made me fall in love with you."

He laughs.

I feel relieved to know that in a small way I've made progress in my search, and I'm closer to what I am looking for.

Will's decision and our conversation helped me to see that I'm not ready to separate love from motherhood. I'm not ready to become a single mother at this point in my life. I still need to grow and make discoveries about the way I experience romantic relationships before I'm ready to begin my family. Maybe as the window of my fertility starts to close, I will come to feel differently. But right now, I feel relieved.

# 5
## &

# The Sweetness of Doing Nothing

It is freezing outside, one of those February days when the city sidewalks shimmer and seem warmer than the air. I'm sitting by the window in my apartment, staring out at a pink and orange sunset over the glassy buildings of Hoboken, New Jersey. Flocks of pigeons swoop down in circles over the rooftops of the West Village. It's windy, and whitecaps dot the thin slice of the Hudson River that I can see from my window.

I usually love this view, my tiny sliver of the world—especially at this time of day, when the golden light warms the faded red brick of the old AT&T building. When I'm anxious or sad or have a big decision to make, watching the light and the water calms me.

But today this view is not making me calm. I'm stressed and overwhelmed; my sliver of the world feels claustrophobic. A few days earlier, Will and I were talking on the phone, and I told him how down I was feeling. It's not because of the sperm issue—I'm feeling pretty resolved about that for now. It's because

I'm tired of all this thinking about family and the future. I'm fed up with dating and the pressure I've put myself under to create a family on a tight schedule.

Will was sympathetic. He told me that he and two of his friends were heading down to the Osa Peninsula of Costa Rica in a few weeks, and he asked me if I wanted to join them as a way to chill out. But I don't really feel comfortable with the idea of being the only woman in a group of male friends; I worry that I'll feel like a fourth wheel.

Whenever I feel confused in this way, I usually call my friend Mollie. She is the friend I laugh with the hardest; we see the world through a similar lens of absurdity. She is also the friend who seems to constantly lap me in relationships. In the time that I've been looking for love, Mollie has married, divorced, and fallen in love—twice, I think. She is about to move to New Zealand with her latest love for no reason other than to see what it's like to live upside down like a Kiwi for a while. The way Mollie lives her life is a constant reminder that marriage and happiness aren't the same thing. Mollie's exuberance comes from within her, regardless of whether she's in a relationship or not.

One of my favorite memories of Mollie is a weekend we spent at her parents' house on Martha's Vineyard. One afternoon we paddled plastic kayaks to her favorite spot in the bay to go clam digging at low tide. Mollie's a pro—she was pulling clams out of the ground every minute while I kept coming up dry.

"I'm never gonna find a clam, I'm never gonna find a clam," I griped.

By the end of the afternoon, my bikini was covered in ocean mud and salt. We decided to head back home. But just as I was getting into my kayak, I stepped backward and felt a hard edge. I bent down, dug around in the sand, and pulled up the biggest clam I've ever seen.

"Mollie, look!" I yelled, holding up a monstrous five-pounder.

"Wow! You found the mother of all clams," she said, in a deadpan voice.

We both collapsed into the mud in hysterics.

Mollie is one of those intensely sensitive people who always understands the kind of mood I'm in without my having to explain too much. So today, I call her and say, "I don't know. . . . I'm just feeling constricted and stressed about the future."

She's quiet for a few seconds, then responds. "I think you need to let go of everything, just live your life, and be still."

My immediate question, of course, is, how exactly will I do this? I've never been very good at being still—in fact my entire personality is the opposite of still. Ever since I was a child, I've been a thrill seeker and an adventurer. My father's theory is that it's connected to when I was six months old and my parents woke up me in the middle of the night to catch an early plane to Puerto Rico. "You just loved the excitement of being up and moving when no one else was."

That's the way I've been for as long as I can remember—thrilled by the great unknown. Climbing a glacier in the Trinity Alps of Northern California, staring into a marble mine in western Portugal, kayaking on the Sea of Cortez, camping in a thunderstorm on a black sand beach on the big island of Hawaii, or dancing in the desert under a pink parasol at the Burning Man Festival in the Black Rock Desert of Nevada—these are the times when I've felt most alive.

But since I moved back home to New York and began focusing on my career, I feel like I've lost touch with my adventurousness, as if it's something I need to abandon in order to become more serious, focused, and adult. And all of the time I've spent trying to find Mr. Right hasn't helped either. Dating with intent is definitely a huge time suck.

I realize, ironically, that what she means by being still is that I need to remember how to live in the moment again and let go of worrying about the future as if marriage and children are the only routes to becoming a legitimate adult woman in the eyes of my peers. I tell Mollie that she's right. I need to start enjoying being single, looking at it as a positive experience of freedom instead of getting bogged down and beating myself up for not having achieved the things that are supposed to be the keys to a happy life.

And who knows, after all, if the keys to happiness even work? The divorce rates in America are staggering, after all, and I know plenty of women—single friends, widows, divorcées—who seem perfectly happy to be on their own. I push our phone conversation in this direction after Mollie reminds me that she discovered after her divorce that marriage with the idea of creating a family was not the be-all and end-all. Even if you think you've found Mr. Right, she reminds me, there are no assurances that life after that will go according to plan.

Mollie's right, of course. While I believe personally that life is sweeter in love and partnership, lots of other women seem to feel differently—especially after choosing the wrong partner.

And there is, in fact, a good deal of evidence that achieving the so-called happy life—a monogamous partnership and children—may not make us so happy after all. In his book *Gross National Happiness*, Arthur C. Brooks argues, based on extensive research and number crunching, that although people who are married tend to report that they are a little happier than people who are not, having children makes them *unhappier*. "The evidence is that marital happiness takes a nosedive as couples move from childlessness to having their first baby, and it continues to plummet until about the time the oldest child starts school." He also finds that a couple's happiness plummets again when the kids become teenagers— and only rises back to pre-child levels after the youngest has left home. His most important finding, perhaps, is that people who decide not to have kids are just as happy in later life as the people who did have children—and they don't regret not having them.

I tell Mollie that maybe this goal I'm so obsessively focused on might not even be the answer I'm looking for, that maybe I just to need refocus my energies on trying to be happy right now, just as I am.

I start thinking that maybe a trip to Costa Rica isn't such a bad idea after all, and I mention the invitation to Mollie.

"Go!" she says.

Maybe this is my chance to try being still.

~

A few weeks later, my plane touches down on a grass runway in the small town of Puerto Jimenez, on the Pacific coast of Costa Rica. Will and Dan*, his best friend from college, and Pete*, a new friend of Will's from his meditation retreat center, are there to pick me up at the airport. Will has now shaved his head completely; he's clearly moving deeper into his practice.

I get into the four-wheel-drive truck they've rented. Mos Def is blaring from the CD player, and we lumber along a bumpy dirt highway past fields of palm trees and grazing cows into the jungle, until we arrive at a house.

"Welcome," Will says, pointing to a green lawn filled with almond trees, bright red flowers, and an arch of palm trees framing a black sand beach and the bright blue water of the Golfo Dulce.

Casa Bambu, an open-air, solar-powered house made from local bamboo, has a huge kitchen and a screened-in front porch with a hammock. It looks like something out of *The Swiss Family Robinson*. As soon as I put down my bags, I lie down on the hammock and look out over the water. I can hear the lion-like sounds of howler monkeys and the beeps and squawks of jungle bugs, tree frogs, and macaws perched on distance trees.

Over the next week, I spend hours alone, splashing through tide pools, listening to Al Green on my iPod, hiking around jungle trails looking up in the trees for monkeys, or just floating on my back in the water, staring up at the sky. One day, Will and I spend an afternoon jumping off a rock cliff into the water on the beach near our house. Another morning his friend Pete, who is obsessed with fishing, wakes me up at five to kayak into the middle of the gulf to catch lunch.

All of this play reminds me of spending time with my father when I was a child. When I was little, we used to have a daily ritual together called the "do something hour." He would stop working and focus exclusively on doing something with me. One summer he taught me to fly cast in the backyard.

"Reel it in slowly," he used to say.

One afternoon I convince the guys to go surfcasting on a deserted beach a few miles away. When I get a huge tug on my line, the guys taunt me and cheer me on like brothers as I hold the rod between my legs and slowly reel in my catch. But the fish gets loose. Endless teasing ensues, of course, about the one who got away. Disappointed that I didn't bring home the fish,

I am inspired that evening to cook up a huge pot of beef bour-
guignon. I make it with local mora berries and serve it on a
huge palm leaf. That night, while we sit around the table eat-
ing and laughing, I realize that I've stopped obsessing about
creating a family. So long as I'm here, Will, Dan, and Pete *are*
my family. With them I feel more like myself, my *real* self, than
I have in a very long time. I am maternal and nurturing and
sexy and one of the guys—all at once. I am living what the
Costa Ricans call *pura vida*—pure life.

$$\sim$$

My trip to Costa Rica has reawakened my travel bug. When I
return to New York, I decide to go on a dating hiatus—what
my friend Abby likes to call a "hidatus." I'm not totally closed
off to a relationship if it happens naturally; I'm just trying not
to focus so obsessively on finding one. Instead, I'm going to
spend the next year devoting myself to *pura vida*. But I realize
that living in New York—with all of its social pressures—
makes stillness hard. So I decide to spend the spring focusing
on getting more travel assignments, which will take me out of
my own little world.

In the early summer, I start planning a trip to South Africa
to write about a new safari lodge. I'd never been to Africa before. The closest I've come was a giraffe I saw in a cage at the
Bronx Zoo, where my father would take me on weekend outings
as a child. I loved giraffes. So I was over the moon when a friend
of my parents called after returning from a safari in East Africa
to tell me that she had brought me a giraffe as a gift and would
deliver it the next time she visited our house. I imagined a
giraffe living in our suburban backyard. For days I talked about

how I would walk it on a very long leash, pet it from the tree house, and feed it big oak leaves.

When the friend brought the gift, my heart sank. It was a three-inch-tall toy giraffe woven out of some kind of African grass and lacquered so its neck wouldn't flop over. Politely, I played with it for a few minutes. I made it walk around my playroom floor while pretending that a houseplant was a tall African tree. But its stiffness was boring, and soon I left it on a shelf. I decided I'd rather play in my tree house with the fantasy of nurturing and feeding my own real giraffe.

As I grew up, my idea of Africa evolved from the home of my fantasy giraffe to other people's fantasies that gave the place texture and color. It was the place where Peter Beard photographed Turkana tribespeople living side by side with Nile crocodiles; where elegant men in khaki would take their fur-coated blond wives on glamorous safaris in Ralph Lauren ads.

It also was the place where my heroines went. In high school and college I read Isak Dinesen's *Out of Africa* and learned about Dian Fossey's work with gorillas and Jane Goodall's study of chimps. These women inspired my sense of adventure. Their unwavering devotion to their causes taught me to follow my passions. These women had deep love affairs, but they never allowed the relationships to consume or control them. Their romantic lives were always shaped by their own dreams and relationships with the land and with animals. Africa came to represent for me the ultimate freedom and independence.

Before I even arrive in South Africa in September, I discover that South Africa is in the midst of a gender revolution. In a country where until 1979 it was illegal for a woman to vote, get divorced, or go into a bar alone and for a man to pour a drink in front of a woman, female entrepreneurs are now running their own businesses, creating new jobs, and acting as the primary leaders of community projects in the developing black townships. I learn this on the plane from New York to Johannesburg, where I meet a talkative Zulu woman who tells me that she runs her own public relations business with a white female partner. As a result of increasing economic independence for women, many are living on their own, and getting married and having children older. She herself is in her mid-thirties and single.

After landing in Johannesburg, I meet up with Erik, a guide with the South African tourism bureau, at my hotel. He has red hair and the slightly absurd formal manner of a Monty Python character. For a few days, he shows me some of the city's restaurants, former townships, and the new Apartheid Museum. As we drive around, I see young girls, black and white, playing on soccer fields. I also notice that South African women have adopted Western fashions, like low-rider jeans.

From Johannesburg, we hop a flight to Cape Town, where I spend a few days exploring the city, including one spectacularly memorable afternoon watching penguins near the Cape of Good Hope. Early the next morning, we fly to Durban and then drive a few hours south to the Safari Lodge in St. Lucia, a wetlands park near the Indian Ocean. There, we meet up with Hayden, a tall and fiercely macho safari guide.

A few days after I arrive at the lodge, I end up drinking late into the night with Hayden and Erik in the hotel bar. I tipsily commit to going on a walking safari the next day in the Hluhluwe Game Reserve, a local park filled with elephants, impalas, lions, and giraffes. The park also happens to contain the largest number of endangered black and white rhinos in all of Africa.

It's an unusual—and not entirely safe—way of seeing game. Most tourists see the African wilderness through the lens of a camera while riding in a jeep or minibus. We, however, will be on foot with a Zulu animal tracker. We will be walking in the trails of animals like traditional hunters whose skills have been passed down for generations.

"It breaks down the barriers between you and the animals," Erik explains.

I'm nervous, but I think about my giraffe. Now I will be in its backyard, as close as possible to that ideal of mine, the freedom of Africa.

The next day, we set out at dawn and meet up with our animal tracker, Mr. Zwane, a Zulu man, at the entrance to the game reserve. He has a large potbelly, which Hayden tells me is a sign of wealth and leadership among the Zulus.

It's a clear day, and the sun is just beginning to warm the ground. It's the beginning of spring in the southern hemisphere, and the first leaves are just beginning to appear on the Umbrella Thorn trees.

Erik hands me a waiver and tells me to sign it. The waiver says, basically, that the park is not responsible for anything that happens to me while I'm on safari here.

"Like being attacked by a lion?" I ask.

"Yes," says Erik, frankly.

I must look nervous, because he assures me that most of the "human predators" tend to stay away from the walking safaris. He also tells me that Mr. Zwane is the best of all the trackers in the area, and that he knows how to keep us downwind from the animals so that they don't catch our scent. I'm feeling reassured, but then Hayden tells me to put on a thick jacket, so I will be better protected from being scratched by branches—or worse.

I dig through my bag and put on my jean jacket. I'm nervous, but I decide that I have no choice but to leave myself in the hands of fate. If this isn't pure life, I don't know what is. I know I have to stop trying to control everything all of the time.

Before we set out on the trail, Mr. Zwane tells us that if we do happen to see a threatening animal, we should remain absolutely still.

"No matter what, do not run away, and don't get too close," he says.

He also tells us to remain absolutely silent at all times. This will be hard for me. I'm about as bad at being quiet as I am at being still. He says that if we need to alert him to anything, we should click our tongues twice in the center of the roofs of our mouths.

"African nature is not your friend and not your enemy, but any mistake in it and it's unforgiving," says Hayden. "It's usually the people who lose respect for it who lose control."

We set out on a narrow trail made by impalas, which are small antelopes with a reddish brown coat and a black streak running down the middle of their backs. The grass surrounding the trail is filled with yellow and pink proteas, pint-sized flowers that look like prehistoric pincushions. We walk silently. I make sure to stay right behind Mr. Zwane. I keep my eyes firmly glued to his game rifle and the big copper bullets in his ammunition belt.

Occasionally, Mr. Zwane casually stops and points to different types of animal dung on the trail. He whispers the Zulu words and then translates them into English. *Indlulamithi*, giraffe. *Indlovu*, elephant.

At one point, Hayden points to a tree. From its branches dangle hundreds of reddish bird nests that looked like knitted socks. He says that the male builds the nests and if the female doesn't approve of it, she can make him rebuild it over and over until she is satisfied, up to ten times.

"That's the way it should be with humans," I whisper to him mischievously.

He rolls his eyes. "My wife would agree."

After about an hour, my nervousness subsides. The heat is coming up, and my mind begins to wander. I think about the cute guy I flirted with—and wished I had kissed—over a nightcap at the hotel in Cape Town, the e-mails I need to answer, bills I need to pay, how far away I feel from the crowded sidewalks of New York.

Suddenly, Mr. Zwane stops walking, clicks his tongue, and points just ahead.

"*Imkhomb,*" he whispers.

I look ahead of him. About twenty yards away is a white rhino grazing in an open field. I see its thick prehistoric hide and its massive horn and then look at the copper bullets in Mr. Zwane's belt, which suddenly seem very small. I freeze.

The rhino senses our presence and turns its head to look in our direction.

"Very aggressive," Hayden whispers.

My body goes completely numb, and my intestines feel like they are turning inside out. I'm breathing so heavily that I can no longer hear anything outside. I've never been this scared in my life.

The rhino begins to circle us, pausing now and then to hoof the ground as if about to charge. Mr. Zwane points away from it, explaining with his hands that we need to move downwind.

I suddenly feel an almost irresistible urge to start running. It is as if the most primitive part of my brain has taken over and is telling my body to flee.

Hayden grabs my hand and pulls me toward him.

"Don't worry," he whispers. "If he charges, just climb a tree."

"But I don't know how to climb a tree," I whisper back.

"You'll learn."

I look around at the trees and see none sturdy enough to climb. I am suddenly infuriated that this macho crew has allowed me to get into this situation. I whisper that I'm going to run back to the safety of our car.

"No," says Hayden, firmly. "If you run, the rhino will chase you or you will run into another."

I want to defy his authority. I want to run. But charging rhinos move faster than running humans, and I know Hayden's right. There's nothing I can do but stay still. I place my shaking hands in prayer position.

I hold my breath as we slowly walk downwind. I can't stop shaking or take my eyes off the rhino's massive horn until I know that he is not going to charge. But after about five minutes of pure panic, he trots off in another direction, and I finally let out my breath.

When we are safe, Hayden tells me that I should feel proud, that 90 percent of women in that situation give in to the urge to run, and that it is a sign of my strength that I didn't.

We continue walking. My racing heart begins to slow, but I'm feeling high off the adrenaline from the encounter. Soon, though, I begin to feel a part of the African bush. As we continue walking along the trail, I notice that my breath slows, and eventually it is in tune with the wind. Gradually, I become calmer, and my eyes begin to wander away from Mr. Zwane. On the hillside, different shades of green and deep purple are emerging, and my eyes begin to play tricks on me, making distant trees look like impalas and rocks like sleeping rhinos.

We are climbing up a small hill when Mr. Zwane stops abruptly and points ahead. I follow the line of his finger and see a giraffe chewing docilely on the leaves of an Umbrella Thorn tree.

"I give you a giraffe," Mr. Zwane says, in broken English.

I watch the giraffe in silence. I admire the elegant curve of his neck as he bows down to reach the low branches. His patterned hide is golden in the morning sun. He is completely unaware of our presence.

I am still.

I am happy.

~

When I get home, I consciously stop talking—and complaining—about being single, and instead I start to relay my travel stories to my friends. I begin to notice a shift in our conversations. Instead of asking me, "How's your love life?" "Who are you dating?" the questions become, "Where are you going next, world traveler?"

Italy is the next place. This time the assignment is more hedonistic than adventurous. I'm spending four days on an eight-hundred-acre estate called Villa Montagnola in Umbria, the earthy middle province of Italy that links the north and south. Here, a company called Italian Days runs retreats that combine yoga and Italian cooking—two of my great interests.

Italian Days is the idea of Anastasia Bizzari, an irreverent forty-year-old Italian corporate type turned yogi. One of the first things she tells me when we meet is that she loves authentic Italian food so much that she once smuggled a coveted round of quality mozzarella into the United States by telling the customs agent it was her silicon breast.

"Ayurveda stresses pure food," she explains. "And so does Italian cooking, which is about simple natural ingredients. So much of life is around preparing meals, going to market, connecting with other people, and through this getting in contact with the self. And in yoga, as in preparing a good meal, mindfulness is a very important quality."

Villa Montagnola is an ivy-covered estate that is home to a distant branch of the Medici and Borgia families. The Medicis were the first family of artistic patronage during the Italian Renaissance, and the Borgias are most famous for Lucrezia Borgia, a fourteenth-century woman legendary for her use of poison in political intrigues.

Vittoria Iraci Borgia, a distant descendant and a young mother of three in her late thirties, now runs the villa as an olive oil farm. Twenty-five members of her extended family either live in the villa or use it as their country estate. Anastasia and Vittoria are old childhood friends, which is how this villa has become the setting for her retreats.

My temporary home is a former tobacco storage house that has been converted into a small apartment with a window that overlooks a forest of deep green Cyprus trees, twisting fig trees, and blooming olive trees.

Our small group includes Lindsay Unger*, a high-strung Parisian who works at the George V Hotel in Paris; Laura*, a wine salesperson from New York; and Ann*, a shy administrative assistant at an investment bank who is taking a rejuvenation vacation from her husband. It also includes Vittoria's mother, Caterina Medici Tornaquinci, a formal matriarch who clips her hair back in a low silver ponytail and speaks to us only in Italian; and Ippolita Medici Tornaquinci, Vittoria's wry, chain-smoking aunt who teaches cooking and etiquette in Florence.

Every morning I wake up, walk up a dirt road to the villa, climb a winding staircase, pass through a corridor filled with frescoes of Roman goddesses, and arrive in a sparse room. There, Cathy*, a salty former speed skater from Long Island whom Anastasia recruited from New York's Reebok Club, leads us through a strenuous two-hour yoga class. After yoga class, our group heads to the kitchen for a cooking class lead by Carmela, the house chef. Anastasia joins in waxing on about the connection between cooking and yoga.

"In cooking, you have to be patient," she says.

"Watch Carmela. She puts all her energy into kneading. She is being patient and, look, there is dough. She is rewarded."

It seems kind of hokey, but as the week passes, the yoga practice seems to focus me in the kitchen. My senses become more open, and everything starts to taste better. I start to better appreciate the flavors in the food and the details around me, like the smell of jasmine and the distant sounds of church bells wafting into the yoga room.

Dinner in the formal dining room is the day's big event. We dress up and eat on elegant china. One evening, we have a three-hour feast that starts with lasagna with fava beans. Cheryl* tells us about her adventures in Southeast Asia. Lindsay admits that she is considering leaving Paris and moving to San Francisco to have a more balanced life. Ippolita tells me a story about the time that she got so mad at a boyfriend that she threw all of his clothes out the window.

In the next few days, I start to feel more in the present moment. One morning I watch while Vittoria's daughters curl their hair up into buns and decorate them with glitter in preparation for a swimming exhibition. One afternoon there's a conversation about voters in France and the Netherlands rejecting the European Union constitution. On the day of Infiorata del Corpus Domini, which honors a Bohemian priest by carpeting the streets in flower petal patterns, I meditate over a peach gelato in the town of Torgiano.

Instead of focusing on what I don't have, I've decided to appreciate what I do have. Here I am in a noble villa in Umbria, bonding with a multigenerational and geographically diverse group of women. After my more macho adventures, it's really nice to be in the midst of this feminine and nurturing sorority, lounging in the garden, sharing stories, and learning to cook recipes that have been passed down through the generations of Vittoria's family. We aren't overly focused on men—we have pushed aside serving them to serve ourselves and come together as a grand party, finding common links as a kind of modern family.

~

When the week is over, I decide to go to Florence for a day before leaving for New York. I immediately head for the Uffizi Gallery. Given my radical change in attitude, I figure that standing still in front of some Renaissance paintings will be good for me. I find myself, on my last day in Italy, staring at Cupid and Venus in Botticelli's *Birth of Venus*. Pondering it, I realize that I am beginning to understand the kind of love I'm looking for. Cupid, the adorable archer with those little wings, symbolizes lustful and earthly love—the kind of love, I realize, that I experienced in all those wonderful flash-flood love affairs of my twenties. Venus represents a more noble and romantic kind of love, which isn't about instant gratification. Her love is more sophisticated and built on mutual respect and friendship that transcends base desire.

In that moment, staring at this timeless masterpiece, I know that this is the love I want as the basis for my family. And I know that it is worth waiting for. I'm going to sit still for a bit longer, rather than worrying about what will come. I am madly in love with this life I've chosen, I realize. I appreciate afresh my mother's advice: "Find your passion. Find yourself."

# 6

Adventurous SWF
Seeks Hottie

I return from Italy resolved to hold out longer for real love—and thus ignore the deadline I set for myself to pursue single mother-hood when I turn thirty-six. Instead, I decide to give myself the present of a puppy. I know I am once again gambling on my eggs in order to fulfill my romantic dream, and I figure a furry little friend will give me warmth and help me through my occasional bouts of loneliness. Most of my friends are thrilled by my decision, but one reacts differently, and won't stop making fun of me.

"You're going to carry around a puppy in a bag like a baby?" she asks, mouth agape.

I take her point. Clearly, I would be using the puppy to ful-fill my need to nurture something—and to have company. But what's wrong with that for now? I'm not intending to become a crazy dog lady, the kind of woman who lives with five giant dogs and doesn't know how to relate to real people. I just want a creature to take care of, wake me up in the morning, and keep me in the present moment.

I tell my friend that I promise not to carry it around in a little handbag.

~

Although I am going to wait for love, I'm certainly not going to do it passively. I decide to start dating again, and in a strange moment of serendipity, I receive a call from an editor at *Outside* magazine asking if I might be interested in taking on a new and somewhat challenging assignment. She wants me to go undercover to research a new dating website called SingleAndActive.com.

I love doing things outdoors, and I figure it will be a good way to have fun and throw myself back into the game. I worry a bit that my dates will turn out to be tree-hugging hemp lovers who want to massage me with patchouli oil—but it's just an assignment after all. And there is the possibility that it might lead me to meeting someone in a real way. So I tell the editor I'm in.

At the end of October, a month before my thirty-sixth birthday, I log on to the site. I choose "Cosmo Camper" as my screen name, figuring that this is a good way of making it clear that while I enjoy walking safaris in Africa, surfing, and yoga, I also I love art galleries, martinis, and a great pair of heels.

"On a recent walking safari in South Africa," I write, "I learned that I fall into the 10 percent category of women who don't run when face-to-face with a white rhino. When I was twenty-one, I trekked to sixteen thousand feet in the Himalayas to bring my boyfriend a beer on his birthday."

For the finishing touch, I uploaded a photo of myself in a snowboard jacket at the base of Snowbird Mountain in Utah.

Within a few days, I receive my first e-mail from a New Yorker.

"Do you like the trapeze?" he asks.

In the past, guys have asked me to watch the Playboy channel with them or take a spin through the vibrator section of Toys in Babeland, but this trapeze thing is new—and kind of freaky. But after a moment I realize that he's being literal. At Trapeze School New York, you can don a harness and take lessons on the art of circus catch and release. I figure that a man's ability to catch me flying through the air might be a good test of his trustworthiness, so I reply and say the trapeze thing sounds fun.

"First, could I see a photo that shows a little more of you?" he writes back.

I'm a little freaked out that he wants to check out my body before meeting me in person, but then decide to send him a picture taken on my trip to Costa Rica, right after I almost reeled in that big fish. I'm wearing a sun hat and a bright blue bikini and holding my fishing rod.

He never writes back. Maybe it was too suggestive?

In the next few weeks, I scan past a hunter from Denver who poses in camouflage with a rifle, a hiker from Seattle who instead of a picture of himself posts a photo of a prairie dog wearing a wig, and a flycaster from Colorado who drops me a line and tells me to check out his profile page, which has a picture of the gaping mouth of a large fish.

"Do you really think this will attract a woman?" I e-mail him.

"Doesn't that look like a moist and inviting pair of lips to you?" he writes back. "If you look long enough, you may just start to develop affection for the cute little fishy!"

Ick. I don't respond.

Next, I have a long exchange with a doctor in Katmandu who tells me he found me by randomly typing in my zip code. He doesn't seem to mind that I live half way around the world.

"Your profile is superb, and it is the thing that pulled me toward you!" he writes. I respond—he's so sweet, how can I refuse?—and tell him that during college I spent a month living in a village in southern Nepal studying meditation with a holy man.

"You are my type!" he writes back. "I used to do simple meditation. Have you heard of that young man in Nepal who has been meditating in the forest for six months without food or drink?" The doctor sounds way too enthusiastic about the idea. The movie reel in my head projects a new scene. *I'm starving in the Himalayan outback surrounded by yaks and a chanting, skeletal husband.*

So I decide to stick a little closer to home.

One unseasonably warm winter morning, a note arrives in my inbox from a backcountry skier with the screen name Rutabaga*.

"I ski a lot," he writes. "How about talking about adventures while having a martini?"

Rutabaga also sends two photos, one showing him tearing down a powdery steep. I can barely see his face, but the action shot is sexy. The other reveals a slightly balding guy with a boyish face and charming blue eyes. I e-mail him back, saying that a martini sounds great and suggesting that we meet the next night at Raoul's, a gritty SoHo haunt favored by New York politicians and reporters.

My date is waiting at the crowded bar when I arrive. He's wearing a bright orange shirt that screams "bachelor for too long." I'm already thinking of exit strategies but decide one drink can't hurt. He's from New Hampshire and once worked as a ski instructor in Colorado; now he's a freelance film editor. As the martini buzz comes on, I start feeling a faint attraction. I like the way his arms look.

"There's nothing more romantic than watching the sun go down over the river and the lights come up on the Manhattan skyline," I say, overtaken by the drink, and the idea that this might make great copy.

"How about kayaking the river at sunset?" he proposes.

Perfect.

The weather stays warm all week, until the day before our date, when an arctic front sweeps in. By the time I show up at the Manhattan Kayak Company on a pier off the West Side highway, the temperature is 30 degrees, the coldest day of the year so far. Instead of gazing longingly into each other's eyes over Irish coffee in front of a fireplace, Ruty and I are shivering in full wet suits, orange life vests, and wool hats. While the fast-talking, silver-haired owner of the company and guide, Eric, is describing our mile-long round-trip excursion in a double kayak from 23rd Street to the Port Authority ferry terminal on West 38th Street, I'm praying that we don't capsize.

We head north under a chemical orange and red sky, barely crawling against three-knot currents. I'm up front. Ruty is in the back, breathing hard and struggling to steer us past the twisted, rusty iron pier that used to house the New York Department of Docks.

"It just happens that the exact time of sunset is when the currents are the strongest today," Eric yells to us.

The currents are so strong that they're pulling us backward into a whirlpool that looks like it's going to suck us under. My date is barely speaking to me. I can't figure out whether it's because he's the strong and silent type, or because he's so scared and winded he can't talk.

We're definitely in a bad spot. Where the river squeezes through a small vent near the Verrazano-Narrows Bridge, it collides with the force of the Atlantic Ocean, creating a powerful counterclash of currents. The dynamic appears to be unfolding directly beneath us.

The first thing I think is that it may be a good test of our potential.

"The double kayak has a long history of being the marriage boat or the divorce boat," Eric yells across the waves. "If the person in the front isn't setting a good pace then the person in the back has a hard time staying on stroke. You have to stay synchronized. You have to work as a team."

"I think it's too hard!" I shout.

"Let's not give up!" Ruty shouts, emerging from his silence.

Eric points us toward what he's dubbed "the nest of ferries," a technically challenging 250-yard paddling sprint across the major ferry thoroughfare between Manhattan and New Jersey. To avoid getting caught in the wakes—or, worse, running smack into one of the giant vessels—crossing this section of water must be carefully timed.

"Only half a dozen people can successfully make it across at rush hour," he announces cheerfully.

Ruty and I do our best, weaving through the wooden pylon remains of an old dock.

"Watch to your left!" Eric shouts.

I look left and see a huge wave—the wake from a monster ferry—crashing toward the side of our boat. I momentarily panic, imagining the headlines in the *New York Post*. *Single*

*White Kayaker Struck and Killed on Internet Date—"She could have done better," witnesses say.*

I paddle hard to the right, Ruty does the same, and we turn the kayak just in time to face the approaching water, then gently surf over it. The ferry captain sticks out his hand to signal that he sees us.

"This is getting fun," Ruty says.

An hour earlier, the gray fortress of the ferry terminal seemed impossibly far away, but now we've actually reached it. Eric directs us to turn around and head back to the kayak company. We steer south, catch a swift current, and effortlessly glide on the water. The sky has bruised to deep purple. Glimmers of reflected light from the Empire State Building and the chrome spire of the Chrysler Building skip off the jet black water. Even though we're only a few blocks from the blaring horns of Times Square, it's absolutely silent by our boat.

Eric congratulates us back at the dock. "You guys worked well with each other."

Ruty smiles at me and asks if I want to grab another drink.

Even though we've done well on our adventure, the shot of adrenaline hasn't inspired any real sense of romance in me. He's nice, but flat—and besides, it's hard for me to really connect with him when the reporter in me is thinking constantly about what great copy the date will make. But we did just accomplish quite a feat, so I think we deserve a celebratory martini.

We head back to Raoul's, where several of my friends are gathered for dinner. After a few glasses of wine, however, I begin to find Ruty downright annoying. He's a far better paddler than conversationalist, it turns out. The date reaches a tipping point when he grabs my ass under the table. I shoot him a nasty glance, and he clearly gets the message, because the next morning I get an e-mail from him:

"I really enjoyed kayaking with you, but I don't think we have the romantic kismet that it takes to date," it says.

On November 25, I turn thirty-six. Instead of calling a sperm bank, I call a dog breeder upstate. I plan to get a red female King Charles Spaniel because I love their big brown eyes. I'm going to name her Nellie after Nellie Bly, one of my favorite female adventurers. Bly was a journalist who worked for the *New York World* in the 1920s. She became famous for feigning insanity in order to gain entry into the Women's Lunatic Asylum on Blackwell's Island and went on to expose the staff's brutality and neglect of the patients. In 1888, Nellie suggested to her editor that she take a trip around the world, mimicking Jules Verne's book *Around the World in Eighty Days*. A year later, she left New York on her 24,899-mile journey, which took her seventy-two days, six hours, eleven minutes, and fourteen seconds, breaking the world record.

The breeder tells me that she has a new litter and that I'll be able to come pick up my puppy in mid-March, as soon as she is weaned from her mother. My brother buys me a cute green leash and collar for Christmas.

A week after my birthday, I get an e-mail from a man on SingleAndActive.com who says he likes the way I look. He tells me he loves climbing, skiing, and biking. I flirt back to say hi. A few hours later he writes something more substantial, describing himself as "a fairly successful, well-traveled, cultured, overeducated math Ph.D." He reports that his most recent odyssey involved hiking to the Blümlisalp Swiss Alpine Club hut in the Alps.

I have a hard time picturing myself locked inside an SAC hut with an intensely rational and slightly cocky postdoc, but I'm intrigued. So on a sunny Saturday, I meet up with the mathematician and go for a walk along the river, near my apartment. His name is Art*, and he's an angular guy with dark brown thinning hair. He spends most of our time together talking about his job, which is predicting the future of stocks at a Manhattan hedge fund.

I'm not physically attracted to Art—he's too cerebral and skinny—and I suspect there will be no baby-making in our future. But I think he's a nice guy, so when he e-mails and asks if I'd like to meet him on a Tuesday night at an indoor climbing gym, I say yes. But first I make sure to tell him that I've gone climbing only once in my life. I was eleven and at sleepaway camp in Vermont. At the critical moment—when I was supposed to lean back and rappel off the top of a twenty-foot rock face—I had a massive panic attack. I stood there for an hour before I could let go and rappel down.

"So you have trust issues?" Art asks.

When I don't respond, he sends a follow-up.

"I've been climbing for two years, so I'm sure you'll be fine under my mediocre tutelage," he writes. "But you should probably make sure you've got an up-to-date tetanus shot."

We meet at a climbing gym on the Upper West Side, a bare-bones place with a hipster vibe and a climbing wall built into an old racquetball court.

Art shows up late and doesn't offer to pay the $15 for my climbing session. He does bring me a small bottle of water, though. The room booms with the sounds of industrial rock and the occasional Santana tune. Twenty-something yoga girls and climber geeks are splayed every which way on molded plastic faux rocks precariously stapled into the walls. I wonder if he was actually serious about the tetanus shot.

Art tells me he'll belay me and hands me a harness. Once I've cinched it around my waist, he grabs the front of it and yanks it tight, making my hips thrust toward him.

"OK, climb!" he says, pointing to a fifteen-foot wall. I feel like I'm in a French S&M film.

I grab onto a lower rock and start climbing, making it up halfway pretty easily. I look down and smile at him for approval. I've already decided that I don't really like him—so far he's talked only about himself, showed up late, and been cheap. But he does seem to know something about the climbing, so I figure I'll take him as a coach, albeit a slightly sadistic one.

"Don't let me fall," I call down.

"I won't let you fall, because I don't want to lose my membership," he yells.

"So this is about you," I retort, stepping onto a tiny green foothold and hoisting myself to the top of the wall.

"Life is about self-interest," he shouts back.

Art, it turns out, has a robotic side. When I get down from the wall, he tells me about his climbing schedule. Three times a week he walks here from his office in Midtown, climbs for a few hours, ambles around the corner to Taco Express on 9th Avenue, orders a grilled chicken burrito—always the same kind—and eats it at home. He likes climbing because it's pure physicality—the opposite of his brainy analytic job.

"Climbing is about being in your body in the moment," he tells me.

I know something about that myself, and I wonder if maybe I'm being too standoffish, not letting myself fall into this experience. But then he motions for me to follow him to an area called The Cave, and I realize that I'm not the problem here.

The Cave consists of a bunch of mats lying on the floor beneath an inclined ceiling stapled with rocks. The object is to lie down on the mat directly under the lowest part of the ceiling, grab a rock and climb the slope to the higher part of the ceiling—all while hanging upside down.

We lie on the mats for a moment, side-by-side.

"It took me six months to master this," he says, latching on and scampering effortlessly up the incline.

I look at him dripping with sweat and feel repulsed at the idea of him climbing on me. Then I try it myself and can't even pull myself up on the first rock. Recognizing how hard this exercise is, I'm impressed by his acumen. But it doesn't make up for his total lack of social skills.

At last, the torture ends, and we put our sweats back on to leave. It's obvious to both of us that there won't be a date #2, but I decide nevertheless to accompany him on his burrito run.

Standing in line at the joint, I suggest he find a woman who is a bit more cerebral. I'm really thinking, *someone just as self-centered and robotic as you*, but I don't want to be that incendiary.

"I think in the final analysis I'm looking for a female version of myself," he tells me. "I'm ultimately doomed in that respect, because they broke the mold with me, baby."

I cringe and politely make my exit.


By late December, I have outdoor-dating fatigue. I've responded to fifty e-mails and haven't heard from anyone who sounds remotely like my better half. I'm convinced these adventure men care more about their sports than they do about female companionship. The only creature I want to curl up with is my impending puppy.

The upside of all of this Single-And activity, however, is that I'm feeling totally in my game. I've been working out, going on dates, flirting, and in general putting out that inexplicable vibe that makes men hover around you the minute you get engaged or show up at a party with someone new on your arm. Call it kismet or pheromones. Whatever it is, it's working.

Then one night in the dead of winter I get a phone call.

"Hi. My name is Jacob*," says the boyish voice on the other end of the line. He tells me that he got my name and number from an online dating/networking site for graduates of elite colleges. I'd joined years earlier, but no one from the site had ever contacted me, and I'd forgotten all about it. I realize that the profile he's seen must be really, really old.

Jacob tells me that he is an architect, thirty-six, Ivy League educated, Jewish, and a native New Yorker. He was raised in Mamaroneck, on the Long Island Sound, not far from where I grew up. I sense his warmth immediately while we make small talk about the places we've worked and how we both used to live in California. He tells me that he's recently joined forces with a well-known female architect and they've started their own firm. They're working on a high-profile building uptown.

While we're on the phone, Jacob e-mails me a picture of himself. I completely melt over his gorgeous green eyes and thick black hair.

I'm trying to remember what I had put in my profile on the site, even what picture I'd used. So I ask him what in my profile attracted him to me.

"Well, I liked your picture, and what you said," he tells me.

"What in particular?" I ask, digging.

"You wrote: 'Thirty-two. Very pretty journalist. Looking for a smart, ambitious guy who's not afraid to keep the love swimming forward.' You were referring to the famous Woody Allen line about how love is like a shark and if you don't keep it swimming forward, it'll die, right?"

"Yes." It's coming back to me now.

"Well, that sounds pretty good to me," he says. "Are you free this Tuesday?"

I'm really excited to meet him but realize it could be a disaster if we meet and he learns how old my profile picture is. I go for full disclosure and explain that I'm thirty-six and that the profile is from four years ago.

He falls silent for a second.

"Well, OK," he says. "So I'll call you Tuesday."

That Tuesday, we meet at the Olde Castle, an Irish pub in the theater district. When he walks into the bar, he immediately knocks over the chair next to mine by accident, and laughs. Clearly not a single and active guy, but comfortable enough in his own skin that he recovers quickly.

"Well, that was quite an entrance, wasn't it?" he says, with such self-deprecating irony that I laugh.

We chat over stiff scotches and discover that we have a million things in common—we both love traveling and skiing. And, despite his clumsy entrance, he also loves outdoor adventure—he tells me he once climbed Mount Kilimanjaro. And even though we met online, we actually know some of the same people, which instantly makes me feel more comfortable with him than I normally would on a first date.

Over the course of the evening, I become increasingly smitten. He's terrifically upbeat and positive—like a character from a 1950s teen movie. Unlike most of the people I meet in

New York, he doesn't seem jaded or cynical. I like the way he talks about his career in a passionate way. I like that he has a close relationship with his family; like mine, his parents have been married for almost forty years. But the success of his parents' marriage doesn't seem to make him unrealistic. Later in the evening, he tells me how much he loves the movies, but that he doesn't believe in "movie love."

"Marriage is about hard work," he says.

This is music to my ears. My gut tells me that Jacob will be my next boyfriend, but as the romantic fantasies start to unspool in my head, I force myself to stop.

After sharing a big plate of nachos, he says he has to go back to work, but offers to walk to me to the subway. Standing in front of the station, he leans over to hug me—he feels warm and strong. I pull back and look at him, and something in his eyes inspires me to kiss him. It's quick, and I'm embarrassed by my assertiveness, but he smiles as if he likes it. He says he'll call me, and I run down the steps to the station.

*Be still. Stay in the moment*, I think.

The next morning, I get an e-mail from Jacob asking me out on Saturday night. Over dinner at my favorite hamburger joint in the West Village, we talk more about our relationships with our families. We agree that the closeness is wonderful, but sometimes oppressive as well. We figure out that we both moved to California to get some distance from all of it.

I've never felt this in-sync with a man so quickly; I find myself telling him things that some of my closest friends don't know. Then, as the evening winds to a close, he tells me point blank that he wants to get married and have children "soon." I like the way he reaches across the table, looks me in the eyes, and grabs my hand in a commanding way when he tells me this. I try not to swoon.

"You are very pretty," he says, staring at me intently. "Foxy, actually. You have such a beautiful smile." I feel embarrassed, almost uncomfortable in his close gaze. No one has ever looked at me this way.

I take his hand and pull my things together, and he stands too. Outside on the street, he kisses me passionately, and I start to feel the love bugs fluttering in my stomach.

"You're so emotionally generous," he says.

I invite him up to my apartment, and we make out on the couch. He doesn't try to have sex with me that evening, and I'm charmed by the high school innocence of it all.

On our third date, he takes me to an apartment he is thinking about buying. It's on a high floor and has a beautiful view over a small park. I think about the male bird I saw in South Africa making his little nest for his mate to approve. I approve.

The film begins running in my head—this time I can't stop it. I imagine Mollie giving the maid-of-honor speech at our wedding. "Mollie, I can't find a clam. I can't find a clam," she'll say, imitating my voice before telling all of the guests about how I finally found my enormous clam—just when I stopped looking.

~

On our fourth date, Jacob and I decide to date exclusively. It's time for me to cancel my SingleAndActive.com membership, finish writing, and hand in my story. Even though the website didn't lead me directly to Mr. Right, I realize, the confidence I gained from the experience paved the way for me to establish this amazing connection with Jacob. It occurs to me that a lesson I learned while traveling also applies to dating: sometimes you have to change your perspective in the physical world in order to change your emotional one.

Around Valentine's Day, Jacob and I start planning a trip to Los Angeles in March. We talk about bike riding at the beach and hiking in the Santa Monica mountains. The only problem with the trip, I tell him, is that I'm going to have my puppy by then, and so I will have to find someone to take care of her while we're gone.

When I tell him this, his jaw drops slightly.

"Didn't I tell you I was getting a puppy?"

"Didn't I tell you I was allergic to dogs?"

# 7

## The Instant Family

The next day I make the difficult call to the breeder. I tell her that she's going to have to find another home for the puppy. She's worried and unhappy because the dog is getting older and it will be harder to place the puppy with someone else. I feel terrible, like a mother who has just abandoned her child. But I rationalize the decision: I'm spending almost every night with Jacob now—how could I get a puppy knowing that he would be awake all night sniffling and wheezing? I can't do that to him, and it could be a huge interference in our budding relationship. So I decide to sacrifice Nellie and put Jacob first.

I know I'm making the right decision. It's been more than four years since Alex broke up with me at The Cloisters, and finally I've found a guy who seems right for me. Jacob is amazing, and I can't believe how happy I am with him. He's the perfect combination of friend and lover, and I feel totally myself around him. He's one of the first men I've dated who really appreciates me and my work. I can remember too many boyfriends who just tuned out whenever I told them about my latest assignment, but when I talk to Jacob about the stories I'm working on he listens intently and then tells me how sexy he thinks it is that I'm a writer.

Jacob also gets my sense of humor. One night at dinner with some straight-laced banker friends of his, I make a willfully provocative statement about how Manhattan has lost some of its gritty charm because artists and writers can't afford it anymore now that all of the ultramaterialistic investment bankers have moved in. The comment falls with a thud; I've clearly made Jacob's friends feel uncomfortable.

"Rachel loves to stir the pot!" he says, smiling and simultaneously kicking me under the table. Walking home after the dinner, he scolds me for embarrassing him but then grabs me and kisses me and tells me that he loves how free-spirited I am.

I love Jacob's energy and his sense of humor. I love his odd obsession with comic books, the way he piles them by his bedside like a teenage boy, and how superheroes have shaped his moral universe. Superficially, he can seem a bit uptight, but when we're alone he relaxes and becomes irresistibly playful. He brings amusement to even the most mundane errands by turning everything into a movie scene: he brings the characters we see to life by taking on their voices and imagining what kind of personalities they have. Sometimes he even starts singing like he's in a musical.

I'm much more interior than he is—I live more of my life in my own head. I'm more likely to make references to a book or a film than to someone who passes us on the street. When I wrote out my description of my ideal partner, I said I wanted a man who complemented me. Jacob does that. And sometimes he also wears turtleneck sweaters.

On Easter weekend, in late March, I introduce Jacob to my parents, brother, aunt, and uncle over dinner at the Boat House in Central Park.

"He's perfect for you," my uncle whispers.

And that's exactly how I feel, like all this time I've spent searching and working on the life I wanted for myself has finally brought me to the right relationship, to real love. It was worth the wait.

~

By late summer, Jacob is preparing to move into the apartment he showed me early on. I'm feeling pretty convinced that he is the one. It doesn't seem premature to me—I'm nearly thirty-seven, and I've had enough bad relationships along the way to recognize how great this one is. Even though it's been only six months, Jacob and I are really serious about each other. We talk every day, we know all of each other's friends, and we're organizing our schedules around seeing each other as much as possible.

I resolved early on in our relationship not to let my imagination get ahead of me, but at this point I don't feel I am. Jacob told me that getting married and having a family is a priority for him as well, and at our ages it doesn't seem too early to begin thinking about what that might look like. There have been a lot of stories about couples our age who get married within a year of meeting and have children soon after—or even before: The *New York Times* ran a story in 2005 with the headline "Here Comes the Mother-to-Be." Couples in their late thirties are putting baby first, marriage second.

"Brides are not only not hiding their pregnancies, but they are showing them off, celebrating the upcoming birth in vows and toasts, wearing gowns that flatter their bump, and, in short, refusing to give up any elements of a traditional wedding just because there is a baby visibly on the way," wrote reporter Mireya Navarro.

A few years ago, I might have mocked these insta-couples—how could these unions possibly be real? Surely, these women were just desperate for babies and settling for whoever comes along. But now I see it differently. What Jacob and I have *is* real, and it's hard-fought. I've learned a lot about myself in the course of all of my failed relationships. I've also learned a lot about what it takes to make a relationship work. Jacob isn't just someone who showed up in the right place at the right time. I've done a lot of work to get here.

My pragmatic side, however, tells me that I should research the insta-couple phenomenon before considering it too seriously myself. When I tell my mother how I feel about Jacob, she suggests that I go talk to Jane Harnick, the daughter of her friend Barbara Barrie. Jane, my mother explains, met her husband, Adam, when she was thirty-eight. She was pregnant within the year.

A few days later, I go to Jane and Adam's apartment for tea. They live in a one-bedroom on the Upper West Side. Barbara is also there.

"I'd been dumped—again," Jane begins, telling me the story of how she met Adam.

An earthy redhead with relaxed gestures, Jane is a photo editor at a fashion company. She explains that by the time she turned thirty-seven, ten years of dating in New York had turned her into what felt like a walking *Cathy* cartoon: serially dumped by emotionally unavailable guys and about to age out of her own fertility.

Jane's mother offered to pay for her to go to a weekend dating seminar. Jane went, she got some insights (she had to stop being drawn to emotionally withholding men like her father) and then got back online. This time, she decided, she would make online dating a project. She even set a deadline. If she didn't find the right guy by the time she was thirty-eight, she was going to have a child on her own.

"I said I'd help her," Barbara tells me.

Every night, Jane sat at her computer—sometimes until three in the morning—e-mailing every man who looked remotely promising. "I totally blitzed it," she says. "I would say to myself 'one more page, one more page,' until I got back to the beginning."

For two months, Jane went on two to three dates a week. Then one Saturday afternoon she had a picnic date in Central Park with Adam, a warm and funny thirty-seven-year-old PR director for ABC Sports. He was five years out of a divorce and living alone with his dog in a studio on the Upper East Side. Jane liked him immediately.

"He brought the right kind of food," she says. "Hummus, bread, and cheese. Mangoes and avocado salad. I was impressed. I asked him if he wanted to have kids. I didn't want to beat around the bush."

The relationship took off quickly.

"Right after we met we stopped using birth control," says Jane.

"After you met?!" exclaims Barbara. She turns to Adam. "But you hadn't asked her to marry you yet!"

"We weren't actively trying to get pregnant," Adam explains. "We basically decided that if it happens, it happens."

Seven months later, Adam—and his dog, Vinnie, moved into Jane's place. By February, they were engaged.

Jane tells me that Adam showed an openness that she had never experienced before with a man, and that she knew quickly that he was right for her. And because of their age, and their past experience—Adam had gone through one marriage and learned a lot from his mistakes—the pieces fell together quickly.

Seventeen months after their first date, Jane walked down the aisle eight months pregnant in a white, size 46 stretch-jersey dress. Jane and Adam's daughter, Roxie, is now ten months old.

"In a perfect world, I wish we'd had more time alone before she was born," she says. "Now we're so busy and tired, it's hard to find time for each other."

But the days of her feeling lonely, anxious, and serially rejected have been replaced by a sense of comfort and stability. "Now the baby goes down at 7:00, Adam and I have dinner, and then we go to bed. I'm thrilled."

They'll celebrate their two-year anniversary by going to Paris for their honeymoon. "Adam assures me that Roxie will remember us when we get back," Jane says, smiling and looking over at her husband. She rolls her eyes. "Of course I'm convinced she's going to walk and we'll miss it."

I leave Jane's place feeling optimistic; maybe my desire to move forward with Jacob is not rushed, but defiantly pragmatic—and natural for a woman of my age. Jane and Adam seem so comfortable together, and truly in love with each other. I wonder if the older you are and the more you know yourself, the easier it is to see what's right sooner. For Jane and Adam, it seems that committing and conceiving in a flash was not an act of desperation or instability. Quite the opposite—it was a leap of faith toward a more stable future.

That night, I meet up with Jacob and his sister Allison*. He refers to Allison as his best friend, so I take it as a big step that he wants to introduce us. Allison and I bond immediately. She works in development at an art gallery. She has a big mass of curly auburn hair and a squeaky, high-pitched voice that belies her tough disposition. For example, when Jacob makes a slightly entitled comment about the service at the restaurant, she shoots him a knowing glance that quickly shuts him up. She is clearly the family diplomat.

After dinner, part of me wants to tell Jacob about my meeting with Jane and Adam. But I know it might sound like I'm putting pressure on him, so I decide not to. Be still, I tell myself. Or at least *pretend* to be—I'm madly in love with Jacob, and I can't stop my mind from racing ahead.

~

Although there are no broad-based studies examining the success rates of insta-couples, the available data suggests that for many people, quickie weddings may work just fine. Ted Huston, a professor of psychology and human ecology at the University of Texas at Austin has tracked 168 marriages since 1979. He has found that the relationships in which couples were engaged within nine months have a better chance of surviving to the seven-year mark. "Early bliss makes people stick it out longer when the marriage runs into problems."

Studies have also found that living together for a long period of time before getting married increases the risk of divorce. A 2002 study conducted by demographers at Pennsylvania State University found that the longer a couple had lived together before marriage, the more accepting they were of the possibility of divorce. They also grew less enthusiastic about marriage and having children.

As much as I enjoyed the legitimatization of hearing about Jane's success story, and the confidence it gives me about my own relationship, I realize I owe it to myself to learn about the dark side of insta-marriage as well. A friend of mine refers me to Joanne*, an acquaintance of hers, whose insta-family fell apart.

Joanne, a mother of two, lives in Brooklyn. When I call her, she tells me that when she was thirty-six she married, bought a house, and had her daughter within a year and a half of meeting her husband, a successful documentary producer. She was feeling pressure to get married and felt like he was the one. She had her son only sixteen months after her daughter was born. "The decision to have kids quickly was not an accident," she says. "I knew I wanted to be a mother, but it was my husband who pushed it."

Although Joanne played along, she tells me that part of her knew she was rushing; that she was almost convincing herself that she loved this man completely because she was so eager to achieve the trifecta of adulthood: a husband, a house, and children. But a year after their second child was born, her husband became distant and the couple began fighting over everything from the way they should raise the kids to who should make dinner. The reality of their challenges made them forget the early bliss, and eventually he left the marriage for another woman.

Looking back, she says she thinks she got married too quickly. "It made sense on paper, but I was too caught up in the things that I was accumulating," she says. "If we had moved slower and had more of a courtship, I would have seen certain things in his personality that were going to cause problems." Still, she is grateful that she had her children—and she says that she would make a fast decision again. "It's always a risk, and now I'm wiser from the lessons I learned the first time."

～

Joanne's story makes me want to know more about the downside of insta-families, so I call my friend Rob Stein, a Manhattan-based marriage and family therapist. Rob sees a lot of insta-families in his practice, and over lunch he tells me that these marriages can be extremely fragile—no matter what age you are.

"If you have a shaky sense of self and try to solve it by getting married quickly and having a child, when things get challenging, you're going to start to question the relationship quickly," he says.

I press him for more. He says that often couples have "fairy-tale expectations" and make promises to one another early on, during the honeymoon phase, that change later. For example, in the throes of early love, the man tells the woman that he wants to be an equal in the child rearing. But when reality sets in, and the kids are born, he fails to meet these expectations, resentment grows, and cracks begin to appear in a foundation built out of the original fantasy that propelled the couple to commit.

Another warning sign, he says, is a person who has never had a serious sustaining relationship in the past who suddenly jumps into marriage. He tells me about a man who wanted to replicate his parents' seemingly perfect marriage with the first woman he fell in love with. He quickly asked her to marry him, and she agreed. But as they spent more time together and grappled with issues of real intimacy, the stuff that causes some pain and bumps, he got scared that the ideal was not working and began to sabotage the relationship out of fear.

"Another mistake is committing out of fear," Rob tells me. "A person may make a decision out of anxiety—baby panic, because your friend or sister got married, financial insecurity—or a sense of not being safe in the world. What happens when the fear subsides, and you're left with a less than ideal relationship?"

In the wake of my conversation with Rob, I try to assess if I myself am falling into any of the traps he's described. I know that I can be hopelessly romantic, and that I'm easily prone to constructing fantasies about the future. And certainly I have fantasies about my future with Jacob. But those aren't the basis of our relationship, by any means. We both know that marriage isn't easy, that it's about hard work. We both agree that the trick is to find someone you love so much that you want to *do* that work. And it's not as if Jacob and I are living in some silly fantasyland in the way we interact with each other. We haven't really talked about our future or made any promises to one another. We're living day by day, learning more about each other and enjoying what we have.

I do think seriously, though, about Rob's comments about fear. Of course it's true that I'm worried about my biological clock, and I have to guard myself against letting this anxiety propel me too far forward too quickly. I also need to make sure that it's not blinding me to any red flags. It is true that Jacob hasn't been in a lot of long-term relationships. He's never lived with anyone before, and his last serious relationship was in his late twenties and only lasted a year. But when he tells me that his relationship with me is the most serious he's ever had, I take that as a huge compliment. Jacob is an extremely discerning person; it's not hard for me to imagine that he's had trouble finding someone who lives up to his ideals. After all, I've had the same problem myself.

~

Biological pressure, not surprisingly, plays a huge role in the decision of many couples to start an insta-family. But as I speak with more couples, I learn that it's not the only thing that spurs these couples to move forward quickly. Many of these men and women have, as they've gotten older, simply redefined—or at least refined—their ideas about what love is and should be. After a decade or often more of dating experience, they no longer see the point of a long courtship: you just know if it works. Pragmatism has replaced grand passion as these couples fulfill their practical desire to get on with the next stage of life.

Bela Schwartz and June Zimmerman, another insta-couple I meet through a friend's recommendation, exemplify this spirit of pragmatism. Seven years ago Bela, a baby-faced financial executive, turned forty and looked back at the previous decade of fourteen-hour workdays and weekends in the office. "I just kinda said it's time to grow up and get a life, have kids, and, you know, figure it out," he explains.

Six months later, he was dating June, a sporty redhead who was living in a small studio in Midtown, preoccupied with the financial pressure of trying to keep up as a freelance medical writer. "I wanted a sense of home," says June. "I no longer wanted to depend on luck, or that idea that you're destined to meet the right person. In your forties, if you're not in a relationship, you get a sense that you could be alone for the rest of your life."

She also admits that biological pressure was weighing on her. So when she went on a date with Bela, the first person she met on Match.com, she began to change her attitude. June admits that she was casting her net more widely than usual due to her intense desire to settle down. "Ten years ago, if the profile said New Jersey, I might have moved on. I would have been a snob."

After six months, Bela asked June to marry him. June immediately made an appointment with a fertility specialist. She was about to turn forty. "The doctor told me that I was in the last inning in the World Series and that I better start now," she says. Immediately after the wedding, June went through her first IVF cycle and got pregnant with her son on the first try.

On a humid day in August, the pair, now both forty-eight, arrive at a local playground, unpack the car, and settle down under an oak tree. Their five-year-old son, Isaac, runs off to the play equipment. They now have three children—their towheaded twins, Alysia and Margarita, were born through IVF when June was forty-five.

As the kids sit quietly drinking from their juice boxes, June reflects on the upsides and downsides of her insta-family.

"The obvious negative is that you haven't had the ten years to nurture your relationship and you don't have the memory base to keep retrieving," says June. "We don't remember what life was like when it was just the two of us. We should probably put it on the to-do list to have more alone time!"

But June also points out that because she and Bela didn't spend years together before having children, family life is all they know as a couple. "We don't have to mourn the freedom that we lost because we never had it."

~

One weekend, Jacob invites me out to drinks with his parents at an Italian restaurant on the Upper West Side. I'm excited because this will be our first introduction; I recognize that this is a serious step for Jacob.

And as soon as I meet Jacob's parents, I'm completely besotted. They have a folksy suburban glamour. His mother is a warm and slightly eccentric social worker—she's wearing a jacket with feathers and an eclectic antique brooch. She asks me lots of questions about my career, but I can tell she's trying to not pry too deep to make me uncomfortable. We talk a bit about my life in California and a story I just wrote for the *New York Times* about an anthropologist who studies the chemistry of love. His father is more quiet and controlled—an entrepreneur who sells 1920s artifacts. He doesn't talk much, just seems to be taking it all in. It's clear to me that Jacob's mother is the fierce glue that holds this family together.

After dinner, Jacob and I walk back to his apartment. He tells me that his parents clearly adore me; while I was in the bathroom, he reports, his father told him that I seemed like a lot of fun. I tell him that I liked his family because they remind me a lot of my own. They've clearly accepted me as someone important in Jacob's life.

Our relationship accelerates as we become more entwined with each others' families. Jacob regularly comes home with me for dinner with my parents, and soon I'm included in most of his family events. I join them for nights out at the theatre, parties with their friends, and a celebratory dinner when Jacob finally closes on his apartment. A future together is beginning to seem inevitable. My family has more or less adopted him, and his family me. If we were twenty-four, I wouldn't be thinking this way—but given our ages, it's hard not to imagine a wedding in our future.

~

Then one morning I wake up at Jacob's apartment and realize that my period is a few days late. As I trudge to the drugstore to buy a pregnancy test, I'm a little concerned, but it's not an unfamiliar feeling. In my twenties, I had a number of trembling episodes sitting on the edge of the toilet praying that I would not see two little red lines appear on a pregnancy test.

I was lucky; I never saw those lines. But if I had at that stage of my life, I know I would have had an abortion. Like so many of my liberal, agnostic, forward-thinking friends who did have abortions in their twenties, I would have gone through a scary, painful process of mourning. But like them, I ultimately would have rationalized the decision by telling myself that by waiting to have a child until I was more stable and secure, I would ultimately be a much better mother.

But this morning it's different. As I wait for the results, I'm not panicked. Instead of praying that I won't see the two red lines, part of me hopes that I will. When the test comes up negative, I'm disappointed rather than relieved.

"Not this time," I tell Jacob, half-smiling, when I emerge from the bathroom. I want to see his reaction before I tell him about my own feelings.

Jacob looks nervous. "Well, if you did get pregnant, you would have an abortion, right?" he asks. "There's no way we could have a baby so early in our relationship."

His question hits me like a blow. Part of me understands that this is a normal reaction after spending only six months together, and that at a different stage of my life I would have responded exactly the same way. But after talking to so many couples who just *knew* when they met the right person, I can't help but wonder if my sense of the strength of our relationship has been completely misguided—or is at least one-sided.

I realize that I'm also really disappointed by Jacob. We're so in-sync about so many things, and he understands me better than anyone else has. So why doesn't he understand that as I approach thirty-seven, having an abortion would be very, very hard for me? I've told him many times how important it is to me to have a family, and I feel tremendously let down by his knee-jerk reaction. I wonder if this is a small sign that he is the type of person who will always think first about himself and his desires.

But instead of saying any of this to Jacob, I just nod.

"Yes, of course that's what I'd do," I say mechanically.

Reflecting on the conversation later that day, I resolve to be extra careful about birth control. I'm ready to have a child, and my biological clock is only getting louder and more insistent. At this stage of my life, there is no way I could have an abortion.

~

One weekend, Jacob and I go away with some of his friends to the Berkshires. The evening we leave, I get a call from my mom, who tells me that my ninety-nine-year-old grandmother has fallen and broken her hip. Mimi is in the hospital and will need surgery. I know that surgery carries a huge risk for someone her age, so I ask Jacob to drive me to the hospital.

I get there just in time to talk to my grandmother before she's wheeled off to the surgical ward. I show her a picture of Jacob because I know it will give her strength to imagine me with a man I love. Ever since I was a child, she's talked about how happy she will be at my wedding. As she looks at the picture, she gives me a knowing smile.

Mimi makes it through the surgery, but two days later she refuses to eat or accept a feeding tube. Within a week, her blood pressure drops and her body begins to shut down. The doctor suggests that we move her into hospice and start saying our good-byes.

On the morning Mimi dies, my mom calls me from the hospital in tears. I'm lying in bed with Jacob, and as he holds me I feel the generations shift. Soon it will be my mother's turn to be the grandmother, and me, the mother. But as the tears roll down my cheeks and Jacob strokes my hair in silence, I can't help but wonder how soon that will be.

# 8

## Talking Past the Elephant

On a brisk Sunday morning in late November, I wake up feeling sad. It is the day after my thirty-seventh birthday, and the romantic in me had hoped that Jacob might give me an engagement ring. Instead, he gave me a beautiful shawl and cashmere sweater and came to dinner with my family. But still, I'm slightly disappointed and a little anxious because I'm a year older.

Jacob's still asleep, so I get out of bed, make myself a cup of coffee, and sit down to read the paper. My cell phone beeps. I look down and see a message from Jacob's sister Allison. We're having dinner later in the week, and she's sent me the names of a couple of restaurants she'd like to try.

"P.S. Did you see *Modern Love?!*" she writes at the end of the note.

Allison is a year older than I am, and a few months ago, just before her thirty-eighth birthday, she broke up with her boyfriend of a year because he wouldn't commit to marrying her. She's been down because she really loved him, but also because she is worried about her fertility. Because Allison and I are in such similar positions, we've talked a lot about the challenges of the New York dating scene and the pressure of our biological clocks. So it's not surprising that she would mention the story in that morning's *Modern Love* column in the Styles section of the *Times*. It's titled, "In the Grip of Nature's Own Form of Birth Control."

"I don't know how I got to be so old without having children," journalist Wendy Paris begins her piece. "When I was 28 and my cousin had her first child, at 31, I thought, 'I certainly won't wait that long.' But then my freewheeling, career-centric life lasted another decade."

Paris goes on to describe her later marriage and first pregnancy at thirty-eight, which, "still felt too soon." But that feeling ended after she miscarried two weeks later. Paris writes that she then consciously decided she was going to take this miscarriage in stride, let go, and just try again. She was not going to become one of those obsessed "older urban women professionals who were accustomed to controlling the factors leading to their success."

And then eight months later, she got pregnant again. And miscarried again. Eventually, Paris and her husband, David, registered at a fertility clinic and started "what feels like an endless cycle of tests and appointments, determined to do whatever I could to succeed. Suddenly I have a new appreciation for those neurotic would-be mothers I had criticized before. Obsessive vigilance is a natural reaction to the shocking realization that you are not in control."

The experience made her change her tune about waiting to start a family. A few weeks later, Paris found herself at a party advising a friend to "focus on finding a real partner and creating a family sooner than later. 'You don't have to do what everyone else is doing,' she says. 'It's much harder, actually, to start a family when you're older.'"

The friend's response is a phrase I've also heard a million times. "I have a friend who just got pregnant at 42."

The article sets my wheels spinning, of course. I want to run screaming into the next room to tell Jacob that we need to start working on the next generation right now! After all, I just turned thirty-seven! But I know this is the last thing our relationship needs. It's a stressful time. He's settling into his new apartment, and we're both working really hard. And while he's starting to involve me in decorating his apartment and refers to the place as "home"—as in "I'll meet you at home"—we are also facing some bumps.

I've begun to notice some of his flaws—and he mine. After the first few months of bliss, I've come down to earth slightly. One of my close friends, a woman who is intensely emotionally intuitive, told me a few weeks earlier that she's suspicious of Jacob's tight-lipped smile; that he seems fake and secretive and she wonders what he's hiding. I defended him, of course. But perhaps her comment primed me to take more notice of his behavior, because certain ticks of his have begun to irritate me. For instance, sometimes when I reach out to hug him, he pushes me away like a sulky little boy. Once when he did this, I got visibly upset. He explained that he's always been like that, that he's never been entirely comfortable with expressing affection openly, and that a past girlfriend used to cry when he did the same thing. I'm somewhat relieved to know that it's not me causing his reaction, but nevertheless it does feel rejecting.

It's also becoming clear to me that Jacob and I have different ideas about what we should be to each other. A couple of months after my grandmother died, he told me that he found me too needy and that it stressed him out. I tried to explain to him how much she had meant to me, and that I was in mourning and feeling especially vulnerable, but he told me that I expected too much of him in the weeks after her death—regular phone calls even when he was away on business, more emotional support than he knew how to give. The conversation irritated me at the time, and worries me still. In a life together, we would inevitably encounter much tougher blows than the death of a grandparent—could I count on him to bear those blows with me?

Jacob and I have had some good conversations recently about trying to compromise more—I know I need to be more respectful of his need for space and privacy, and he agrees that he has to try harder to make me feel safe and cared for. Already, I've noticed him trying to be more affectionate. And I'm trying not to overwhelm him.

But there's still a big elephant in the room. Even though we've been together for close to a year, Jacob and I still haven't said "I love you" to each other. I'm usually spontaneous, and when I'm in love, like when I was with Alex, I tend to broadcast it. I *am* in love with Jacob, but part of me feels self-protective since he's not spoken the words yet. I also know that Jacob is a rationalist—he rarely says anything without thinking hard about it first. I reassure myself that "I love you" means something different to Jacob than it means to me—once he even intimated that he didn't want to say the words until he was certain he wanted to make a complete commitment to me.

So I look to other things for evidence that our relationship is heading toward marriage. For instance, the fact that he invites me to a surprise fortieth anniversary party for his parents.

That night at an Italian restaurant in Westchester, I sit next to his mother, and she and Jacob introduce me to all of their closest family friends. At one point, his mother puts her arm around me and introduces me to one of her best friends.

"This is my . . ." she hesitates, as if she wanted to say more than just "Jacob's girlfriend." But before she can get the words out, the friend looks at me, smiles, and says, "I know who you are."

Moments like this reassure me that I really am a meaningful, and potentially permanent, part of Jacob's life. And for now, I realize, that's as good as it gets. Given that he's already criticized me for smothering him, the last thing I can allow myself to do is pressure him for assurances about our future.

So on this particular morning, the day after my thirty-seventh birthday, I put the paper down, take a deep breath, and remind myself: *pura vida*. Then I walk into the bedroom and lie back down in bed, so I can be there to smile and say good morning when Jacob wakes up.

~

I know that taking things easy with Jacob is the right thing to do, but it's also terribly difficult for me not to think about starting a family with him and therefore think about my age. Even though all signs point to my fertility cooperating, it's hard not to feel sensitive—especially when I hear and read about other women's scary stories. I'm aware of every passing month, and wonder how long we can gamble before we start trying to get pregnant if we do decide to commit to each other.

Wendy Paris's article has raised in me a particular fear of miscarriage. It's a sensitive subject for me because I experienced the pain of losing a sibling when my mother was thirty-eight and I was seven. She was pregnant with a little girl; she and my father had named her Rebecca Lillian before she was born. Her middle name was in honor of her would-have-been godmother, Lillian Hellman.

On December 2, 1976, my mother's doctor decided to induce labor because she was two weeks beyond her due date. But first he prescribed an amniocentesis—a relatively new procedure in 1976—to ensure that Rebecca was really ready to be born, that her lungs were mature enough.

Shortly after the amniocentesis, a nurse in the room discovered that she had lost Rebecca's heartbeat. My mother was rushed into surgery for an emergency C-section. But it was too late. Rebecca, who also had her umbilical cord wrapped around her neck, had suffered blood loss. My baby sister was alive for only a few minutes after she was taken from my mother's womb.

Amniocentesis is typically performed using a needle guided with ultrasound. In my mother's case, however, the test was done without ultrasound because the doctors were in a hurry. In hindsight, the doctors think that the needle might have somehow displaced the placenta, thereby putting the umbilical cord in a bad spot. But no one can know for sure.

That night, when my father came home from the hospital, I asked him if I had a brother or sister. He just looked down, put his hand on my head, and told me that my baby sister had died.

Over the next few weeks, I spend a lot of time thinking about and researching the dangers—as well as the advantages—of getting pregnant in my very late thirties or early forties. I know the numbers—at age thirty-five, about 66 percent of women will conceive within a year; 44 percent will at age forty.

But while I take some comfort in these statistics, I really want to hear about older parenting from individual women who have been there themselves. I want to know the dilemmas they faced and the decisions they made. Were they frightened by the possibility of miscarriages or birth defects? Do they feel like they have enough energy to raise young children into their forties and fifties? Are they glad they waited, or do they wish they'd had children earlier? How did they—or do they—balance their careers and family lives?

On the positive side, I discover that in each woman I speak with there is a voice that says, *I'm so glad I waited. I'm a more confident and stronger mother now.* This is what my mother told me about the birth of my younger brother, Noah, when she was forty. In 1995, researchers at Leicester University in England published a four-and-a-half-year longitudinal study. The Leicester Motherhood Project report found that the personalities of women who intentionally delay childbearing differ from younger or "average-age" mothers. They are more likely to have had mothers who started later and are more likely to have fulfilled themselves prior to becoming mothers.

My mother isn't the only older woman who reassured me. At a cocktail party, I talk to a family friend about these issues, and she tells me that high-achieving women have been having babies in their forties for generations. She suggests I call Ruth Gruber.

She had her first child at forty-one in 1940 and never thought twice about it. Gruber finished a Ph.D. on the novelist Virginia Wolfe when she was twenty, and then she won a Guggenheim Foundation Fellowship to study the lives of women under fascism and communism in Eastern Europe. In her thirties, she became the first foreign correspondent allowed to fly into Siberia to interview prisoners in Stalin's Soviet gulag. In 1944, Harold Ickes, the secretary of the interior, appointed her as his special assistant, and at that post she traveled all over the world. On one assignment, she secretly escorted Jewish refugees from Germany to the United States.

"I was very busy," says Gruber, who is now ninety-seven years old.

At forty, she fell in love with Philip Michaels, a lawyer and a social activist. They married quickly.

"I always knew that I wanted to have children," she tells me. Despite warnings from her doctor of the risk of birth defects, Gruber tried to get pregnant, and after months of trying, she succeeded.

"Instead of Down syndrome kids, I had two ordinary Jewish geniuses," she says.

Looking back, she believes that waiting until she was older was a good choice. "I think I had more of an understanding of who I was and what life throws you. Many of my friends regretted not getting themselves firmly established in careers for the rest of their lives. They always sensed that they had lost out."

More recent studies bear out Ruth's opinion. Brian Powell, a sociologist at Indiana University, told me that through his research he has discovered that children of older parents are significantly better off. Since we live in a culture that places a premium on youth, and therefore assumes that younger parents will have more energy to give to their children, these findings surprised him. Powell thought that he would discover that there were certain advantages for older parents and other advantages for younger parents.

"We thought there would be more tension between having more energy and more resources," he says. "But it turns out that in almost every area that the researchers looked at, older parents were more involved in their kids' lives. They not only spend more money on their kids, but also spend more time with them. They are more likely to belong to the PTA and go to parent-teacher conferences, and they are more likely to know their children's friends and the parents of their children's friends."

In her 2005 study, Princeton University sociologist Sara McLanahan discovered the same thing. She found that families with mothers who had the most economic independence—the highest education and income level who delay childbearing—are proving to spend the most time with their children.

"These mothers are leading the way," she says. "Not in single motherhood, but in establishing stable marriages that are based on more equal sharing of parental responsibilities."

These discoveries gave me a sense of peace. Maybe starting later isn't such a disaster after all—that is, if my biology cooperates or I decide to take an alternative route. These extra years I've spent focusing on my career and my finances will help me be a better mother. Instead of regretting my years of exploration and self-discovery, I'll remember that they will be an asset to my children. I've been feathering a more stable nest.

That said, there are real dangers to advanced-age pregnancy. We know definitively that after the age of thirty-five, the risk of chromosomal disorders increases, and the risk of miscarriage increases to 20 percent. At forty, the risk of miscarriage rises to 33 percent. There is no arguing with these numbers, and many women who get pregnant in their late thirties or forties have a nagging voice in their heads saying, *I'm too old for this. It's too risky.*

But these anxieties are nothing like they used to be for older mothers.

When I had tea with Jane Harnick and Barbara Barne, Barbara told me that she couldn't believe the difference between her daughter's pregnancy at thirty-nine and her own at thirty-seven. When Barbara was pregnant with her son in 1965, she and her friends, who were also older mothers, only whispered their fears.

"We had no amniocentesis, CVS tests or sonograms. [Chorionic villus sampling tests are typically done around the tenth week of pregnancy. A small sample of cells is taken from the placenta and tested for genetic diseases.] I don't remember the baby or my husband and me being tested for dangerous diseases," she tells me. "We tried not to think about the consequences. We just had to take our chances. And pray."

Technological and medical advances since then have transformed the field of obstetrics. Before Jane's baby was born, she could hear her baby's heartbeat and have definitive answers about its sex and genetic health.

Still, even with better tests and more information, later-life pregnancies remain extremely stressful. The Leicester Motherhood Project revealed that due to the higher miscarriage rates in women over thirty-five, older mothers experience fewer feelings of attachment toward their unborn baby at mid-pregnancy, though this disengagement disappears by late pregnancy. Mothers who are over thirty-five are also more anxious when their children are young and have more fear of losing a pregnancy.

I learn a little more about what goes on inside the heads of an older couple trying to have a baby one afternoon over tea with my friends Tamara* and Sam*.

Tamara, who has just passed through the first trimester of her pregnancy, is a quirky bohemian girl from Long Island with a quiet brilliance. She is thirty-nine and just finishing her first book. Sam is a muscular and warm former war correspondent from northern Illinois. The two had been married for only a few months when they learned that Tamara was pregnant.

Sam and Tamara have a familiar story. They attended the same law school but met for the first time in New York three years ago, both in their mid-thirties, both having given up practicing law and become writers. Tamara was thirty-five and had divorced three years earlier. Even though Tamara knew that the marriage was a bad choice within the first year, she had a hard time leaving it precisely because she was worried that she might miss her chance to become a mother.

"I was totally freaked out because I wasn't sure I was going to find someone I loved enough during my biological childbearing years," she says. "I went to the doctor to have tests to see if my ovaries were OK. I looked into egg freezing. I was looking into Single Mothers by Choice."

As Tamara talks, I start laughing because she is telling me my own story.

"Did the single mother thing turn you off?" I ask.

"At that point, it did," she says. "I have this brilliant professor friend with great psychological insight. We had dinner when I was in one of my despairing moments. She turned me on to the idea that it's OK not to have kids. She said you're using this as a way to beat yourself up. I think she was also talking about society and having children being the only way of women expressing themselves."

"Those ideas really took hold in me," she continues. "I think it was only after that talk that I got to the point where I was able to leave my marriage. Until that point, it seemed like too much to leave a marriage childless. I had this idea that life would be gray and cold without children, and I somehow came to understand that I was totally wrong and that I had all the freedom in the world."

Once she left her marriage, Tamara relaxed into her new life as a single woman in New York. Then one night she went to a party and met Sam, who was a year older than her. The party was a send-off for Sam, who was on his way to Iraq to report on the war. He was single and had spent the last ten years of his life as a UN peacekeeper and journalist in war zones like Somalia and Rwanda. While commitment and family were always in the back of his mind, they weren't his main focus. But when he met Tamara, he says, everything changed. The two talked only briefly, but Sam instantly knew that she was the one.

"I left the next day, and I e-mailed her from Kuwait and, you know, I'm like, 'Can I see you when I get back?'" he says. "And then I started to conduct myself in a way that I had never done in the field, which was to be really careful. I think as a function of age and knowing that the window of normal marital age was closing, I started to think about things a little differently."

When Sam got back from Iraq, unharmed, a month later, the couple quickly settled into a relationship. They spent a little over two years together before they got engaged, and once they did, they immediately started trying to get pregnant.

The first pregnancy, a few months before our meeting, ended in a miscarriage, but Tamara remained optimistic, and the couple dusted themselves off and started trying again after a few months. Sam, however, is still feeling pretty shaky about everything.

"I've been having sex since I was sixteen and every fucking time, it was like please God don't let her get pregnant," he says. "So then you finally make this decision and kaboom!

Now it's the exact opposite obsession. Every time, you're like, *I hope we get pregnant.*"

The source of his anxiety surprised me. It was not Tamara's chances of getting pregnant at her age, but his own fertility. One day, he Googled "over forty, father, birth defects" and found over a half million links that spoke of increased birth anomalies from Down syndrome to dwarfism.

The first study that caught his eye was the one done using the Israeli military database. The researchers discovered that children of men who became fathers at forty or older were more likely to have autism disorder than fathers who were younger than thirty.

"This is what really caught my eye," he says. "'Cuz, this isn't, like, you know—and God bless all my feminist sisters—but it isn't some feminist diatribe coming at me. This is the Israeli army telling me."

Sam also found a number of other studies. One conducted at the University of California's School for Public Health revealed that offspring born to men in their middle and late forties might have increased chances of being born with autism—and schizophrenia. Another carried out in Israel found that the risk of schizophrenia was 1 in 141 in children of fathers under twenty-five, 1 in 99 for fathers aged thirty to thirty-five, and 1 in 47 in children of fathers fifty and older. Recent studies have also been published citing men's age as the culprit in first-trimester miscarriage.

"I know a lot of guys who say it's better to be older and have a much younger wife, and there's no downside for the male. Now I know that's not true," says Sam.

In a 2007 story in the *New York Times* about this new data on men's fertility, Roni Rabin wrote that these studies might in fact "level the playing field between men and women in the premarital dating game." She also quotes Pamela Madsen, the executive director of the American Fertility Association, who says, "The message to men is: 'Wake up and small the java. It's not just about women any more, it's about you too.' It takes two to make a baby and men who want to become fathers need to wake up, read what's out there, and take responsibility."

Dr. Harry Fisch, the director of the Male Reproductive Center at New York-Presbyterian Hospital/Columbia University Medical Center and author of *The Male Biological Clock*, told me that sperm quality declines as men age due to mitosis, or cell duplication. Even though men manufacture new sperm continuously, the cells that make the sperm also replicate and divide continuously. Each of these replication and division cycles creates new possibilities for abnormalities to enter into the original genetic code. Mitosis occurs over 20 times a year, climbing to 380 times a year by the age of thirty, and 610 times a year by the age of forty. So even though a man may become more distinguished-looking with age, the reality is his silver swimmers slow down a little bit every year.

"I realized this is a bed that I've made," Sam continues, "because I reached forty and didn't do all this earlier. It's not like God imposed this on me. I screwed it up myself."

I'm surprised to hear this regret, especially from a man. Because as much as I think about how lucky I am to have had so much freedom over the course of my twenties and thirties, I definitely have a self-loathing streak that leads me to blame myself for having let myself get so old without having children.

"You look at it as screwing up?" I ask.

"Well, I do regret not getting it all together before now. I feel like I'm in this situation because I made mistakes . . . I just waited too long."

Hearing about Sam's sensitivity to these issues is refreshing. Rather than dumping all of the responsibility on Tamara to deal with advanced-age pregnancy, he's taking a lot of responsibility himself. I can't help but wonder if Jacob would show the same level of maturity. There was that brief silence during our first phone call, when he learned I was thirty-six and not thirty-two. But since then, age hasn't come up as an issue in our relationship. We've even talked about how many people we know who are having children in their forties. On the other hand, his reaction to that pregnancy scare was quite insensitive. Starting later on a family is clearly stressful, and I feel like both Jacob and I should be keeping that in mind as we think about the possibility of a future together.

When Tamara got pregnant for the second time, she remained calm.

"I really wasn't worried about problems with the baby," she says. "Even though the chances were higher because we were older, I still felt that the stats were in our favor and it was going to be fine. If it wasn't, we'd try again."

Sam and Tamara agreed in advance that they would have an abortion if the test results showed the baby had a genetic abnormality. But for Sam, at least, waiting for the test results was excruciating. He compares the long stints in the ob-gyn's waiting room to the experience of passing through military checkpoints as a UN peacekeeper and correspondent.

"You're totally passive," he says. "There is nothing you can do anymore. That feeling like it's life or death reminded me of how I felt in the field at those checkpoints, faced with some kid jacked up on crack with an AK-47. It's just pure faith that you'll get through."

Checkpoint two was the sonogram at ten weeks to find a heartbeat. Checkpoint three was a date with the genetic counselor at twelve weeks and a battery of blood tests looking for genetic predispositions to chromosomal anomalies. Checkpoint four was the decision about whether to face their increased risk of Down syndrome by getting the CVS test at ten to thirteen weeks or amniocentesis at fifteen to eighteen weeks. Sam found the logic brutal.

"CVS comes earlier in the pregnancy, meaning a potentially earlier termination if the result were bad," he explains. "But CVS tests carry a higher risk of triggering a miscarriage than an amnio."

Sam and Tamara chose to wait for the amnio at seventeen weeks. And then at twenty weeks, they elected to have an additional test that is often recommended to older parents: the climatic "structural" sonogram, which not only evaluates the fetus for structural malformations but also searches for the sonographic markers of fetal Down syndrome. The absence of any marker on a second trimester scan conveys a 60 to 80 percent reduction in risk of Down syndrome.

Many people who go through IVF for various infertility issues, or to create embryos to freeze for later use, can also pay for an extra test called preimplantation genetic diagnosis, whereby an embryologist tests a sample embryo for various genetic abnormalities such as cystic fibrosis and certain diseases linked to sex. The most common abnormality doctors look for is aneuploidy: when an embryo carries a discordant number of chromosomes, which tends to contribute to miscarriage. Other common abnormalities are single-gene defects that both parents carry, such as Tay-Sachs disease, Canavan disease, Down syndrome, or cystic fibrosis.

A few days after meeting, I get a call from Tamara, saying that she made it through the second trimester and knows that they are having a healthy boy. I ask them how, at this point, they think about the advantages of waiting to start a family versus the risks and anxieties that decision engenders.

Tamara, who actually had the opportunity to start much earlier with her first husband, is very happy she didn't.

"I've now experienced being in the wrong relationship, being alone and thinking that I might never have a child, and being in a good relationship, older," she says. "Being in the wrong relationship is absolutely the worst. And I know that if my ex-husband and I had a child together, then it would have been that much worse, not that much better, as some people say. I think I would have felt that much more trapped."

Sam is more conflicted.

"Well, I mean no, I couldn't be happier about how it's all worked out, though of course now all I think about is that we have less of a window to have number two," says Sam.

"What if you had been more educated about male fertility when you were twenty-nine?" I ask him.

He doesn't hesitate. "I would have started earlier."

~

After talking to Sam and Tamara, I realize that I need to at least start a conversation with Jacob about our future. I'm aware that our relationship is only nine months old, but we're already all but living together, and we've molded our lives and our schedules around each other. If I were five years younger, I would probably wait longer to initiate this conversation. But at this point I need to be proactive so I don't lose out on the possibility to have children. If our relationship isn't going anywhere, I'd like to know that sooner rather than later so I don't waste my increasingly precious time. And if our relationship is headed toward marriage and children, Jacob and I can't wait indefinitely before considering the timing issues.

And so a few weeks after my conversation with Sam and Tamara, I take an opportunity to bring up the subject. One morning, lying in bed at Jacob's new apartment, I'm reading the *New York Times* wedding section, and I see a picture of a friend of mine. Jacob is still half asleep, but when he rolls over to say good morning, I read aloud to him from her wedding announcement. She and her new husband are exactly our age, and they've gotten married after being together for only eight months. He shoots me a knowing look, gets out of bed and goes into his office. This is something he does when he wants to avoid tough conversations. I get up and follow him.

"You're putting too much pressure on me," he says with his back to me. "I'm not ready to commit," he says.

I tell Jacob that I'm sorry if he feels I'm putting too much pressure on him. In my twenties, I say, I might have just let this relationship take its natural course. But I explain to Jacob that at this age I need to be more conscious about making the right decisions so I don't foreclose the opportunity to have a family before my fertility expires. Then I drop the conversation, feeling like I've said my piece.

But after thinking about it for a couple of days, I decide that I need to take the conversation further. We need to address this issue head-on. And so over dinner one night, I tell Jacob about some of the facts I've learned in the course of my research. I also tell him about my sister's death, my fears, and how important it is to me to become a mother. I suggest that by our one-year anniversary, which is in three months, we should decide whether we are going to commit to getting married with the intention of starting a family. If we don't, I tell him, given my age, I'm going to have to seriously think about all the other options that I've been exploring.

After a long pause, he says, "OK. I think that's a mature decision."

It's a hard conversation, but I'm glad that I've set these boundaries. For the next three months, at least, I can focus on living in the present.

# 9

## Letting Go

I've never been a particularly religious person. My parents focused on raising me with "values" rather than subjecting me to a mixed religious education of my inherited faiths: Judaism from my mother and Episcopalianism from my father. We celebrate hybrid holidays: in December, we light candles on a menorah and place it on the mantle of the fireplace, and we gather around a Christmas tree.

Jacob was raised in a conventional Jewish family and never had a Christmas tree. (He did once admit to me that he loved my "shiksa" side—in the same sentence in which he confessed that his mother once bought him a secret Christmas present when he was a child because he felt left out at school.) So it means a lot to me that, despite some initial resistance, he agrees to spend Christmas Eve with my family, because he knows how important these kinds of traditions are to me. I also take it as a positive sign for our relationship—after some bumpy weeks, Jacob and I are getting along much better. I still have some reservations, but I'm feeling more confident about our future.

We have a wonderful time on Christmas Eve. We gather around the tree and drink hot chocolate, and my uncle plays jazzed-up carols on the guitar. My mom as usual entertains with a sense of irony. I think this makes Jacob feel more comfortable. He even admits to me that he actually enjoys the rush of opening all the presents at once instead of having them parsed out over the eight days of Chanukah. That night, he tells my father how much I make him laugh; my father tells him that laughter has been the key to the success of his marriage. He says that laughing together, even when things are really hard, has always reinvigorated his relationship with my mom.

A few days later, Jacob and I spend New Year's Eve together. I've come down with a nasty cold and can barely get out of bed. Jacob comes over and sweetly makes me chicken Milanese while I sniffle and doze right through the moment the ball drops on television. We blow each other a midnight kiss because I don't want him to catch my cold. It's not the most romantic New Year's Eve, but I appreciate that he has chosen to spend it with me even though I'm sick. It makes me feel comfortable and safe, which is almost more romantic than if we had danced all night at some fabulous party.

January is a tough month for us—or at least for me. Despite the wonderful time we had together over the holidays, Jacob still makes no move in either direction. I become increasingly anxious as the days pass, but remain careful not to pressure him. I know he's thinking about it, so I keep my counsel as I watch him look down every time a TV commercial comes on involving a wedding or an engagement ring.

But in the last week of January, I decide I can no longer keep waiting in silence. We're sitting in the dimly lit living room of his new apartment at opposite ends of the couch when I nervously initiate the conversation. I tell him that I know he's been really distracted by work, but that he seems to be avoiding the subject of what our future holds.

"I know," he says. And then he admits that he is really confused. He has questions about whether or not he can spend the rest of his life with me. My heart races.

"I love you," he says.

It is the first time he's spoken these words in our year together.

"I wish I didn't," he says.

Now I'm totally confused.

He then admits that the idea of committing to me makes him anxious, that there are some aspects of our dynamic that make him anxious. I ask him what in particular, but he tells me he can't really explain it, though he says that he thinks our relationship should feel more like a honeymoon at this point; he worries that it's a bad sign that we've already had some big bumps so early in our relationship. I tell him I disagree. After all, how we get through fights is an important test of our compatibility, and we seem to have gotten through a number of them. I tell him that one of my male friends recently told me that he and his now wife fought a lot more in the beginning, but they grew much closer as they learned how to compromise.

As I'm talking, though, a feeling of panic overtakes me. It's not unlike the feeling I had standing in front of a rhino in South Africa. I feel vitally threatened. I also think that maybe he's met someone else—that he's just making excuses to buy time while he figures out if some other woman would be better for him.

"Is there another woman?" I ask.

He says there isn't and tells me he's furious that I even have to ask.

Now I'm angry too. All of my anxieties—about my age, my fertility, my doubts, his coldness, and, mostly, my disappointment with his ambivalence, suddenly tumble out in a cacophony of tears and accusations.

Jacob reacts in turn. He tells me that by insisting on a deadline I'm putting "a gun to his head." He denounces me as "desperate" and "hysterical."

"When I first responded to your profile, I thought you were thirty-two!" he complains, even though this has never come up since the first time we talked on the phone. "I feel like it's more important to you to have a baby than a relationship with me," he continues. "I'm just the guy who came along at the right time to give one to you."

I deny it. I tell him that I want a commitment for other reasons as well, that I love him for him, for the kind of life we could build together, for the way we laugh together. I don't just want him because I want a father for my children. But there is the cold reality of my biology, I explain. My window of fertility is closing, and the longer I wait the harder it will be to have children. We've both said from the beginning that children are important to us, and if he's serious about that, then he has to take the issue of my fertility seriously as well.

He tells me that he wishes we could just live in the present moment of our relationship, rather than focusing so much on the future. He tells me that he thinks all of the research I've been doing for my book has fed my panic about children and that it's putting too much pressure on our relationship.

"You're not letting our relationship take its organic course," he wails. "I feel like I have no free will."

I tell him I've been following my organic course since I graduated from college. Now I have to think about the future. I have to be practical—it's the very opposite of hysteria, I tell him.

"I've had all this freedom to come this far in my career, and I've finally found myself," I explain. "And as a result, I found you. But now I don't have control over my biology! It's a reason to cry!" I'm bawling at this point. Maybe he's right; maybe I am hysterical. After all, the Greek root of the word "hysteria" is *hystera*—womb. And isn't all of this about just that?

"It's nature's cruel joke on women," he says, calming down a bit.

"What can I do for you?" he asks, after long minutes of silence broken only by my anguished tears. But he stays at his end of the couch as he speaks, rather than reaching out to hold me.

"You could show some empathy," I say. "You could try to understand how hard all of this is for me."

Jacob puts his head in his hands. When he looks up, he tells me that he needs more time. He tells me that he doesn't want to waste my time, but that he needs to figure out also what he wants for himself.

"I want to do the noble thing," he says. Then, more quietly, "I'm afraid."

We don't come to a conclusion that night. I tell Jacob that he can take more time, realizing that love requires mutual respect; I need to honor his timeline as well as mine.

The next day I decide to take a plum assignment for the multimedia series I write for *MSN Money*, to write about luxury trips to India; my friend Abby will be shooting the video. It will include one week on safari and then another in a posh Ayurvedic spa. By going, I will be giving Jacob some space and time to think, and giving myself a chance to contemplate life without him. It's a different kind of leap of faith—I need to jump into the unknown, and trust that either Jacob's or someone else's hands will catch me on the other side.

~

Before I leave, I check in with Dr. Schiffman and tell her where things stand. Immediately, she suggests that I freeze my eggs or, better yet, ask Jacob to freeze embryos with me. We could sign an agreement stipulating that I will not use them if our relationship doesn't work out. By doing this, Dr. Schiffman explains, I will be able to allay my biological anxiety and take some pressure off our relationship.

It's not a bad idea, but I decide it's not the right time—I don't want to add this extra element to Jacob's confusion or ask a man who can't even commit to me to commit to an intense, and rather cold, legal negotiation on behalf of our relationship. He already thinks I want to be with him just because I'm ready to have a baby; I don't think it would be particularly tactful at this point to ask if I could borrow a couple of vials of sperm while I'm waiting for his answer.

A few nights before I leave, Jacob and I have dinner in the West Village. We are sitting in the corner booth of the vegetarian restaurant that we always go to when we have something important to talk about. But this time I don't want to have another heavy talk. I just want to enjoy him. I want to try to remember what made us fall in love in the first place.

Throughout dinner, he stares at me—not in a romantic way so much as a contemplative one. It reminds me of the look he had on his face a few weeks earlier, when he was trying to decide whether to buy the blue or purple towels for his bathroom. I feel strange in his gaze, but also comfortable just being together.

At the end of the meal, as he pays the check, he tells me that he's questioning whether our relationship has the right qualities for longevity. I ask him how he knows what the right qualities for longevity are, since this is the most serious relationship he's ever been in. He says he doesn't really know. He tells me that he asked his father a few weeks earlier how he knew his mother was the right woman for him. His father said that he asked her to marry him because he knew she would be a good mother.

"I think you're going to be a great mother," he said. "But that answer didn't make sense to me."

I tell him that I don't really know what the right qualities for longevity are either, except for what I've learned from my parents' forty-year marriage.

"Throw out all your romantic illusions," my father said to me a few days earlier, when I sought his advice. "Love is just the base, and everything else is work and communication."

Now, walking through the West Village, I don't worry about my love for Jacob, but I do worry about the communication. *Maybe this is the communication*, I think to myself. Maybe this is just the really hard part, the anxious part of real intimacy that couples often hit before they slide into the quiet and peaceful solidity of commitment. Maybe all of these tears and arguments are the beginning of the noble, real love that I'm looking for.

We walk to the subway entrance and then stand there not really knowing what more to say to each other. He reminds me to notice the changing light on the Taj Mahal and to try to visit his favorite place in the world: Fort Neemrana, an old palace estate on the edge of Rajasthan. We then we kiss good night and say good-bye.

~

Three days later, I'm on a flight from Delhi to the central Indian state of Madhya Pradesh. Before the flight takes off, the man sitting next to me—a chatty businessman in a blue baseball hat—turns to me and asks if I would like to meditate.

"Why not?" I think. So instead of making boring plane small talk, we sit together in silence with our eyes closed.

Of course, the minute I close my eyes all I can think about is what will happen with Jacob. But a picture emerges that surprises me. Rather than thinking about all his wonderful qualities that I fell in love with—his ambition, generosity, and sense of humor—I begin to think about all the qualities that irritate me: his narcissism, his rigidity. His comic-book view of the world is no longer charming to me—it's immature and too black and white. *Adulthood*, I think, *is about seeing all of the many shades of gray.*

Instead of clearing my mind in meditation, I find myself getting angrier and angrier at him. Angry, in particular, at his lack of compassion during our emotional conversation at his apartment. A better man, I think, would have understood how confusing and painful it was to hear that the person I love may not want a future with me—and would have understood that if the relationship didn't move forward, I would be back at square one and a year closer to infertility. It wasn't as if I was crying "hysterically" over a burnt dinner. I was mourning over what felt like a real and enormous loss.

My anger at Jacob, however, mingles with its opposite—
happy Hollywood endings in which he picks me up at the airport
with an apology, a sparkly ring, and a promise to do the work
that it will take to keep our relationship swimming forward.

We finish our meditation, and the flight takes off. As I stare
out the window, I realize I'm in a strange purgatory. This adventure, this airplane, this moment I've spent meditating with
a total stranger is a weigh station between two possible beginnings: commitment and starting a family, or a new life alone
with some hard decisions about my future.

Just before we land, my meditation partner offers to read my
palm. I acquiesce and lay my hand on the plastic tray table.

"You will live until you are eighty and make lots of money,"
he says, studying my hand carefully. "You will have two great
loves."

I ask if I will have children.

"It's unclear," he tells me. "I don't have a magnifying glass
to read the smaller lines."

"Why is family so important?" I ask him when he looks up
from my palm.

He looks at me with bemusement, as if the answer is obvious
to all.

"It is the traditional system," he says. "It's the way we survive."

A few hours later, I'm in a car with Abby and a guide driving
along a bumpy highway on the way to Bandhavgarh National
Park, a former royal hunting reserve where the first wild white
tiger was ever found. We pass through bustling postindustrial
towns with satellite dishes on rooftops and billboards advertising American toothpaste and villages with public squares decorated with flower-adorned busts of Gandhi. I watch women

with babies wrapped to their backs in purple, blue, and red saris carrying silver pails of water across verdant fields of grain. Men with ruddy skin huddle over checker games in front of disheveled storefronts. At one point, we get stuck in a traffic jam created by a herd of sacred white cows.

On my second day in Bandhavgarh, I decide to hike to a mountaintop temple that is home to a sadhu, an ascetic priest of Hinduism. Karen, our twenty-six-year-old safari guide tells me that this hike is a common pilgrimage for women who are having trouble getting pregnant—which I suppose I am, albeit not in the sense to which Karen is referring.

We arrive at the base of the mountain and walk through a tenth-century stone gate at which a statue of Vishnu, the god known to be the preserver of the universe, reclines. We slowly ascend the mountain on a stone path. Every few thousand yards, we round a corner and meet a statue of a god. At the first turn is a fish, the second a snake, the third a turtle, and the forth a monkey. Karen explains that each statue represents a different incarnation of Vishnu's creative forces.

"It's like Darwinian evolution," she says. "At the top, we'll reach a temple and see a man."

The sadhu is Mehesh Prasad Mishran, an elderly man in his eighties with a worn, peaceful face and deep-set eyes. He is wearing a white tunic. I walk to him and offer him an orange and a bottle of water. Then I lean over and let him dot my forehead—considered the seat of wisdom and mental concentration in Hinduism—with red powder. He then points me to the back of the temple, where there's a tiny shrine dotted with red handprints of children.

"If you put your hand there, the lord will bring you a child," he says in Hindi as Karen translates. "You just have to have faith."

I approach the temple and put my hand over one of the tiny prints, close my eyes, and pray.

I am not really a person who prays. My dad once asked me if I ever prayed, and I admitted to him that the only time I do is in traffic. There is something about being stuck, unable to move either forward or backward, without any control of when things will start moving again, that makes me want to invoke a higher power. Of course, my situation right now feels like a metaphoric traffic jam. But the higher power to whom I pray isn't exactly God—just a vague and amorphous idea of something more powerful than myself.

Ten years ago, my mother was diagnosed with a rare form of non-Hodgkin's lymphoma. Whenever someone asks her if she believes that God has kept her in remission for all these years she says, "No, science has." I agree with her. Part of the reason that I'm exploring fertility science is that I'm fascinated by how scientific advancement can change the course of human life. I think again about Jacob's words that night we fought. He said that all this research I've been doing on the science of fertility was making me too anxious; that I just need to let nature and our relationship take their organic course. But nature, by and large, does not want women to wait until their late thirties to have children. Science has intervened and allowed us not to control nature but to help it along significantly.

But nature, in the end, will decide whether I have children or not; science can go only so far. The forces of the universe are more powerful than anything Jacob and I could conjure, even if we decide to commit totally to each other. And so it seems like a good time to pray to those forces, whatever they may be.

The next day we drive to Pench National Park, where an elephant safari will take us deeper into the jungle. We pass through the dense teak forests and flower-filled valleys surrounded by majestic cliffs in an open-air truck. I'm sitting up front with Ratna Singh, a petite, tomboyish woman with black eyes. Even though she has a university degree in international law, she decided to come back to her home state to become one of a very few female safari guides in all of India.

Ratna is a Rajput, which is the Indian warrior caste. She proudly tells me that her grandfather was a freedom fighter against British rule, and that her grandmother was quite wild.

"She smoked and hunted," she says. "I'm like her; in school I was captain of the judo team and I broke my nose twice. It was a source of a great deal of worry for my grandmother because she would say 'if you're a cripple, no one is going to marry you.'"

Ratna points out bright green parakeets in mating dances hopping between the branches of pink flowering trees. She tells me to listen for the chatter of langur monkeys, which means that a tiger could be just around the corner.

At twenty-seven, Ratna has been married for four years and has no intention to have children anytime soon.

"I have never been told I have to be a certain way because I'm a girl," she says.

Even though her family arranged her marriage—in India 90 percent of marriages are still arranged—she says that she was not forced to marry the man they chose for her. There was no pressure, and luckily she liked the man who became her husband. He works as a software designer in the United States, and they see each other every few months.

"My parents expected us to have children right away," she continues. "My mother got married when she was seventeen, and by the time she was twenty-seven, she had three children. I don't want to have children for at least four more years. I want to keep doing this, and my husband says it's my choice. My mother is worried that I won't be able to conceive."

I find myself feeling envious of Ratna because she has the freedom to make her own choices and also the security of a strong family system that ensures her protection and survival. I briefly consider e-mailing my parents to get to work on my arranged marriage in case things don't work out with Jacob. But then we come upon a group of elephant herders, and within less than an hour I'm sitting cross-legged on the head of a female elephant and looking into the bright green eyes of an eighteen-month-old tiger cub.

*I got myself here, and I'm happy in the moment, I think. I will also get myself to the other places in life that I want to be. Breathe. Have faith.*

After a week in the jungle, Abby and I board a train heading to the northern state of Uttar Pradesh. We will be spending a week at Ananda, a luxurious holistic retreat and spa nestled in the foothills of the Himalayas.

Stepping off the train in the town of Haridwar, we are greeted by Bobo, a gentle Sikh chauffeur in a red silk turban. He drives us through the town and explains that the spring awakening holiday of Holi—the Indian version of Easter—is getting into full swing. All over the streets, revelers are throwing blue, pink, and red powder at one another (instead of painting Easter eggs, they paint themselves), shooting colored liquid out of water guns, and getting staggeringly drunk. A red water balloon bursts on our car as Bobo whisks us through town. We continue along the edge of the Ganges, past gypsy colonies, up a winding mountain highway toward a distant yellow castle. The spa is located on the hundred-acre castle estate belonging to the maharaja of Tehri Garhwal, who has leased the land to the owners of Ananda.

When we reach Ananda, a private guard opens the iron gates, and we pull into the circular driveway of the castle, which is decorated with Italian Renaissance columns and Rajasthani *jharokhas*, which are overhanging balconies originally created so that women could watch events without going outside. As we get out of the car, two young Indian women in silk saris greet us by placing *mala* necklaces over our heads. A mala necklace is made with 108 beads that are used to keep count while reciting prayers. They also bless our foreheads with red powder.

Ananda, which Abby dubs a "spashram," is populated by a motley assortment of Russian princesses in Chanel glasses, spaced-out honeymooners, and Euro-Buddhists. Everyone walks around in white pajamas and wearing austere expressions that make them look as if they might attempt to levitate.

Over the next week, I sink into a routine of total pampering. One day, two South Indian women sing me prayers and slowly drip hot herbal oil through a copper pot over my third eye in order to relax my knowledge chakra. Another day, I wake up early in the morning for a hike to a goddess temple to see snowcapped mountains; on another I participate in the evening Aarti prayer at a local ashram, where I chant with monks in orange robes and make an offering to the Ganges River. I place a little boat made out of a palm leaf and filled with flowers in the water and wish that whichever way my life goes, it will feel right.

Every night, a guru of Vedanta philosophy leads a seminar. Vedanta (the Sanskrit word means "the end of all knowledge") is a Hindu spiritual tradition concerned with self-realization.

Thought by believers to be a rational science of living, Vedanta is in practice a kind of intellectual yoga, an Eastern version of psychoanalysis derived from ancient texts called the Vedas that are passed down through master teachers. Sree Sreedharam, a visiting professor from Vedanta Academy in the southern state of Kerala, has traveled the world with his master, lecturing at universities like Oxford and Cambridge. He's even given lectures about management based on the principle of Vedanta at Harvard Business School.

Professor Sree's evening classes range in topic from love to anger control to ego management. One night's lecture is titled "Love and Other Mysteries"—a subject on which I am, of course, eager to attain enlightenment.

"Love is the most distorted word in the world," Sree begins. "The *Bhagavad Gita* says that true happiness is 'as poison in the beginning, but is like nectar in the end.' The nectar is 'good' pleasure, born from the serenity of one's own mind. To accommodate the interests of your partner in the beginning is difficult, but if you work on it, it becomes nectar. There is no such thing as the perfect one."

The next day I book a private session with Professor Sree to learn more. Somewhat absurdly, we meet at the first hole of the spashram's golf course to begin our discussion of Vedanta philosophy, and how I can apply it to my life.

As we walk, I tell Sree about my relationship with Jacob, and about the situation I am in now.

"He sounds like a child who you are forcing to go to school," he says. "He's got the fear of the unknown. If he's not ready then you have to move on. You can't influence him to come."

This isn't really the answer I want. I tell Sree how important it is to me to become a mother, that I am worried I'm going to lose the opportunity to have a biological child. I also tell him how I broke down talking about all of this with Jacob, and how he called me desperate and hysterical.

"You broke down because he didn't understand your feelings," Sree tells me. "It seems he was more concerned with the fact that you were crying so hard and wishing you weren't instead of looking at his role in trying to understand the reason for your crying."

I ask him if Jacob is right to think that the arguments we've had mean that we're not right for each other—that the first year should be a honeymoon.

"The idea that it initially has to be a honeymoon is a distorted concept of love because you have not disturbed the real waters," he says. "It is in the adversities that you know to what extent you love each other."

I think about all of this silently as we walk back toward the lodge. Before we part ways, Sree says to me, "If he loses out on you, he'll be a thoroughbred idiot."

This is exactly what I want to hear, of course. But it doesn't alleviate my anxiety.

"If he doesn't want to commit, how will I become a mother?" I ask.

"Give up this desire and it will come searching for you," he says. "Don't get in the mood that you are thirty-seven or think about what will prevent you. You can always adopt a child."

For the first time since I left New York, I feel hopeful. Not that things will definitely work out with Jacob—I'm under no illusions—but because I accept that I have other choices. I decide that if Jacob and I break up, I'll get my fertility tested and use some money I inherited from my grandmother to freeze my eggs. I like the idea of using her inheritance to preserve her

genes. Just thinking about freezing time this way brings me
something close to peace of mind.

On our way back to Delhi for our flight home, Abby and I take
a few extra days to visit the Taj Mahal and Gwalior, a fort town
just to the south of the Taj Mahal.

One night, we go shopping in the main market square of
Gwalior, where we wander through sari shops and pass women
praying in temples for the Durga festival, a week devoted to the
goddess with eight wild arms. Suddenly, we walk past an Indian
wedding procession. The wedding party is fenced in by a chain
of lights supported by poles carried by men. It's moving along
with the traffic in the middle of the street. The groom rides on a
white horse, and the bride dances, dressed all in red. Two men
dressed like soldiers play huge tubas while another lights a fire-
cracker that explodes in front of the procession.

As I stand watching, one of the guests grabs me and pulls
me into the crowd. All of a sudden I find myself dancing among
the trumpeters, guests, and fireworks. Professor Sree's words ric-
ochet in my head as my body moves to the strange rhythms of
the music. *Give up the desire and it will come searching for you.* I
plunge into the party, spinning in circles and throwing my
hands into the air.

~

Instead of a romantic reunion at the airport, I emerge from JFK
into an ice storm. I consider calling Jacob as I stand in line for a
taxi, but ultimately decide against it. He knows that I'm coming back today—I texted him as the sun set over the Taj Mahal
and told him that I missed him and looked forward to seeing

him. He never responded. I'm pretty sure that our next conversation won't be any fun, so I leave my cell phone in my bag while I stand on the curb.

Two days later, he e-mails me and asks me to meet him for a drink that night. I agree and spend the next few hours in a state of total dread. We meet at the Film Center Café in Midtown. Jacob shows up late and gives me a half-hearted hug, tells me how great I look, and asks if I want to get a booth and something to eat. We sit down across from each other. I still have cotton in my head from the flight, and my brain is still stuck in a traffic jam of rickshaws and sacred cows.

We order our food and then sit in silence. I'm nervous, so I start telling him a little about my adventures: seeing the tiger cub in the wild, the crazy guests at the spashram, my Himalayan hike. I'm hoping that my stories will make him laugh and bring us back to the reasons we like to be together so much. He listens, and smiles occasionally, but says nothing. He's clearly relieved when the food arrives and he has something else to focus on.

"I don't have an agenda," he finally says, digging into a bowl of macaroni and cheese. More silence. Then, "I missed you."

"I missed you too," I say.

Then, finally, he begins to speak. He tells me he still feels confused, undecided, that he's not sure our love is "enough." But he doesn't want to break up, either. He asks me to come out with him the next night to talk some more.

I'm not sure where the conversation can go at this point—I've been away for nearly a month, and he doesn't seem to have progressed at all in his thinking. I think of how helpful Sree was to me, and I feel like Jacob and I need a guru to guide us. So I tell him that the next time I speak with him, I want it to be in front of a therapist who can listen objectively. He agrees to go along with that idea.

A week later, I meet him at the office of a couples therapist on the Upper West Side. We get into a fight in the lobby. He's talking on his cell phone when I arrive and doesn't get off to greet me. He doesn't even look me in the eyes. I stamp my foot in frustration. He closes his phone and explodes at me for behaving like a child, but at the same time he's grinning. We've always sparred a bit like siblings and gotten a kick out of provoking each other. My frustration melts away, and we are both smiling when the doctor greets us at the door.

"You rarely see couples walk into couples therapy with such big smiles," says the doctor.

Maybe it's because we are indeed in love. Despite all of the tension, we really do like each other a lot.

"We're on the verge of breaking up," Jacob begins. "I've come because she asked me to."

We go back and forth trying to explain why we are sitting here. I'm too needy, he complains. He pushes me away, I shoot back. The deadline. My fertility. His inability to make a decision. We don't seem to want to break up, but we can't seem to move forward, either. We haven't slept together in a couple of months, I tell the therapist. And yet he says that he loves me; he stares at me deeply, like he loves me.

"I do love you," he says. "But I think you can love someone and not want to spend your life with them."

"So this is your decision?" the doctor asks, cutting to the chase.

Jacob is clearly reluctant to answer, so he changes the subject.

"I really respect that she goes for what she wants," he says. "She is like a train. I remember she kissed me first on our first date, and I thought it was so hot. But now she's pressuring me about family and commitment, and I don't like it."

"You are the one who told me that you wanted to get married and have kids soon on our second date," I remind him.

"I do want to get married," he says.

We dig a little deeper into our relationship, and the problems quickly bubble to the surface. His mother is overbearing; sometimes I remind him of her and it makes him anxious. He is emotionally unavailable, which reminds me of my father, who can be emotionally remote and chilly. All of it strikes me as the normal stuff that so many couples face—the poison that, with work, can become nectar.

Jacob says that he is heartbroken, but worries it's still not enough. I'm mystified by this concept. How does anyone know when something is "enough"?

"Why don't we freeze my eggs?" I suggest after a few moments of awkward silence. "That might buy us more time and help alleviate some of my anxiety over this commitment."

"I think you should freeze your eggs regardless," he says. "Whether you end up using them with me or with someone else. I think you should do it on Monday."

I laugh over his naïveté—as if freezing eggs were as simple as freezing leftovers.

"Would you consider freezing your sperm?" asks the doctor.

"I don't need to," Jacob answers smugly.

The time is running out, and the doctor asks us if we want to come back.

"I'm not sure," I answer. "It feels like we're on death watch."

"I want to come back," Jacob says.

I'm surprised by his response, since it seems like he is the one who is moving away from us.

We set a time for the next week.

After the session, I ask Jacob if he wants to get a drink. We talk about the session like we are still a couple.

"I liked him," he says.

"Me too," I say.

We order drinks and flirt and talk more calmly and deeply than we ever have before. I find myself talking about my first serious boyfriend, Andrew, how when we lived together I wrote in my journal that I knew it was not my real life. I tell him that I finally feel like this is my real life. I've become who I want to be, and I think by merging the worlds that we've built as individuals, we could make a really interesting life together. He stares at me with a look of deep love, but tells me again that he's not sure if it's enough. When we part, we agree not to see each other over the weekend so we can think, and to meet up again for our next session.

The weekend is endless. We talk once. I spend a few hours writing down my thoughts. I want to organize my values and beliefs and desires. I want to be clear and rational. Before the appointment, I'm more nervous than I've been in a long time. I stop to get tea at the local deli, sit on the steps, and pull out the piece of paper with my notes to rehearse the words I want to say. I wonder if it's healthy to have to rehearse my relationship.

Jacob and I meet on a bench in front of the therapist's office. He is on the phone again, talking about work. I sit down next to him. He doesn't get off the phone. Again, he doesn't look at me. But this time I say nothing. I just hand him a jacket that he lent me for India.

"I washed it for you, twice, because it smelled like an Indian train," I tell him when he ends his call.

"Did you put it in the dryer?" he asks anxiously.

"No," I say. I can't believe that in the midst of all of this he's worrying that I ruined his fleece jacket.

We enter the office in silence. And it's not broken until the doctor asks how we are.

"I'm OK," he says.

"I'm not," I say. "I'm really sad."

"I'm really sad too," he admits.

"How did you feel being away from her this weekend?" the therapist asks Jacob.

"I viscerally missed her. It felt good when she sat down next to me on the bench."

Then it's my turn. I pull out my piece of paper and start talking. My hands are shaking.

"As I see it, we're in love," I say. "I saw this look of love in his eyes in the bar after the last session. And to me love is a very precious and rare thing. We miss each other."

*These words vaguely sound like vows*, I think to myself.

"I'm very loyal and I don't give up on things very easily," I continue. "If we were married for five or ten years and we came to a difficult place, like we are now in our relationship, I would do everything in my power to help us get through. I'm not afraid to look at myself. And if I need to change behaviors or bad patterns in order to make our relationship run more smoothly, I will do it."

"I know you would," Jacob says, gently interrupting me. "I don't want you to have to change."

But he is less gentle when he turns to the therapist.

"Don't you see that it's too much?" he asks. "She loves me too much! It's too intense. She's crazy!"

I'm shocked by his comment. Mechanically, I pick up my notes again and start reading.

"As I see it, the issue that has gotten us here is that we both want . . ."

But then I trail off, realizing mid-sentence that I am again trying to fix a problem, control something that's out of my control. The forces of nature—my nature, Jacob's nature—are more powerful than anything I can possibly say.

Jacob suddenly bursts into tears. It's the first time I've ever seen him cry.

"Look at this amazing, beautiful woman," he says. "I know there is some other man out there who will love her."

I don't know what to say to this. I think about all of the "mights": It might be that we're scared. It might be that we need more time, that the instant is not enough; it might also be that our relationship is wrong. It might be that I am overly romantic in thinking we can make this work; it might be that he is overly romantic in thinking that he will ever know when he's found "enough." It might be that there is a better love for him, one that begins with a honeymoon that never ends. It might also be that there is a better love for me. Someone who doesn't push me away, someone who accepts my gray areas, perhaps is even charmed by them.

At this moment of mights, I know only two things for sure. Love is rare. And I have to take care of myself, and of my own time line.

I grab the keys to his apartment from my bag and hand them to him.

"I need to move on with my life right now," I say. "I've said everything I can." I get up to go.

"I'll ship you your stuff," he says.

"I wish I were younger," I say, half to him, half to the therapist. "I feel like this is a death."

"Do you feel like you can take care of yourself?" asks the doctor.

"Of course," I reply. I've never questioned that.

Jacob and I walk out of the office together. We're both crying. We sit back down on the bench.

"So are we going to keep in touch?" he asks.

"I can't talk to you."

"Why?"

"Because I'm in love with you," I answer. "What are we going to do, chat on the phone about our dating lives?"

He looks down, and then leans over and kisses me half on the cheek and half on the lips.

"I'll let you know if I want to do the work," he says.

I nod and put my hand up against his chest.

"Take care," I say.

And with that it's over.

# 10

❧

# Gelato, Science,
# and a Crystal Ball

As the spring blossoms and New Yorkers once again pour onto the streets and fill sidewalk cafés, I'm lying immobilized on my couch hiding under a blanket. The first couple of weeks after the breakup are horrific; I try to sleep through as much of it as I can, in hopes that when I wake up the heartache will be gone. My friends are incredibly supportive. They bring me food and solace and tell me how proud they are of me for honoring my own time line, and for walking away from Jacob's endless indecision.

And inevitably, my friends start telling me all of the things they really thought about Jacob but bit back on while we were together. He didn't pass the handshake test, says the husband of one of my friends. Another friend tells me that she always thought he was more interested in his own image than in other people. My mother is furious, and feels betrayed. "He wasn't who he showed himself to be to us. I think you dodged this phony's bullet."

But all I can think about is how much I miss him; love is indeed mysterious

In early April, my friends Sam and Tamara offer me their beach house on Long Island for a few days, thinking a change of scenery will help me get out of this rut. The experience proves to be exactly what I need. Every morning I get up, breathe in, breathe out, go to the garage, grab a pile of wood, make a fire, make coffee, and then take a long walk along the beach. The dunes are dotted with new flowers and the trees along the roads with tiny cherry blossoms. Then I come back to the house, sit down at my computer, and write.

After a few days, I begin to stop feeling the loss in every inward breath. My passion for my work, and my strong community of friends and family who call me every few hours to check in, are helping me heal. It begins to sink in that the strength and wholeness I've cultivated on my own will sustain me through this and whatever else life throws my way. Finally, one morning I wake up happy—with the faith that I will find love again and somehow find my way to family.

Hindsight is always 20/20. I loved Jacob's many desirable qualities, and if he had asked me to marry him at a time when our relationship felt solid and happy, I would have said yes. We might have learned to better compromise—turned the poison to nectar—and our love might have grown stronger and stronger. But I'll never reeally know. My mother may well be right that I dodged a bullet. Jacob's behavior, particularly at the end, made me question whether he truly had the emotional maturity to swim forward in the deeper and more challenging waters of commitment and parenthood.

Within a few weeks, I find myself not missing Jacob as much as I imagined I would. I've missed other boyfriends in my past for a long time after we broke up. But now I feel almost relieved to be free of all of the coldness and ambivalence. It becomes clear to me that, in large part, I'm really mourning over the death of my fantasy of starting a family soon, and over the crucial time I've lost in my quest to achieve that goal.

Thinking back over it all, I realize that I was so intent on moving toward children that I let myself remain blind to Jacob's more serious failings. If I'd had the same relationship when I was thirty, or even thirty-two, I probably wouldn't have been so tolerant of his behavior, or pushed so hard to make it work. And, to be fair to him, maybe my baby panic did undermine the relationship. I can't imagine that it would be easy for any man to live with a woman who is researching a book on motherhood after thirty-five.

There are still days when I feel angry at Jacob and feel sorry for myself. On other days, I kick myself for holding on to him too tight and for too long. And then on other days, when I'm at my best, I realize that this is what mature love is: the ability to overlook flaws, remain loyal to the relationship, and work on problems. Maybe it wasn't a waste of time; maybe it was a trial run. Even if Jacob didn't want it in the end, I've learned that I am ready for a real partnership, for the real challenges of love, life, and family.

~

In the months after the breakup, I don't feel like jumping back into the dating scene. I need some time to be alone, sort out the mistakes I made in the relationship, and think about how I can make better choices next time. Instead, I decide to focus my energy on further investigating egg freezing, because

I now think this choice could assuage some of my anxiety so that my fertility doesn't distort another relationship.

At the beginning of the summer, I schedule a visit to Dr. Zhang of the New Hope Fertility Center for an antral follicle ultrasound. I figure it can't hurt to know where I stand in terms of my fertility. Dr. Zhang sees eight follicles in each of my ovaries, which he says is a good reserve. He tells me that I can wait at least another year before my fertility will begin its decline to the point where it might threaten my chances to have a biological child. Of course, he reminds me, there are no guarantees. But inasmuch as I've just ended a relationship and am in no way ready to start another one, this news is very reassuring.

Since I last explored egg freezing, three years earlier, the technology has been improving rapidly, Dr. Zhang tells me. Since 2003, an increasing number of babies have been born from frozen eggs every month, which is the most important indicator that the technology is beginning to hit its stride. I'm still skeptical; I know the marketing machine for the technology is so strong in the United States that it might be overselling its success. I decide that for a completely honest perspective on the viability of the technology, I should go to the original source, the Italian scientists who invented the technology.

In early October, I fly to Bologna, Italy, to meet with Dr. Rafaela Fabbri, the biologist behind the invention of the cryopreservation process, and Dr. Eleanora Porcu, the clinician who works with and studies the patients' results. Both work in the Department of Obstetrics and Gynecology at the University of Bologna.

I stay in the old part of the city, in a little hotel overlooking a tiny alley filled with fruit stands and fish vendors. I'm happy to be back in Italy, wandering through the winding streets and meditating over creamy *gelato*. But I'm here for a different reason this time—not to relax and live in the moment, but rather to plan for my future and my family's.

I first meet with Dr. Fabbri, the biologist, in her basement office at the university. She is an attractive blond in her mid-fifties. Dr. Fabbri has moved away from research on egg freezing and is now focusing on ovarian tissue cryopreservation, an even newer technique in which part of a woman's younger ovarian tissue is taken out and frozen, and then can be put back into the ovaries to start generating eggs later on.

Dr. Fabbri tells me that when she and Dr. Porcu started working together in the 1980s, they never envisioned the technology as a way to fulfill women's desires to "have it all." Rather, they were searching for an alternative to freezing extra embryos that women facing infertility and undergoing IVF chose not to have implanted or wanted to save for the future. At that time, the Vatican was considering placing a ban on the freezing of embryos, because Catholic law dictates that life begins at conception. Since many frozen embryos end up being discarded, the church wanted to stop this practice. Dr. Porcu and Dr. Fabbri saw the possibility of freezing unfertilized eggs as a way to sidestep this proscription. If they could successfully freeze eggs, it could give women and couples a new tool for procreation that didn't breach religious law.

Dr. Porcu joined forces with Dr. Fabbri to explore this difficult scientific challenge. Eggs have a delicate internal machinery, and since they contain a lot more water than sperm or embryos, they are much more difficult to freeze. During the freezing process, there is a higher risk that ice crystals might form and destroy the delicate spindle that contains the egg's cytoplasm. The two doctors believed that if they could solve the problem of the ice crystals, then they could make egg freezing a viable option.

In the beginning, Dr. Fabbri tells me, the two began by freezing eggs with the same mix of chemicals used to freeze embryos. But they found that when they thawed the eggs, their survival rate was very low. Dr. Fabbri started experimenting with different procedures, such as trying to freeze an egg without the cell membrane around it in order to look more closely at what was causing the ice crystals to form.

One day, she decided to increase the amount of sugar in the cryoprotectant, the chemical that takes the place of the water after the egg is dehydrated. This replacement allows the egg to freeze and therefore stay preserved at the same metabolic age over a long period of time. This small change in the sucrose level did the trick. Because sugar is a larger molecule than $H_2O$, it doesn't penetrate the cell. She quickly discovered that the sucrose even helped to pull some of the water out. These sweetened eggs froze without ice crystals and therefore thawed undamaged.

As the technique improved, so did the success rate of fertilizing and implanting unfrozen eggs. By 2004, seventy-eight babies had been born through an ongoing research study conducted by Dr. Porcu's lab.

After the scientific explanation, Dr. Fabbri tells me that she and Dr. Porcu no longer work together as a team. In fact, they are now at odds with one another. Dr. Fabbri believes that Dr. Porcu does not want to share credit for the discoveries they made in the advancement of egg freezing. But the tension between them is due primarily to their very different views about the commercialization of the technology. Dr. Fabbri believes that it offers all women a wonderful opportunity to extend their fertile years. That is why she continues to work with MediCult, the Swedish company that makes the freezing equipment and chemicals used by many clinics, including those in the Extend Fertility network. Dr. Fabbri even demonstrates the technique on a CD-ROM that is meant as an education tool for labs.

"I don't think it's a good idea for a woman to have a child at sixty or seventy," she says. "But I think it's important if a woman wants to have a child at forty."

Dr. Porcu disagrees—or at least she did three years earlier, when I began e-mailing with her as part of my research on egg freezing. Then, she told me that she did not support the commercialization of egg freezing because the technology was still so experimental.

"These companies can earn a lot of money, and they have high prices to maintain so they have an incentive to promise things that are apart from the true possibility," she wrote me. "Selling this technology as a method to ensure hypothetical fertility in the future is not fair. It's one thing for people who have no alternatives, such as patients with cancer or patients who want to store eggs instead of embryos for moral reasons, but this experimental treatment should not be paid for by patients."

I'm curious whether her position has changed as the science has progressed. That afternoon, I go upstairs in the same building to meet with her. Dr. Porcu is a stout brunette with a rational manner. The two of us sit down to talk in her sunny office overlooking a courtyard.

She begins our conversation by telling me that her clinic has now achieved a 28 percent pregnancy rate from frozen eggs, a big improvement compared to the 18 percent rate her team reported two years earlier. In the past three years, she and her team have discovered that the pregnancy rate depends less on the number of eggs inseminated than on the number of eggs that a woman produces. While there are many exceptions, the more eggs the woman produces during an IVF procedure, the more fertile the woman is—and therefore the more likely she is to become pregnant with her frozen eggs. Women who produce a lot of eggs also tend to have more eggs of high quality.

I ask Dr. Porcu whether her position against the commercialization of egg freezing has changed as a result of the improved statistics.

"Absolutely not," she says.

She tells me that most of the numbers that Extend Fertility and its partner clinic promote are still exaggerated, but she emphasizes that this is not the only reason she objects to the widespread marketing of the technology. She also maintains a political stance against it. Dr. Porcu believes that giving healthy women the opportunity to freeze their eggs in order to postpone childbearing is in fact very harmful for feminism. She thinks that we need to change society, not our bodies.

"It means that we're accepting a mentality of efficiency in which pregnancy, motherhood, and family are marginalized," she says. "The society should ensure that pregnancy is considered a prestigious accomplishment rather than an inconvenience. The goal should be to make it easier for women workers to become mothers."

"We've demonstrated that we are able to do everything like men," she continues. "Now we have to do the second revolution, which is not to freeze your eggs, and not to become dependent on a technology that involves surgical intervention."

"Egg freezing is not so easy," she says. "It involves general anesthesia and taking heavy hormone shots. Do you really want to do this just to postpone pregnancy because society doesn't want you to be pregnant when you have to work?"

Then she answers her own question.

"We have to change this mentality. We have to be free to be pregnant when we are fertile and young."

Dr. Porcu's argument isn't purely political, however—it's personal as well. She tells me that when she was first starting her career as a scientist, there was no room for her to be a mother.

"Immediately after giving birth, I went to a conference with my daughter. My mother came along, and I fed my daughter in between talks. I did it to avoid criticism from my colleagues." She tells me that if she hadn't felt such intense professional pressure, she would have had more than one child. She hates that women of the next generation are still in the same situation. "Very intelligent, powerful women should have the possibility of being pregnant during their career without risking their power or position."

I find myself torn by Dr. Porcu's argument. On the one hand, I agree that the companies and society as a whole need to do a much better job of adapting to the needs of working mothers. I can see how, on a broad social level, egg freezing allows working women to deny their biological nature and behave more like men. On the other hand, though, I am put off by Dr. Porcu's moralizing. She's not advocating government regulation or laws against egg freezing, she just believes that women shouldn't use the technology as a crutch. I think that like birth control or abortion, egg freezing is a choice, another tool by which women are able to assert control over their bodies, and that the decision to freeze eggs should be a matter of personal conscience, rather than a political statement.

"What about the case of a woman who is divorced and still wants a child, or someone like me who hasn't yet found Mr. Right?" I ask, suddenly feeling defensive about my own circumstances.

"I understand circumstances like yours," she says in a tone of sympathy. "In your case, it is an additional tool to fight against unfair nature. You want to survive as a fertile woman."

She then explains that if I do go through with it, then I must pay close attention to my own biology when making the decision. She says that she receives many e-mail messages from women in the United States in their late thirties and forties asking if it's appropriate to freeze their eggs, and she has to tell most of them that their chances of it working are very low.

"The possibility of freezing and thawing eggs in your late thirties and forties are low because many of a woman's eggs are damaged," she explains. "The success of egg freezing and thawing is strictly correlated to the quality and the age of the eggs."

"So the older and the more deteriorated the eggs are, the higher the chances that they are going to be damaged in the cryoprocess?" I ask.

"Yes," she says. "So if you're over thirty-five you would spend a lot of money and probably have nothing in your hand."

"Of course," she adds, "many women over thirty-five still have a large enough ovarian reserve and are therefore younger from a biological perspective."

I tell her that I recently learned that I had eight follicles.

"That means you're biologically young," she says.

This is the vital piece of information I've been looking for.

I leave Italy feeling more convinced that egg freezing is the right choice for me now, even though I know that there is no guarantee, and that the technology is still experimental.

In the October 2006 issue of the journal *Fertility and Sterility*, the official journal of the American Society for Reproductive Medicine, Dr. John K. Jain and Dr. Richard Paulson of the

University of Southern California's School of Medicine published their overview study of egg freezing based on multiple studies of women between ages thirty and thirty-three. In it, the authors acknowledged that the technology had achieved major advances in the prior three years.

In their research, the authors used two methods of egg freezing. The first is called the "slow-freeze" method, and it is most similar to current embryo freezing techniques. The second, vitrification, or "flash freezing," is a newer method, by which the egg is placed in a more highly concentrated bath of cryoprotectant for less than a minute. There are differing schools of thought regarding which freezing method is superior, though both methods have now had acceptable pregnancy rates.

The 2006 study concluded that "the slow-freeze data showed a gradual improvement in ooctye cryopreservation efficiency over time, with live-birth rates increasing from 21.6 percent per transfer between 1996 and 2004 to 32.4 percent between 2002 and 2004." The vitrification data followed a similar trend, with live births and ongoing pregnancy rates increasing from 29.4 percent before 2005 to 39 percent after 2005. Because of the clear advances over the years, in 2007 the ASRM revised somewhat its position on egg freezing. Its official position remains that oocyte cryopreservation is an experimental technology that should not be offered or marketed as a means to defer reproductive aging; if a woman does elect to undergo the procedure for that reason, she should seek comprehensive counseling. But the ASRM now acknowledges that egg freezing offers advantages to women who are undergoing in vitro fertilization or other fertility treatments and have extra eggs but who prefer not to create and freeze extra embryos.

They also acknowledge that the technology offers opportunities for women who are at risk of losing ovarian function as a consequence of treatment of cancer.

It seems a contradiction that the ASRM committee would approve of and recommend the technology for women with cancer or women using advanced reproductive technology who don't want to create embryos, but discourage its use for women who simply want to preserve their fertility longer. I call Christy Jones of Extend Fertility to find out what she thinks of this position.

"I think my fertility is just as at risk as a cancer patient's. It's a free country," she says. "The right view is to address this through the proper level of education rather than taking a paternalistic view that you just shouldn't do it, or that women should not be waiting so long or be so focused on their careers."

I agree with her position, and, having educated myself about the improved success rates, I set up an appointment with Dr. Noyes to hear more about the results of her study. She tells me that in her research she has now done seventeen egg freezing cycles in women up to age thirty-eight. The mean age of these women is thirty-five. Her patients have produced eleven babies, which include three sets of twins.

Dr. Noyes points out, however, that her research protocol focused on women who elected to get pregnant right after freezing, which means that she and her team harvest the eggs, freeze them, and then immediately thaw, fertilize, and implant them. She notes that no women outside of the research group who have frozen their eggs at the clinic have come back to have them fertilized, so the success rates with eggs that remain frozen for a longer period of time are not yet known.

According to data from the Society of Reproductive Medicine, the New York University Fertility Center has one of the highest success rates in the country for in vitro fertilization in women over the age of thirty-five. In women thirty-five to thirty-seven, 43.9 percent of cycles result in pregnancy; in women thirty-eight to forty, 37 percent result in pregnancy; and in women forty-one to forty-two, 22 percent do. These rates are only slightly lower with frozen embryos.

Dr. Noyes discouraged me from pursuing the technology three years ago; I ask her if she's now changed her position.

"Now I feel very comfortable," she says. "I wouldn't think twice about it now."

I already know from my appointment with Dr. Zhang that I still have a good reserve of antral follicles. Dr. Noyes tells me that I also need to get a follicle-stimulating hormone test because the NYU Fertility Center will not freeze a woman's eggs if her FSH is over 13.5 or her estradiol, another sex hormone created in the ovaries, is more than 70 pg/ml. Higher levels indicate that the brain is working harder to force the ovaries to produce eggs, an indicator of reduced quantity and quality of eggs.

I tell her that some doctors have recommended that I freeze embryos in addition to eggs, because the chances of pregnancy from frozen embryos are higher than with frozen eggs. Some doctors refer to freezing both as "The Works." Dr. Noyes says that at this stage, she is achieving the same rates with eggs.

"I think you need eight mature spindle-positive eggs to achieve a pregnancy," she says. A spindle-positive egg is one that has reached full maturity.

"A mature egg has the best chances for fertilization," she continues. "It works as well as embryos, so why add the dilemma of sperm?"

"What are the pregnancy rates with thirty-eight-year-old frozen embryos or eggs versus forty-two-year-old fresh eggs?" I ask, wondering what the case would be if I just dropped the whole idea and again rolled the dice—even if it meant having to use ART (Advanced Reproductive Technology) in my forties.

"Thirty percent compared to twenty percent," she says.

Ten percent is not that much of a difference, but four years seems like a long time to wait without doing anything. If I'm not going to have a baby now, with a partner or on my own, I want to do something proactive. And every point counts.

I wish, of course, that the percentage of live births from frozen eggs were higher now. I wish that taking such a big step would guarantee that I will be able to have a child for many more years. But I also believe that as more women take this step, the science will become better, and women will have more options. So I decide to put my faith into science and take this step not only for myself and my future child, but for the future of women's choices. Even if I don't end up with a baby, I'll be able to take solace in the fact that I've helped move the technology forward—which will, I'm now quite certain, benefit our lives in the long run.

By December, I've started dating again. I'm seeing an aspiring photographer named Ted*. We disagree about almost everything—he's a vegetarian, I provoke him by making dinner reservations at barbecue joints—but he's flexible and loose and fun to be around. He's the perfect rebound relationship for me. It's clear to me, though, that Ted's not my soul mate and that the relationship isn't going anywhere. So I move forward with my plans to freeze my eggs.

I begin this unintended next phase of my life by getting a battery of blood tests: follicle-stimulating hormone (FSH) and anti-Müllerian hormone (AMH), which strongly correlates with the size of a woman's ovarian follicle pool. Since I'm half-Jewish, I'm also screened for genetic disorders like Tay-Sachs disease and Canavan disease; I'll need to know if I'm a carrier of these if I also decide to fertilize my eggs with donor sperm.

While I'm waiting for my results, I decide I want to visit Maggie Hopkins in Washington, to see what life is like for this new single mom. She went forward with single motherhood because her doctor had warned her that she might need to have a hysterectomy at some point, and it's possible that my blood tests will reveal something that might cause me to follow the same path: if my FSH is too high for egg freezing—that is, if my eggs are deemed to be of insufficient quality to survive the freeze and thaw—the doctors might recommend that I just try to get pregnant right away.

We've never met in person, and when I e-mail her to ask her if I can come visit, she writes back almost instantly.

"I had a baby boy, he is twenty months now, and I am *very* happy with my decision . . . but time is definitely a premium now."

I respond, give her a brief synopsis of the last year, and tell her that I'm more seriously considering single motherhood. I'd be interested in following her around for a weekend to see what it's like. She writes back to say that she's happy to host, but warns me again about her schedule.

"It's so funny to remember what it was like to make plans pre-parenthood!" she writes. "Here's my schedule for this weekend: Friday (I don't work Fridays): Winston* wakes up around 7 a.m. . . . Winston's dentist at 9:45 a.m. . . . Winston's naptime around 2–4 . . . toddler playgroup at local park around 4–6 . . . dinner at 6 . . . Winston bedtime around 8:30 . . . my shower and e-mail and then sleep. Saturday: Winston wakes up around

7 a.m. . . . we are babysitting Henry from 9:30 to 11:30 (either cartoons or park) . . . then try to get Winston to nap around 1–3 . . . drive to Virginia for Single Mothers by Choice party scheduled for 3:30 to 5:30 but will probably last longer . . . if not, may try to stop by the neighborhood Unitarian church Halloween party, scheduled for 5–7 (though I think this is probably too ambitious) . . . Winston bedtime around 8:30 . . . my shower and e-mail and then sleep."

I tell her that I'll be happy to help with anything she needs.

That Saturday morning, I show up at Maggie's small railroad apartment on a tree-lined street.

When a petite redhead opens the door, I'm somehow surprised that she is so small—she has such an outsized personality that I imagined her as someone larger. But I'm even more surprised to see that she is pregnant again.

"You're pregnant again?" I blurt out.

She smiles, saying she thought she told me that she's due to have her second in three months.

"Same situation?" I ask hesitantly, thinking that maybe she's met someone.

"Yes, Alix is the donor again," she says.

We settle down on the couch in her living room. Winston, her darling red-haired, blued-eyed son, immediately starts sharpening pencils in an electric pencil sharpener. The screeching sound is intensely loud and annoying to me, but Maggie doesn't seem to notice it at all.

"After I had him, I was on the fence about having another," she begins. "But when my mom died last year, that was a big decision point for me. I really wanted to have a bigger family. I don't have a lot of friends here, and I don't think it's likely that I'm going to get married. I really don't want them to be alone after I die."

After a pause, she continues. "There are secondary reasons too. I also realize that I have a sort of domineering personality, so I think it'll be good for him to have another child distracting me, so I'm not focused on him all the time."

Again, I'm shocked by her rationality. Yet I'm also impressed that she is so self-aware and conscientious about her son's experience.

Maggie calls Winston over to the table and puts a plate of rice and broccoli in front of him.

This past year, Maggie tells me, she learned that she wouldn't make partner in her law firm. She plans to leave the firm soon, and wants to have her second child while she still has good health insurance and a solid maternity leave policy.

I ask her if she thinks that she didn't make partner because of being a single mom.

"I think that was a factor," she says. "They wanted a much more dedicated lawyer. That's part of the . . . umm . . ."

She turns and puts a piece of lettuce in Winston's mouth.

"Oh, sorry, lost my train of thought," she says. "I'm not going to lose my job—that's different from not making partner. But I don't want to stay at a firm that doesn't think I am worthy of being partner."

Maggie is planning to go solo for more flexibility, even if it means less money and less security.

The doorbell rings. It's Maggie's next-door neighbor, another single mom who is dropping off her son, whom she adopted from Guatemala. Maggie had agreed to watch him for a few hours while her neighbor goes to an appointment. It's a coincidence that they ended up neighbors, and both find it fortuitous that they can occasionally help each other out.

As her neighbor's son settles down onto the couch to watch cartoons, Winston follows Maggie into her bedroom. I follow them down a hallway, past a wall of photographs. There's a frame of photos of Maggie and Winston with his cousins in Texas. Another shows Alix, Winston's donor, and his partner Ricky. Alix is holding Winston. Next to him on the couch, an older woman smiles proudly.

"Is that your mom?" I ask.

"No, it's Alix's mom," she says.

Maggie e-mails Alix photos of Winston regularly, and they talk once a month or so, but according to the way they established their roles before she got pregnant, Alix does not play a primary role in her son's life. When she is exhausted or frustrated by her son, she doesn't seek Alix's advice or emotional support, because she knows that he is busy with his own adopted children. She tells me that now that she's had Winston, she realizes it's not that important to know who the biological father is.

"I was much more convinced then that you knew what you were getting if you knew the person with whom you had a child. Now I'm much more convinced that it's all a total crapshoot."

"Maybe it's better for Winston to know his biological father rather than have him be some anonymous sperm donor," I suggest.

"I don't think it's that complicated," she says. "He'll deal with it. It's not ideal, but we're dealing in a world of nonideals."

Later, when I talk to Alix by phone, he tells me that his mother was more excited about Winston's birth than she was about the adoption of his own child. "She was like, 'Send me pictures, send me pictures!' And she was never that way with my kids. I think because he looks so much like me, it reminds her of when she was a young mother."

"Do you feel paternal?" I ask Alix.

"No," he answers. "I feel biologically connected. Winston is too young to need me to spend a lot of time with him. In the future, as he gets older, that might change. It's really going to be up to Winston. I want to be as helpful and open as possible. As he gets older, I want to be there for his needs."

I sit down on the floor and play blocks with Winston while Maggie finishes folding her laundry.

She tells me that when she was first thinking about becoming a single mom, she decided to do a test run by taking care of her friend's three children by herself for a week.

"One of my notes after that week was: 'You'll never get done what you think you're going to get done in a day. You'll never get them to daycare on time. Never, ever.' It didn't matter what time I got up, I didn't get those kids out of the house on time."

Winston and I start to push a ball back and forth on the floor over and over. I realize that unconsciously I'm waiting for someone to come home to check in, to relieve Maggie. But no one is coming.

"What do you do for emotional support?" I ask.

"I have a best friend, Charlene. I met her in law school. She's in her fifties and has a very similar personality. She lives in Texas, but we talk on the phone all the time."

Winston grabs a barrette off the dresser.

"Can I have that please?" she asks him, taking it away. "That's Mommy's."

I tell her that when I think of home and family, I think of something more than just children.

"I've always imagined it as a kind of emotional center," I tell her. "I'm afraid of not having another adult to lean on when it gets hard."

Winston starts crying.

"I don't understand that concern, to tell you the truth," she replies.

"A partner takes part of the weight," I continue. "I have great friends, but I don't think I could count on them 100 percent. They have their own lives."

"Absolutely," she says. "I think it's important to recognize that. That's part of the reason why I'm having a second child. I think single parents put a lot of pressure on their kids to be their emotional support."

I ask her if she ever has sex.

"I haven't been sexually active with a man for a few years. I miss it a lot," she says. "I've gone out to bars, I've gone on dates, but I haven't met someone."

While I find this confession sort of horrifying, I realize that it's not just a problem for single women. I know a lot of married couples who also say they have stopped having sex.

"I really think you can meet someone and have a relationship if you really want it," I say. I realize I'm arguing with her at this point, because she's telling me things I don't want to hear.

"So many women have this fantasy that they're going to get married and have children. I never really had any of that," she says. "For a while, I thought I might meet someone, but I just got to know myself and have now realized that it's probably not likely. I've mourned it and accepted it."

"Are you happy?" I ask her.

"Oh, yeah," she says.

"Are you serious?"

"Yes, it's been delightful. The best thing I've ever done."

I tell Maggie that I'm going to go outside and take a walk. Once I'm out of the house, I burst into tears. I could never live this life, nor raise a child without believing that someday I would have a partner for myself. But at the same time, I admire Maggie for knowing what she wants, and for going after it. I want to be that person as well.

Once I calm down a bit, I realize that Maggie and I are very different people. I think Maggie is fundamentally uncompromising—I see it even in the way she schedules every minute of her day, and Winston's. I suspect that this makes it very hard for her to form relationships. I reassure myself that I am more flexible, that I will be more open to adapting my life if I meet the right man. But still, I liked the version of the single motherhood story represented by Ann in Iowa much more than this one. I can't imagine family life without that warm living room, without that partnership.

In the afternoon, we go to a Halloween party thrown by another single mother by choice in a small apartment complex on the other side of town. The host is dressed as a slutty maid and has decorated her place like a haunted house—complete with a sound machine making spooky noises. The room is filled with other single mothers and toddlers dressed in clown and bunny costumes. Talking to other single mothers, I'm relieved to find that most of them are still intent on finding Mr. Right.

One woman, who had her daughter on her own at forty-one with a donor's sperm, asks me why I look unhappy.

I tell her about my conversation with Maggie.

"One person's stories and opinions can't dissuade you," she responds. "It's all about your attitude. As I explained to my friends and family, I needed to do this first. But, oh, I plan to meet someone."

Toward the end of the party, a sporty blond woman shows up at the door with three children: a seven-year-old boy, a two-year-old girl, and a five-month-old boy. I'm shocked that a woman would have three on her own. But I quickly learn that she only had the two-year-old with a sperm donor. She had her five-month-old with the man she met and fell in love with a year after her daughter was born, and the seven-year-old is her husband's child from his first marriage.

"Well aren't you the ultimate modern family!" I say after listening to her story.

"Yes!" she says, beaming.

At that moment—here in this tiny apartment in the midst of all these cooing and screaming children, bobbing apples, and bowls of candy corn—I resolve to continue working on myself, and continue working to find my perfect love. I won't give up on that, even if the test results come back indicating that it's now or never to have a child. I would have that child, but that doesn't mean I would commit to living my life alone. Giving up on part of the fantasy of having a child with the perfect man doesn't mean giving up on the whole. I think: *I have faith that it will all fall into place in its own sweet time.*

~

When I get back from D.C., I call Dr. Noyes, praying that my results will allow me to freeze my eggs. She immediately assures me that my FSH is a 4.6 and my estradiol is a 24, so even though I'm older than thirty-five, biologically I'm young enough to make the cut.

"Am I crazy for doing this?" I ask her, feeling a bit overwhelmed as this new frontier of family planning starts to become my reality.

"If someone comes in and I think they're insane, I won't let them go through with it," she replies. "You're not at all crazy. You're being self-protective. You are living in the real world, and you should not be denied the chance to have a child because Mr. Right couldn't commit or hasn't come along."

"So you think I should do it?"

"Based on your numbers, I *think* you're going to be fertile until you're forty-one," she says. "And if I look into my crystal ball, I believe that you're going to have a baby at thirty-nine with Mr. Wonderful. But if that doesn't happen, then you'll have the option to use frozen eggs."

I'm ready to take the leap of faith—or, more accurately, the leap of science.

# 11

# Freezing Time

On December 17, I attend my first egg-freezing class at the NYU Fertility Center. Standing in front of a large PowerPoint projection of the female reproductive system, Jennifer Giordano, a nurse at the clinic, explains every detail of the process I'm beginning. The drug protocol differs for each woman depending on her hormone numbers and her individual biology, but the directions of the basic recipe are the same:

Step 1: Stimulate the growth of eggs.

Step 2: Trigger the release of eggs.

Step 3: Retrieve eggs.

Step 4: Freeze eggs.

In the first phase, I will shoot myself up with a stimulating hormone called a gonadotropin. Follistim, the brand name for "follitropin beta," is a manmade form of follicle-stimulating hormone (FSH) that is used to stimulate egg production. It is manufactured through a new biotechnology called recombinant DNA technology. By recombining the DNA sequences of cells cloned from a Chinese hamster ovary cell, scientists re-create the FSH molecule.

Jen points to an ultrasound image of a woman's ovaries filled with large dark circles. Each circle is an antral follicle that may contain an egg within it. In a natural menstrual cycle, it takes approximately two weeks for an antral follicle to grow one egg. In the first few hours of her period, the woman's body begins to naturally release FSH, which will stimulate the release of the single egg during ovulation.

"When we give you gonadotropins, each ovary will absorb the drug and stimulate a larger number of follicles to grow so you get more than one egg," Jen explains.

The first step will take ten to twelve days. I'll give myself shots of Follistim into my belly with a 27-gauge needle, which is smaller than a needle used to take blood. As the follicles grow, they release estrogen, and with each shot, my estrogen level will rise. Estrogen is measured in picograms (one trillionth of a gram) per milliliter. During a normal menstrual cycle, estrogen typically peaks shortly before the point of ovulation, reaching levels in the blood at between 50 and 200 pg/ml. When stimulated with Follistim, my estrogen level should reach ten times the level achieved in a normal cycle by the time the follicles are big enough to release eggs—between 500 pg/ml and 2000 pg/ml.

Jen uses the analogy of an oven to explain why the process has to move slowly.

"If you turn the temperature up too high, it will burn," she says. "If your estrogen gets too high, you will get sick."

Jen then demonstrates how to do the shots on a medical dummy. That's when I start to get a little more nervous, because I'll be giving myself the shots.

During the time when I'm taking the shots, I'll go into the clinic every few days for a blood test to check my estrogen levels. The doctor will also measure the size of my follicles with an ultrasound. When the follicles are the right size—between 18 and 20 millimeters—it will mean that my eggs are mature and ready for retrieval.

I'm not to do any strenuous exercise during this period, because my ovaries will be larger than usual and I might run the risk of twisting them. I should also cut back on alcohol. Most important: I'm supposed to abstain from sex for two weeks before the retrieval. That's because I'll be extremely fertile and could get pregnant with, say, quadruplets.

"If you do have sex, use triple protection," she says.

I ask Jen how the hormones will affect my mood.

"Estrogen is a feel-good hormone," Jen says. "You will have a lot of energy and feel happy. The number one side effect is that you will feel bloated."

Just before the egg retrieval, I will take what Jen refers to as the "trigger shot." Human chorionic gonadotropin (hCG) is a peptide hormone naturally secreted by the bloodstream. During pregnancy, the placenta begins to produce it after the embryo has implanted in the uterine wall. A synthetic form of hCG introduced into the bloodstream in the presence of mature follicles also stimulates ovulation, so I will inject myself with it exactly twenty-four to thirty-six hours before my eggs are to be retrieved. This shot is a little scarier because the needle is larger.

Step 3 is the part I'm most nervous about: the surgical retrieval. Jen flips to a slide illustrating the procedure. Using a transvaginal ultrasound with a small needle on the end of it, Dr. Noyes will guide the needle through my vaginal wall and remove the eggs from the follicles. It takes about twenty-five minutes, and I will be under light anesthesia when the surgery is performed. Once the eggs are removed, Dr. Noyes will put them into a test tube and hand them off to the embryologist.

In Step 4, the embryologist counts the eggs, separates the most mature ones by using a type of microscope called a polscope. The most mature eggs are what doctors call "spindle positive," which means that a structure in the egg called the meiotic spindle is present. A strong spindle means that the egg is mature and therefore has a better chance for fertilization.

Once the best eggs have been selected, the embryologist will freeze the eggs to minus 196 degrees in liquid nitrogen, using the process invented by Dr. Porcu and Dr. Fabbri. The eggs will then be stored in little test tubes racked up in a big metal tank that looks a little like an olive oil barrel. The NYU Fertility Clinic will provide free storage for the first year and then charge $400 every year after that.

If I were infertile and going through standard IVF to get pregnant, the eggs would be fertilized with my partner's or a donor's sperm rather than frozen. The embryos would then be transferred into my uterus in two or three days.

In my case, one third of the batch of my eggs will be fertilized with my donor's sperm and also frozen. Even though Dr. Noyes told me that she is getting the same results with frozen eggs as she is with frozen embryos, I don't totally trust this because I've seen other data showing freezing eggs alone to be riskier. But I plan to do The Works only if I make a large number of eggs. Dr. Noyes said I need at least eight eggs to freeze on their own, so if I produce more than that, I will also create embryos for additional insurance.

"If you choose to fertilize your eggs with your husband's sperm later, we can also refreeze them as embryos," Jen says.

I ask Jen how I will feel after the surgery, and she tells me I should expect to be a little tired and a little bloated for a week or two. I'm also concerned about the effects of the drugs on my body, because every time I tell someone I'm thinking about doing this they say, "Doesn't that cause breast or ovarian cancer?"

Jen says I shouldn't worry. Later that day, when I check out PubMed, a database of research collected by the National Institutes of Health, I find a 2005 study published in the *International Journal of Infertility*, in which the researchers surveyed fifteen studies on the risk of developing breast cancer after IVF treatment. The authors concluded that there was no significant association between the treatment and breast cancer. The results on ovarian cancer, however, were deemed a little less conclusive. A 1995 study published in *Lancet* found six cases of ovarian cancer after examining 10,386 women who went through IVF between 1978 and 1982. "Although there was no significantly increased risk of ovarian cancer, the small number of cases limits the conclusion that can be drawn," the study concluded.

I have Jen's phone number and plan to call if I have any other questions. But for now, I have to wait to get my period, so I can start my cycle.

I also have a Step 5. Since I've decided to freeze embryos in addition to eggs, I need to choose a sperm donor. At first, I'm resistant to the process—it seems so sterile, the furthest possible thing from creating a child out of love. It feels simultaneously sad and empowering that I have this freedom. But I know I can't overthink it. After all, I haven't committed yet to having a child with donor sperm—I've only committed to freezing embryos so it will be one possibility further down the road.

So the evening after my NYU Fertility Clinic class, I click onto the website of the California Cryobank to begin yet another online adventure. At first, it feels no different from signing up for an online dating site, except this time I don't have to fill out a profile about myself, and I know that I never have to meet any of these men in person. I sign up for an account and hit a button labeled "Power Search." This function allows me to select everything from race to eye color to height to weight to religion to temperament to hair color and even hair *texture*. The computer will then search for the closest match. I scan through the list of options and quickly discover that the traits I'm attracted to in a donor are not all that different from the traits I like in a lover. I enter 6'2", green eyes, brown hair. There is no match.

I know that I want an open ID donor because I want my child to have the option to find his or her biological father in the future. And an excellent health history is a really important aspect of my choice as well. I've learned that I have a very specific concern: my blood tests revealed that I carry the gene for Canavan disease. Most frequently found in Ashkenazi Jews from eastern Poland, western Russia, and Lithuania, Canavan disease is a neurological birth disorder caused by a gene mutation in the nerve fiber of the brain. When both parents carry the gene mutation, there is a 1 in 4 chance that their child will be affected with the disease. The disease manifests from early infancy; early symptoms include feeding difficulties, abnormal muscle tone, and an unusually large, poorly controlled head. The disease progresses rapidly, and generally the child doesn't live past the age of four.

Dr. Noyes told me that I must be careful not to pick a donor who carries the same gene. It's a strange factor to consider—with the same knowledge, would I really not date any Ashkenazi Jews? If Jacob and I had decided to get married and I found out on the eve of our wedding that he was also a carrier, would I have changed my mind? Of course not.

In real life, I would never ask for a medical profile before falling in love with someone. That pregnancy via sperm donor allows for such considerations is one of the many strange—and confusing—aspects of the process. Of course, given the option, I will choose a donor who doesn't carry the Canavan gene—or have any other significant health problems. What woman wouldn't? There's a huge potential upside here in terms of eliminating, or at least reducing, lethal diseases. But as I contemplate the complete range of choices available to me in the process, I can't help but think that it verges on a kind of eugenics. It's one thing to screen donors for a history of breast cancer or Alzheimer's, but is it wrong of me to be considering genetic traits like eye color and height and hair color? I suppose unconsciously I make these choices anyway when I choose the men I date, but there's something about the literalism of this process that makes me feel vaguely uncomfortable.

But I'm here for a reason, so I start sorting the profiles. As I enter my preferences into the search engine, I start to imagine the mix of my genes with the different profiles I run across: a blued-eyed, 5'9" Hindu Indian; an agnostic, curly-haired Russian Jew with an "artisan" temperament; a tall, fair-skinned Episcopalian with soft hair; a heavy-set Chilean Catholic with hazel eyes.

In the middle of my search my mom calls.

"What are you up to?" she asks.

"Oh, just shopping for some sperm," I say, laughing out of discomfort.

When I got back from Italy, I had told my parents—and a handful of my friends—about my plans to freeze. My parents said they were happy I had made a decision that made me feel better; and my friends, the ones who didn't cringe when I talked about needles, were proud that I had made a proactive choice.

But this is the first time I've described my part of the process to my mom. I'm a little worried that she's going to think I've gone off the deep end. But she doesn't.

"Remember when you had those shoes made at the mall and you could pick the fabric and style?" she asks, also laughing. "What you're doing reminds me of that kind of fashion customization."

She's right, of course. On a certain level, I'm sitting here designing my potential child.

"How do you make the decision?" she asks.

"I don't know," I say. "Do I go outside of my gene pool or stay inside? Do I pick traits from your side or dad's side?"

"Do they have half and half?" she asks.

"Actually, yes!"

Within an hour of looking through the website, I feel utterly overwhelmed. So a few days later, I find myself back in Dr. Schiffman's tiny office. I haven't seen her since just before I left for India, almost a year earlier.

"So how have you been?" she asks.

I tell her about breaking up with Jacob and that I'm dating someone new, but it's only been a few months. I tell her about my visit to Dr. Zhang, to the doctors in Italy, and how I came to the conclusion that I would freeze eggs and also embryos made from donor sperm. NYU actually requires a meeting with Dr. Schiffman before it will fertilize any donor eggs for their patients. They want to evaluate whether the patient is going to be responsible and has considered the short-term as well as the long-term effects on the child. "I would use embryos only if the eggs don't work," I say. "If I find myself in my forties and I really just want to have a child. Then I'll have embryos made with my younger eggs. But there's also the possibility that I can go through an IVF cycle in the future with my partner, right?"

"Right," she says. Then she asks if I'm finding donors that meet my criteria. I tell her that I've been asking myself whether I'll go outside my gene pool or stay inside of it.

The question has made me start thinking a lot about my genealogy, I tell her. I've been leafing through the papers my grandmother left behind and talking to some of my more immediate family members about our family history.

My mother is an Ashkenazi Jew. Her dad was a chemical engineer, born in Grodno, a town in western Russia. In the summer of 1930, my grandfather came to stay at the inn my great-grandparents owned, where he met my grandmother. She was twenty-three and he was thirty. Her parents were away on a trip that week, and my grandparents had a whirlwind romance. When my grandmother's parents got home, she announced her engagement. My grandmother once told me this story over dinner at the golf club in New Jersey, where we used to meet up every so often. She thought it was so strange that people in my generation were now meeting through computers. I can only imagine what she would think of my latest search.

My father is a mix of German Protestant, Jew, and Scottish Episcopalian. The Lehmanns (an eighth of my ethnicity) were possibly Sephardic Jews who left Spain in the fifteenth century. The Haupts were German Lutherans from a town in eastern Germany called Stettin, which is now in Poland. Therese Haupt, my great-grandmother, was a poet and playwright. Carl Friedrich Ferdinand Lehmann, my great-grandfather was a professor of ancient history, and familiar with some two dozen languages. When they married, they decided to combine their names into one because Therese, the poet, wanted her name to continue.

My paternal grandfather, Hellmut Otto Emil Lehmann-Haupt, was born in Berlin in 1903. My paternal grandmother, Leticia Jane Hargrove Grierson, was a spirited Scot whose father's family came from the Shetland Islands. Her father, Sir Herbert John Clifford Grierson, was a scholar at the universities of Aberdeen and Edinburgh and was knighted for reviving interest in the metaphysical poets. In 1933, she accompanied her father to the United States when he was to receive an honorary degree from Columbia University; she met her husband-to-be at a faculty tea in the Morgan Library. He proposed to her on the Columbia campus; they were married in the university church.

My own parents met because they lived on the same floor of a building in Greenwich Village in 1961. My mom, a poet and editor at the time, told me that she wrote in her diary that she was going to marry a man named Christopher.

"At first, Dad wasn't the slightest bit interested in me," she said. "He tried to fix me up with his brother, who said, 'What's the matter with you? This woman is interested in you, not me!'"

I tell Dr. Schiffman that ideally in this situation, I'd like to find some mix of my ethnicities in my donor. While I might never ask these kinds of questions of a date, and it's not critical that I marry someone with the same religious or ethnic background as me, if I'm going to create a child with a donor, then I want to share a similar background with him or her. When, one day in the future, my child starts to ask about his or her genetic origins, I want to be able to point to a map and say, "We're from here." Having a common background with the donor and with my child feels like a solid kind of foundation to give to a child of a single-mother family.

Dr. Schiffman tells me I should think about the factors that are going to be most important for the child.

"I think if a child could look a little like you that would be a plus," she says. "It's harder for a kid to be confronted constantly by, 'Where did you come from?' So I wouldn't pick a Swede, for example. Not that I have anything against Swedish heritage, and not because you might not be attracted to a Swedish guy. But you don't look Swedish. Your child should look like a member of your family."

I tell her that a lot of single moms have told me that they picked someone opposite to them to offset negative traits. I was thinking about someone a bit more rational and science-oriented, like a doctor. I could then say, "Mommy is really artistic and your donor was scientific."

Dr. Schiffman nods. "For some people, it is very important that the donor has some artistic or athletic or scientific qualities." But then she reminds me: *"You have to remember that these choices don't guarantee anything in your child."*

That evening, I continue my Web search, trying to keep in mind that I ultimately have no control over the life I'm creating. For all the reasons that Dr. Schiffman and I discussed, I've decided to look for some combination of my own genetic history in my biological mate. If I'm not going to be procreating from love, I like the idea of carrying on my family's ethnic traditions. I also like the idea of a tall man. My father is tall. My mother is short. I'm 5'7" and I think height is commanding. I also wouldn't mind finding someone who might balance out some of the things I don't like about myself. I hate my curly hair, and I also think my creative and passionate temperament can sometimes veer toward irrationality.

On the Power Search page, there is a link that says, "Click here to view our list of donors with at least one Jewish ancestor." I click. I scan down the list to an open ID donor with

wavy brown hair and Russian origins. Performing arts. 5'9".
Maybe a little too short. Next.

I scroll down to a Jew with English, German, Polish, and
Romanian roots. He is a 5'10" doctor with seven years of education and fair skin. I add him to my "favorites" list.

The next one that catches my eye is a 5'11" man of English
and German roots. He studied computer science, law, history,
literature, and writing. I add him to the list. I also add a 6'1"
man with English and Scottish roots, wavy brown hair, and a
background in the performing arts.

After about an hour of sorting through at least ten pages,
my eyes begin to glaze over. I decide to take a break and then
look through my favorites in a few hours. I'll order more
lengthy profiles of each of them, baby photos, as well as voice
recordings, so I can hear what they sound like. But I'll have to
pay additional fees for all of this, and I don't have unlimited
funds. I'm already spending close to $10,000 on my freezing
procedure, so I decide to narrow my choices down to the top
three by reading their short profiles, which are free.

In the short profile, the donor is asked to answer questions
about his personality, math and mechanical skills, favorite
sports, hobbies and favorite food, whether or not he likes animals, where he likes to travel, his favorite color, artistic abilities, his ultimate goals in life, and where he sees himself in
twenty years.

This last question seems vital because if my child decides
he wants to contact his biological father, it will most likely be
right around this time. I don't want my child to show up at his
door only to find an unemployed guy smoking pot and watching *Dr. Phil* reruns. Of course I know that life can change
course in an instant, and that many of these donors are only in

college when they write their essays. But still, I want someone who shows signs of ambition.

The 5′11″ English German wears corrective lens. I can barely read his handwriting, which annoys me at first, but he is also one of my only choices who has a baby picture available. I can make out that he likes to sew and cook and do yoga, and that his favorite sport is surfing—for which I give him extra points.

"I don't have a favorite color," he writes. "I prefer black and white combinations and orange. I have a hard time suffering the company of those in the world that want simple self-gratification."

The Jewish doctor loves watermelon, strawberries, cucumbers, ice cream, and steak. He had a 3.4 GPA in college, got 5 on the AP calculus test. He has a few freckles and majored in molecular biology. He's also good at fixing things around the house, which immediately appeals to me. I have to remind myself that I'm not picking a boyfriend—my sperm donor isn't going to fix the cabinet doors in my kitchen. The doctor is also into photography and wants to travel to Alaska for outdoor adventure and visit the Amazon River. He's "outgoing, easy to talk to, passionate." He sounds a little like me. Well, except the part about majoring in molecular biology and getting perfect scores on the calculus test. Ours could be an interesting gene combination, I think. I decide to order more information about him.

The 6′1″ Scottish German with wavy hair is a world literature and art major. He also writes that he scored 650 on his math SAT, is computer savvy, and ran a 5:35 mile when he was fifteen. He speaks English, Italian, and Spanish. He composes music, writes songs, and sings. He wants to travel to Germany to research his mother's ancestry and describes himself as "outgoing, charming, and funny."

"I'm adventurous, nonconformist, and a bit of a rogue," he writes. "At times I can be an intellectual introvert, but I am generally more of a class clown." In twenty years, he sees himself as a successful recording artist and writer.

I think I'm in love.

After an evening of reading, I narrow my choices down to two: the Rogue and the adventurous Jewish doctor who likes watermelon. I decide to invest some more cash in their baby photos, longer essays, and audio recordings. So far I've spent $150. The Jewish doctor has a perfect medical history, but unfortunately he doesn't provide a baby photo. Even though he looks great on paper, I can't live with the idea of not having an idea of what my baby might look like, so I decide to let him go.

That leaves me with the Rogue. I order a long profile, his medical history, and a baby picture. Another $35. My instinct is that he will be a good choice, and I decide that if like what I see, I'm going to go with him and not spend any more money on this process. After all, I'm still not 100 percent convinced that I'm going to freeze embryos.

*You have to remember that these choices don't guarantee anything in your child.*

In his donor essay, the Rogue says that he wants to be a donor because he knows that "many women dream of raising their own biological children" and he wants to help. He says he doesn't have a great relationship with his immediate family, but there is a group of relatives that he loves a lot. Again, he emphasizes how creative he is. He's recorded three CDs and has had an exhibition of his photography. He even writes a message to his future child: "Follow your dreams, regardless of what anyone thinks. Make your own decisions, think for your-self, be kind and polite to others, and be as positive, engaging, and entertaining as possible."

I love this message, and I keep my fingers crossed that he has a good medical history and that he was a cute baby.

It turns out that his medical profile is nearly perfect: no glasses or childhood allergies; he has good teeth and gets regular exercise, and the only time he's been in the hospital was for a simple sinus surgery. He admits he occasionally smokes pot, which is fine with me.

I immediately like his family. His paternal grandfather was fluent in five languages. He says his paternal grandmother was an excellent cook, very warm and charming. He has two sets of twin cousins (a fraternal pair, a boy and a girl, on his father's side and identical boys on his mother's side). There are no serious birth defects in his family's history, though there have been some medical problems: his maternal grandmother and paternal grandfather both had high blood pressure, his maternal aunt had asthma, and his maternal uncle was diagnosed with precancerous skin cells in his early fifties. His maternal cousin was diagnosed with a mild learning disability at age five. A little more worrisome, his mother was diagnosed with rheumatoid arthritis at age seventeen, and it affects her wrists. His paternal aunt had gout, and a paternal uncle abused drugs in his twenties, though the Rogue writes that he went to rehab and is now drug free.

Would I even know all this—or, more important, care—if I were in love with someone?

I download his baby picture, the final test.

The Rogue was an absolutely adorable baby. He has big brown puppy dog eyes, a mop of blond hair, and a little pug nose. Perhaps I'm projecting, but he also seems to have a slightly devilish grin that definitely says "future rogue."

I follow my gut and hit "Add to Cart."

On New Year's Day, I get my period and call the clinic. The nurse tells me to come back in three days. If my hormone levels are OK, I'll be able to start my cycle.

On the morning of Wednesday, January 4, I head over to the NYU Fertility Clinic for a blood test and ultrasound. A few hours later, I get a call from Jen, the nurse who taught the egg freezing class, who tells me that my FSH is 4.6 and my estrogen is 24. She says that these are great numbers and that this is my baseline. She instructs me to give myself 300 mg of Follistim that evening, and then 150 mg in the morning and 150 mg in the evening for the next two days. On Saturday morning, I should come in for another blood test to check my estrogen level.

I meet up with my friend Abby and tell her that I'm going home to take my first shot. She asks me if I want her help, but I've already decided that this is a very personal experience—if I'm not going through it with a partner, then I want to do it entirely on my own. Back at home, holding the Follistim pen needle, I sit down on the couch and read the instructions.

1. Load medicine cartridge into pen.

2. Dial prescribed dose.

3. Clean about two inches around the injection site where the needle will be inserted.

4. Squeeze skin, insert the needle, and push firmly down on the injection button.

I am preparing the shot when my doorbell rings. My friend and neighbor Patricia is stopping by to say Happy New Year.

"Strange timing," I say when I open the door. "I was just sitting down to give myself my first egg-freezing shot."

We both break into laughter over the absurdity of it all.

"I guess a little voice in my head told me to come check in on you," she says.

She asks if I want any help. I tell her I'd love for her to stay for moral support, but I really want to do the actual injection myself. I prepare the needle and swab my belly with alcohol. She cringes as I take the cap off of the needle. I plunge the little needle into my belly and feel a cold sensation and slight soreness. Then it's over, and Patricia and I chat for a while, catching up on life, work, the vacation she is planning to Spain, and the latest between me and Ted—which isn't much. I feel like we are spinning our wheels. He's fun to have around, but I'm no more passionate about him than I was at the beginning. Since he is in his forties and wants to have children, he occasionally drops a hint about getting married or having unprotected sex and seeing what happens. I've tried hard to convince myself that I could make up for lost time by forcing myself to love him, I tell Patricia. But there's no getting around it: he's not even close to a new love.

Over the next two days, I become a pro at giving myself shots. The morning shot easily blends into my morning ritual. Make coffee. Wash face. Brush teeth. Shoot artificial FSH cloned from Chinese hamster ovaries into my belly. Read newspaper.

After three days of shooting myself up with FSH, I feel like Wonder Woman. I have an enormous amount of energy, and I am hyperfocused on my work. Everything I hear and see is more intense: the yellow of my scrambled eggs seems brighter, the songs on the radio sound clearer.

One night, I meet a few friends at a bar in the East Village, and I feel intensely connected to everyone I talk to. I also want to jump every cute guy in the room. I flirt with a thirty-six-year-old oceanographer, who flirts back but then tells me that he recently started dating a woman two years older than him. I immediately switch into journalist mode and start asking him how he feels about the age difference, the issues of fertility and family.

"I wonder, if our sperm expired, would women start choosing younger men?" he asks, half joking. Then he turns serious. "I'm careful and concerned about a woman who wants to have kids. I'm sensitive to the fact that she might be rushing things because she has something that she wants that is very important. But I don't look at a woman and think, 'She's too old, she probably can't have kids so therefore I don't want to date her.' We could adopt. I have nieces and nephews, so I feel like my family has reproduced."

The next morning, I go in for another blood test. A few hours later, Jen calls me to say that my estrogen has shot up to 1000.

"You're responding very quickly," she says. "This could be good or bad. Either way, it means you're very fertile."

She goes back to the cooking analogy and explains that the key to getting a good number of eggs is to take my levels up slowly, like thickening a sauce over low heat. If my estrogen gets high too quickly, and the ovarian follicles grow too quickly, then I run the risk of ovarian hyperstimulation syndrome—burning the sauce. It happens in only 2 percent of cycles, but if it does, I will likely experience severe nausea or diarrhea. If it's a severe case, I could develop abdominal bleeding or fluid in my lungs.

Jen tells me that my doctors are a little concerned; that I need to lower my daily dose to 225 mg and then come back to the clinic in the morning for another blood test and ultrasound to check the size of my follicles.

"If there are a lot of little follicles and your estrogen is high, it means that we took you up too quickly and may have to cancel the cycle," she says. "If the follicles are nice and big, that means you can move on to the next medication and prepare for the egg retrieval as early as the middle of next week."

That night while chatting on the phone with a friend, I prepare another shot.

"I just did it."

"Wow," said my friend. "You didn't even say ouch!"

"It's really not a big deal," I tell her. "It hasn't been hard at all so far."

But it becomes very hard later that night. I wake up at 3 a.m. in a cold sweat, dizzy and totally nauseated. I also have some sort of strange bionic hearing that makes everything sound ten times louder than normal. Suddenly, I'm not feeling so empowered and independent. I feel scared and out of control. But the feeling passes after about ten minutes, and then a wave of calm euphoria follows it. I fall back to sleep.

Early in the morning, however, it happens again. For a moment, I'm not sure I can even get out of bed and make it to my appointment. But the feelings pass, and I jump in a cab.

At the clinic, the attending doctor looks at my ovaries on the ultrasound screen, and her eyes open wide.

"Wow, they're really big," she says. "You're responding really well."

I tell her about the flashes, and she says that my estrogen is really high for so early in the cycle; that's why I'm having these sensations. She tells me that a doctor will call me that afternoon to tell me about the next steps.

I go home and flop on the couch. I'm a little discouraged that I'm not feeling so well. A few hours later, Jen calls to tell me that my estrogen level has shot up to 2475. This is far too high for a woman only four days into her cycle, and my follicles are still only 8 mm. They won't be ready for the trigger shot until they're 17 mm. For this reason, she explains, the doctors have decided to cancel my cycle. The next time around, they'll use a lower dose of drugs.

In other words, I've overheated.

Jen emphasizes that although we had to cancel the cycle, my reaction to the drugs is ultimately very good news. It means that I'm really fertile and will probably produce a lot of eggs when they get the dosages right.

"We're really surprised to see such a profound response in someone your age," she says.

The next day I speak to Dr. Noyes.

"How dare you hyperstimulate!" she laughingly scolds me. "But the silver lining is that you're going to get a lot of eggs, at least twenty-five. You're the best responder ever."

A lot of eggs, I have to remember, doesn't mean that they will all be mature or of good quality, but it's still good news.

Over the next few days, I relay the story to friends. One is shocked that my doctor "overdosed" me, and she wonders why I would put myself through such a difficult experience.

I tell her it's really important to me to have children, and to have them in the right situation. Lots of women get breast implants and have other painful plastic surgeries for reasons of pure vanity. The shots are no more strange or painful than any of that, and I'm doing it for a far better reason.

"Yeah, I guess what you're doing is a little more noble than a boob job," she says.

I have long-standing plans with friends for a trip to Brazil and Argentina, so I can't start my next cycle right away. And it's really nice to get away to the pure hedonism of Carnival in Rio after these stressful weeks that started with shooting up and then feeling let down.

On the first night of Carnival, my friend Rebekah and I head to a club in Lapa to hear some samba music. The streets are filled with vendors selling huge bouquets of cotton candy and revelers dressed in sparkling masks, carnival tiaras, and low-cut dresses. But at around 10:30, a tropical storm hits, flooding the streets. We take cover in a small club, where a band from Bahia is playing. I start to dance with a young Swiss guy in a straw hat.

"Your heart will open so wide after Carnival that you will never be able to go back to your old life," he tells me.

He's wrong. As much as I love traveling, it's different this time. My heart is pulling me back home; the real adventure for me right now lies in the syringes in my refrigerator. It's much less romantic than dancing the samba until sunrise with a sexy Brazilian man, of course, but right now it's so much more important.

I get my period a couple of weeks after I return from my trip, and I begin a new cycle. This time, for the first week, I'm shooting up leuprolide acetate, another gonadotropin. This one actually *suppresses* estrogen and testosterone so I won't run the risk of overheating again. During that week, I have no interest in sex. One night, Ted makes a pass at me; I tell him I want to go home and go to bed—alone. In the second week, I start up the Follistim ritual again.

A week before I'm supposed to go for my retrieval, I make a quick decision not use the Rogue's sperm. It's not that I don't like the Rogue, but after another phone conversation with Wendy Kramer, the founder of the Donor Sibling Registry, I learn that the California Cryobank doesn't put a cap on the number of women to whom they sell any given donor's sperm. Although the American Society for Reproductive Medicine has guidelines stating a clinic cannot sell a single donor's sperm to more than twenty-five women, Kramer tells me that a lot of banks don't follow the guidelines. The idea that there may someday be hundreds of mini-Rogues out there freaks me out. As the reality of actually creating life from these embryos becomes increasingly apparent, I can't help but imagine how my child would feel when finding out that there are scores of half siblings out there.

A friend of mine who is a single mother recommends that instead I go to the Sperm Bank of California in Berkeley. It is the only nonprofit sperm bank in the United States, and it limits each of its donors to ten families. Even though this means that my child could end up with multiple half-siblings, somehow ten seems like a more manageable number.

So I call the Sperm Bank of California and talk to Simone, one of the client coordinators. I immediately like her style; rather than just pointing me to an online search engine, she walks me through the website and even makes some recommendations. The experience feels less sterile than my first online search did.

Simone points me to a new donor, a UC Berkeley student who is also a professional poker player. He sounds interesting, and I feel some vague affinity, since I went to Berkeley for graduate school.

"I like him because he really understood what he was doing," Simone tells me.

Since I'm in the middle of my cycle, and therefore in a rush, she says she will Fed Ex his profile and baby photo to me.

The next day it arrives. He is 5′10″ with fair, rosy skin, light brown eyes, and blond wavy hair. He aced college tests while still in high school, and is a strong athlete. His mother is English and Canadian, and his father is German, Scottish, and English. His family includes a grandmother who was a professional violinist and another who works with the Gray Panthers, a political action group comprised primarily of retired people. His grandfather skied until the day he died, and his sister is a gymnast. Healthwise, everything looks normal—my only concerns are that he had acne as a teen and that there is a gene for color blindness on his mother's side.

I'm mostly impressed by his clever and slightly eccentric essay: "I built various projects as a kid: balsa airplanes, a radio from components. I can tie multiple neckties, and do so on myself or on someone else. Sometimes when I'm walking somewhere, I start running because I am, in my mind, too lazy to wait for walking. I have a penchant for aphorism. I enjoy eclectic diction and phrasing, gliding from *petanque* to badonkadonk, perhaps even in a single sentence." (I have to look up "badonkadonk": it's slang for "well-shaped female buttocks.")

With regard to his goals, he writes, "I think it's the quotidian effort in living by principles that results in remarkable accomplishments. Seizing today is more important than sizing up tomorrow." And he wants to be a donor because "life matters. Philosophically, we need another generation to have a crack at life's big questions and unbounded possibilities." And, like the Rogue, he's also written a message for his child: "There is meaning in every act, thought, decision, and experience. Whatever we bring into this world, directly or indirectly, becomes a unique and irreplaceable corpuscle in the body of human existence, as it reaches across time. It's not our privilege to know the full impact of our lives. So live, as best you can."

I like his essay a lot. He seems smart as well as strong and humble, an unusual combination. My instincts tell me that if my child were to contact this man in the future, he would handle the meeting in a responsible way. And then there's his baby picture: an adorable little boy playfully poking his fingers into plump cheeks with a big wide-open smile.

I fill out the form and submit my credit card information.

On the fifth day of my Follistim shots, the doctors decide to let me "coast," which means not take any medicine the day before my trigger shot. They are a little nervous that I'm going to overheat again. The next day, my estrogen drops to 1100, and I get a call from Jen telling me that my estrogen is now dropping too low and that I need to take more Follistim. If my levels don't rise, it could mean that this batch of eggs is not good quality and so this cycle might have to be canceled too. For the next twenty-four hours, I'm on pins and needles. If they cancel the cycle, I'll have to start all over again, and I'm not sure I can go through this a third time.

The next morning I go in for a blood test, and luckily my level has risen back to 3000. I'm ready for the trigger shot, and my retrieval is scheduled for the next morning. That night, I knock on Patricia's door and ask her if she'd be willing to give me the trigger shot. The needle is really big, and I have to inject the hormones into my butt this time, which is a bit awkward anatomically. After she's given me the shot, she tells me that she thinks I'm really brave for doing this, and promises to help me out if I ever decide to become a single mother. I pour two glasses of Scotch, and we toast the future and take photographs just in case someday I want to show my child the night his or her life began.

The next morning, two days before Easter Sunday, I take a cab to the NYU Fertility Clinic. In the "retrieval" room, I change into a surgical gown and little booties and put a cap over my hair. A nurse takes my vital signs and then leads me into the surgery room where I talk briefly with Dr. Lisa Kump, who will perform the retrieval, since Dr. Noyes is on vacation.

Dr. Kump is forty-one and just had her third child a year earlier. I ask her if she had to use ART.

"No," she says. "I was lucky."

She then points to a nurse in the corner and tells me that she had a baby at forty-six.

"We call her the woman with the golden eggs," she says.

I lie down on the surgery table, and the anesthesiologist places an IV in my arm and tells me to sleep well. In what seems like three seconds, I'm awake and in the recovery room.

"OK, you're done," says the nurse.

The anesthetic has made me feel a little jittery, so I drink a couple of glasses of apple juice while I wait to hear the results.

In the meantime, the freezing process is beginning behind the scenes in a lab. My eggs, still suspended in follicular fluid, are placed in a portable incubator that is set at 37 degrees Celsius, the temperature of the human body. An embryologist hunts for the eggs in the fluid, separates them, and counts them. The eggs are then placed in a petri dish on a surface that is also heated to 37 degrees. The embryologist cleans off the eggs in order to assess their maturity and then picks out the best ones. The less mature ones are set aside in case they're needed, in which case they can be matured artificially.

Half of the most mature eggs are placed in another petri dish, this one filled with six to nine drops of the sugar-infused cryoprotectant, to prepare them for freezing. The others, the eggs to be fertilized with the donor sperm, will be placed in a different dish filled with a solution that essentially mimics the reproductive juices in my uterus. A few drops of donor sperm (150,000 sperm per drop) are then added. The solution in the dish convinces the sperm that they are in the uterus, and they become hyperactive as a result. The embryologist then just lets nature take its course. Fertilization generally occurs after sixteen to twenty hours.

I'm still drinking apple juice when the embryologist comes into the recovery room to report that they have retrieved thirty-five eggs—a very high number. The only problem, she says, is that it looks like only eight of them are mature. Another eleven are what they call M1, which is semimature. These eggs can be matured for future fertilization, though little data has been collected on the thawing and fertilizing of this type of egg.

Because I have only eight mature eggs, she recommends that I don't split the batch—I should choose to freeze either just the eggs or just the embryos. She says that the M1 eggs can be matured and then inseminated with my donor sperm using a technique called intracytoplasmic sperm injection (ICSI), a procedure whereby a single sperm is artificially inserted with a tiny needle directly into the egg. Fertilization rates and pregnancy rates with these embryos are similar to normal IVF pregnancy rates. The catch is that this procedure will cost me another $2,000.

I have only a few minutes to make this major choice—and I'm still slightly spaced out from the anesthetic. So I do some quick calculations of the pros and cons. If I freeze embryos with the mature eggs, I won't have enough frozen eggs to use with Mr. Right. If I freeze eggs, I will have to sacrifice the slightly higher success rates achieved with fertilized embryos. Can I afford another $2,000 on ICSI for immature eggs? Probably not. Plus, deep down, I don't really think I'm going to use those embryos. I really believe that I'm going to find my true love in time to have his genetic children.

I also recall Dr. Noyes's remark that her success rate for frozen eggs is now equal to that of frozen embryos. And I believe that because of all of the research being focused on egg freezing right now, the technology will improve rapidly and the success rates will be even higher by the time I would use the eggs. Again, I just have to let go and take a leap of faith.

"Just freeze the eggs," I say to the embryologist.

She nods and heads back to the lab.

And with that choice, this adventure is over. I get dressed, stop at a local café to get a cup of tea, and go home to sleep for the rest of day. After a few days of feeling a little tired and a little sore, I'm back to my normal routine.

When she gets back from her vacation, Dr. Noyes calls to say that eight mature eggs is a good number. She wishes I had a few more just in case I end up wanting a chance at a second baby, and she suggests I go through another cycle. I tell her I can't afford to do another cycle now, and that, anyway, I feel at this point as if I should just accept where I am and what I have.

"Do you feel less anxious now?" she asks.

"Definitely," I reply. I feel like I've done everything within my control. And I've also learned that I'm still very fertile. Dr. Noyes tells me it's likely that I have a few more years ahead of me in which I will be able to conceive naturally.

"Just keep checking your FSH levels every few months," she reminds me.

I thank her, then hang up the phone and call my mom with the news.

It turns out that you can't return sperm. I learn this when I call Simone at the Sperm Bank of California to tell her about the results of my freezing procedure and my decision to bet on my eggs alone. The conversation goes something like this:

"So it turns out that I don't need the sperm. What's the best way to send it back to you?" I say.

"Well, I'm sorry, but our policy is that once sperm leaves the premises, we cannot take it back or refund your payment."

"But I don't need it now," I say. "Won't it help someone else?"

"Unfortunately, that's our policy."

So I now own two vials of a Berkeley poker player's frozen specimen. It's frozen and stored side by side with my frozen eggs. I guess there is some comfort in knowing that if at any moment I decide I just want to go ahead with having a child, the sperm is just sitting there waiting for me.

Daily life quickly returns to normal. My egg-freezing adventure becomes just one among many in my life. I tell half a dozen friends about what I've done; some are amazed at my bravery, and others just cringe at my description of the surgery.

Freezing my eggs has one important and immediate outcome: it allows me to assess my relationship with Ted more honestly. I accept that I'll never be in love with him—and decide that this rebound relationship has gone on too long. So a few weeks later, I tell him that I don't think we have a future, and we agree to just be friends.

I'm happy that I'm able to begin the summer having taken a proactive and progressive step. Even though the odds are uncertain that I'll ever be able to produce a child from my frozen eggs, knowing they're there has given me a sense of peace. Of course I won't stop thinking about my fertility entirely—it will continue to be a factor in my future relationships. But I think I'll feel a bit calmer the next time love comes my way.

# 12

# The Egg Donor Economy

One afternoon, I meet up with my friend Abby for tea. Abby has a knack for asking disarmingly direct questions. So when the conversation turns to my frozen eggs, she looks at me intently and asks point blank:

"What if they don't work in the future? Would you adopt?"

"I'm not sure what my next choice would be," I admit to her.

When Abby and I went to India, we visited a fort in Gwalior. At the entrance, we met a little beggar boy with a limp who tried to sell us some postcards. Abby and this little boy bonded immediately, and he spent the next few hours following her around the grounds of the fort. When we left, she was sad and told me that she wished she could adopt him and bring him home.

Abby was single when she turned forty a few months later, and she decided to take a step toward becoming a mother by trying to freeze embryos created with donor sperm. But after going through two cycles of shots and spending close to $4,000, her body just wouldn't cooperate. Her doctor told her that her ovarian reserve was too low to produce viable eggs, and suggested that she consider using donor eggs instead.

"Yes, that's great," Abby told the doctor sardonically. "I can use donor eggs and donor sperm and since I really have no desire to actually give birth, maybe I can find a surrogate! And you know what that's called? Adoption!"

Rather than further trying to control the situation with more technology, she decided to let go.

"I realized I was never going to be one of those people who went through IVF eight, ten, twelve times," Abby tells me. "And the truth is, I'd always wanted to adopt—ever since I was a kid. The donor sperm–embryo approach just never felt natural to me."

I ask her why she went through the IVF process if she always thought she wanted to adopt a child.

She pauses for a moment before responding.

"Ego, I guess," she says reflectively. "My ego kicked in, and I decided I really wanted to see what it would be like to have my own genes reproduced. It was more intellectual than biological. I thought, 'Wouldn't it be nice to have a biological extension of me roaming the earth?'"

But as soon as she learned that she would not be able to create a biological child, she decided not to press technology to the extreme to pursue her fantasy.

"I realized what I wanted was a child to take care of and love and adore. What business do I have bringing a biological child into the world when there are so many kids in the world who are in need? I know that's not the way everyone thinks, but for me it makes the most sense. I don't think biology is destiny, at least when it comes to childbearing."

~

A rising number of women and couples in their forties and fifties are turning to adoption to create or augment their families. But at the same time, many women in this age group are going to physical extremes to become biological parents. Using donor eggs has become one of the most popular options for older women.

The choice of using this microscopic egg holds so many questions. Its purchase cracks open a whole new world of social, ethical, and moral choices—everything from the donor the woman chooses, the relationship she chooses to have with the donor, and what she will tell her child about his or her biological origins in the future.

The Centers for Disease Control and Prevention now report that the number of women attempting to become pregnant with donor eggs or embryos has risen from 1,802 attempts (IVF cycles) in 1992, the year I graduated from college, to 16,161 in 2005, which was 12 percent of all attempts and resulted in 5,887 pregnancies. Americans are spending about $38 million to buy eggs each year. The number of paid donors is unknown because, like sperm donation, the industry is largely unregulated.

Becoming pregnant with a donor egg is neither easy nor cheap. It involves buying the eggs of a younger woman, creating embryos with sperm (either a partner's or donor sperm) through in vitro fertilization, and then implanting them in the uterus. The entire process can cost upwards of $40,000. Why do women put themselves through this financial, emotional, and physical stress to have a child biologically, even when that child won't be related to them genetically?

The decision is intensely personal, and the answer differs depending on who you talk to. Some women do it because they can't produce children themselves but want to have a child who is genetically related to their husband. Some women just want the experience of being pregnant, giving birth, and breastfeeding. For many women, these are vital bonding experiences. And buying a donor egg, like choosing a sperm donor, allows women and couples some control over their child's genetic background.

As I think about Abby's question—would I adopt?—I find myself heading in the opposite direction. I think my first choice would be to use a donor egg. I like the idea of being pregnant, of having my body and blood nourish a life. I like the idea of nurturing the biological child of the man I love. I would not experience these things if I adopted a child—a process that can be just as expensive and intensely bureaucratic. For me, the idea of being pregnant seems more important. For the same reasons that I chose donor sperm with a similar ethnic background to my family, I like the idea of doing this with an egg, so that one day I can point to a map and say, "We are from here. We have the same genetic background."

~

In late spring, I fly out to California to visit an old friend from New York who now lives in San Francisco with her husband and kids. She had suggested that during my visit I interview her friend Samantha Long* about her experience of using donor eggs. I had taken her up on it, and called Samantha to make a date.

Samantha is a pretty blond with sparkling blue eyes. She lives in a small, eclectically decorated apartment in Pacific Heights with her husband and four-year-old daughter.

As we settle on the couch, Samantha, who is forty-two, begins to tell me the story of how she bought two eggs through a bank she found during an Internet search and then had them fertilized with her husband's sperm and implanted in her uterus. She is a little over a month pregnant with twins.

Samantha got pregnant with her daughter when she was thirty-eight.

"It was really amazing," she says. "I got pregnant on the first try on my honeymoon. It was a total surprise."

Sixth months after her daughter was born, the couple decided to try for a second baby, and because it had been so easy the first time, Samantha wasn't worried. But after trying for eight months, she still wasn't pregnant.

After a year, she started to worry; then she got pregnant and miscarried. The couple went to a fertility specialist to talk about in vitro fertilization, and he told them that Samantha's ovarian reserve had become too low; she could no longer get pregnant using her own eggs. Her husband wanted to look into adopting, but Samantha said that it was really important to her to experience being pregnant again. She also liked the idea of having some genetic control over who her next child, her daughter's sister, would be.

A day after her doctor's appointment, she Googled the words "egg donation." Thousands of links popped up with pages and pages of information on donor agencies.

"It was completely overwhelming," she says.

Samantha wanted to find a donor that looked like her, so she spent most of her time looking at blond-haired blued-eyed girls. She scanned through these women's photographs, hobbies, and favorite movies. She called the agencies and asked them to send pictures of prospective donors' brothers, sisters, parents, and sometimes grandparents to her.

It turned out that Samantha's husband was even pickier than she was.

"He would say, 'Oh no, this one is too short, or this one isn't smart enough,'" she says. "For me, it wasn't the intelligence so much as personality. I wanted somebody who was outgoing. I was looking for a love-at-first-sight thing."

The couple finally settled on a donor in Los Angeles. She was a beautiful and tall opera singer from Texas with watery blue eyes, cornhusk hair, and an Ivy League education—the ideal that Samantha had imagined. She was part of the agency's "premium" donor program—more highly educated and deemed particularly attractive, and the agency charged twice as much for her eggs as for nonpremium donors.

When Samantha called the agency to inquire about the donor, however, she learned that in her last retrieval the woman had produced only five eggs. So she decided that choosing this donor would be too risky. Samantha notes that the agency continued to advertise her even though she was producing a low number of eggs, which points to the aggressive marketing tactics used in the business of egg selling.

"She's pretty, and that drew me to their site," she says.

So Samantha and her husband began the search all over again. One evening, they were casually cruising the donor sites, and they came across a photo of a girl with long red hair, a wide smile, and big white teeth.

"There was something happy about her, and even though she looked nothing like me we both really liked her," Samantha tells me. "It was love at first sight."

The next morning, Samantha called the agency. The redhead was available immediately.

Samantha and her husband paid $6,500 for the donor's eggs, but with the added cost of travel expenses, lawyers, agency fees, the donor's medication and visits to the doctor, they spent close to $40,000 on the process.

After the donor's eggs were retrieved, they were fertilized with Samantha's husband's sperm. Samantha went through two weeks of progesterone shots, which she will have to continue for the first trimester, to prepare her body for pregnancy.

The day of the implantation felt surreal to Samantha.

"It seemed very foreign to have someone else's genetic material put inside me. I had a picture of the donor, and I kept having these flashes of, *Wow, this is someone else's eggs.*"

"My husband actually really wanted to meet the donor just to see her personality," Samantha tells me. "I didn't want to meet her because I didn't want to put a voice to the face. I'm carrying the children, and I want to bond with them like they're mine."

Before the implantation of two embryos, Samantha met with a psychologist to discuss her future relationship with the donor and whether she plans to tell her children about their origins.

In the end, she and her husband decided that they will tell their twins that they had "a helper."

The ethics committee of the American Society for Reproductive Medicine recommends that parents tell their children that they were conceived with donor eggs. In the eyes of the law, however, the woman who carries a child to term is considered the legal mother—even if the child was not conceived with her eggs. Most agencies require that donors stay in touch for five years, in case any medical problems arise. Samantha and her husband also signed up with the Donor Sibling Registry so that their donor and any other offspring might be able to get in touch in the future.

Samantha wrote a thank you note to her donor, enclosing a picture of the Long family.

"I included pictures of us so she would know who she was giving this to," she says. "I think if I were doing this, I'd be curious to know whether I was giving to people who were going to be good parents."

Samantha now has the blush of a newly pregnant woman. If I didn't know her story, I would never be able to guess how much money, thought, and technology went into this pregnancy. And maybe some women like egg donation for exactly that reason: it allows not only for personal control but also for privacy.

I ask Samantha if she has any regrets, if she begrudges the physical stress or the expense of getting pregnant with two donor eggs.

She shakes her head. "If it's going to give you a family, it's worth it."

After hearing Samantha's story, I want to know more about the other side of the equation—the women who sell their eggs so that other women can bear children. It seems to me that this process is one of the great ironies of the modern age: women spend their fertile years finding themselves, getting educated, building their careers, and postponing pregnancy in order to make money, and then, having run out the clock on their own fertility, they have to spend that money to buy a younger woman's eggs.

I fly down to Los Angeles to meet with Brigid Dowd, the director of the Donor Egg Bank, a four-year-old agency housed in a high-rise in downtown Los Angeles. Brigid, a laid-back California girl with blond hair and a tan, has agreed to walk me through the process of buying donor eggs.

"It's not as easy as 'I want to buy an egg!'" Brigid begins, as I sit down in her small office, which is decorated with optimistic-looking stock photos of blooming flowers. "Not everyone realizes what's involved. And then when they hear about the costs, a lot of them just pass out."

"So how would I begin the process?" I ask her.

"Usually, we would start by asking if there's something in particular that you're looking for," she says.

Brigid takes a white plastic binder off the shelf and lays it out in front of me. I quickly flip through the book. Each donor has a two-page profile. The first page displays pictures of the donor with basic stats like height, weight, hair color and texture, eye color, degree, major, and GPA. The next page goes into more detail: the donor's educational goals, occupation, health information, athletic abilities, favorite types of music and books, whether or not she has ever been diagnosed with a major psychological disorder, and whether any member of her immediate family has a birth defect.

A quick scan through the binder shows a twenty-three-year-old Cherokee-English blond with a medium complexion. A 5'11" redhead says she has eclectic music taste: "My CD collection has everything from Sinatra to Eminem. I actually love '80s rock."

I tell Brigid that I think I would want an egg donor with an ethnic background that's similar to mine in order to have a child who would physically fit into my family.

"Does everyone in your family have medium skin tone?" she asks. "Is height an issue?"

"Yes! I don't want a short child," I blurt out.

Then the idea of making a baby the old-fashioned way pops into my head, and I have to laugh at myself.

"You know, if I were trying to get pregnant with my husband, I don't think I would blurt out 'I don't want a short child' in the middle of sex!"

"I know," Brigid laughs. "It's not like you would interview your boyfriend or husband and ask, 'How tall are your grandparents?'"

Brigid then reminds me that although women and couples who are choosing egg donors have more choice when it comes to traits and genetic history, that can offer a false sense of control—just as I've learned from my experience of choosing donor sperm.

"If you want your baby to have brown eyes, and your donor has brown eyes and both her parents have brown eyes, then you'll probably get brown eyes," she explains. "But there are no guarantees when it comes to genetics."

Brigid says she encourages her clients to be as open-minded as possible, because if they are too rigid or become too obsessed with finding the "perfect" donor, the choice can become more difficult. She illustrates this with a story about a client from China who was initially interested in a donor who was highly educated and half-Chinese, half-Irish.

"Everything about this girl was perfect except that her hair was light brown, and that was holding her back," says Brigid. "She said to me, 'Every other child in China has dark hair, and I don't want my child to stand out.' The doctor explained to her that because her husband had dark hair that most likely it was a dominant gene and would win out. But she didn't want to take the chance."

Brigid tells me that the people who go with their visceral hunch end up happier in the end.

"They read profiles and are like, 'Oh, that's my favorite book' or 'I really love what she says about wanting to donate her time to helping earthquake victims' or 'She has my husband's eyes.'"

But if the search for the right donor becomes too over-whelming, Brigid often refers her clients to Gail Anderson, a psychologist who runs a program called Donor Frontiers. She hands me a flyer with a photo of a beautiful baby on the front. Gail advertises herself essentially as a personal shopper who will sort through all the options and make it easier to find a donor who fits a person's specific criteria. She acts as a liaison between the woman or couple and the donor agencies in order to make the process less time-consuming, and also to help support her clients during an emotionally trying experience.

"Donor recipients are giving up a lot," Anderson explains when we meet up later in the day. "They have to go through a mourning process, the loss of their biological child."

On the back of the flyer is a price list. A search for fundamental criteria—race, hair color and texture, eye color, and height—costs $350. An advanced search costs twice as much and also includes educational background, parents' background, and hard-to-find donors, such as obscure mixed races.

"I try to help them to get to the point where, instead of feeling like they don't have another option, they say, 'Thank God I have this option,'" she says.

Most agencies simply play matchmaker between the recipient and donor. The donor goes through the egg retrieval process, and the eggs are fertilized and implanted in the client immediately. The agency makes money by taking a commission on the donor's fee, which is determined by the agency.

But the Donor Egg Bank is beginning to offer the option of buying an egg directly from the bank, from a stock of eggs that have been frozen and stored; they can be from either previous donor cycles or new cycles. It's a service that allows for a new kind of flexibility: the donor and recipient don't have to line up their schedules so that the recipient will be physically ready for the transfer of fresh eggs as soon as they are retrieved from the donor. It is also considerably less expensive for the recipient. Instead of the recipient paying for all of the donor's expenses, the clinic covers the medical expenses, and the recipient pays a set fee for the transportation and thawing of the egg. The approach removes the cost of the donor's drugs and doctor appointments, and any travel and hotel expenses if she lives in a different city.

The clinic assumes the donor's medical expense, but still makes money because it can charge per batch of eggs rather than per cycle. For example, Brigid tells me that her bank sells eggs in batches of eight for $16,000 per batch. If a donor makes thirty-two eggs, then the clinic pays for one round of shots, but it can potentially make money on four batches of eggs. But of course this process is more risky. The Society for Assisted Reproductive Technology does not yet collect national clinical data on the rates of fertilization of embryos created from fresh eggs compared to those created from frozen eggs (though Dr. Porcu's research indicates that frozen eggs have a 28 percent pregnancy rate). The 2005 CDC report on donor eggs reports a 52 percent live-birth rate from embryos created from fresh donor eggs. And as the technology improves, the use of frozen eggs could democratize the donor option by bringing the costs down.

"Right now it's $10,000 less if a woman uses frozen eggs," says Brigid.

Since the Donor Egg Bank opened its doors in the spring of 2006, Brigid has already seen a huge change due to improved pregnancy rates and more births from frozen eggs.

"Three years ago, we couldn't give the eggs away. Everyone who came by our booth at the Pacific Coast Reproductive Society meeting told us it wasn't going to work," she says. "Now we have the eggs of twenty donors frozen, and all of a sudden we've had this big rush and we need to freeze more."

My next meeting is with Dr. Marylyn Shore, a psychologist who is in charge of evaluating women who want to become egg donors.

Shore is a statuesque blond in her fifties who turned to psychology after years of working as a fashion model and businesswoman in New York. Her expertise in the fashion and modeling business helps her recruit and choose egg donors, since one of the big selling points for any agency is highly attractive donors.

Shore explains that the main purpose of the evaluation, however, is to make sure that the donor is psychologically fit. As I am now well aware, going through a retrieval cycle is not climbing Mount Kilimanjaro, but it isn't a breezy walk on the beach either. This fact, however, doesn't stop many donors from going through five or more cycles.

Shore says that 80 to 90 percent of the donors she interviews want to donate in order to offset some of the cost of their education. While U.S. law prohibits the sale of body parts, donors can be "compensated" for the medical procedure of having their eggs removed. The ASRM's ethical guidelines say that an egg recipient donor agency should never pay more than $5,000 for the services of an egg donor, but some agencies and individual donors charge much more, often up to $50,000.

These high prices have turned egg donation into a big business by creating a new economy of fertility. Ads now appear on Craigslist and in college newspapers offering female students thousands of dollars for their eggs. An ad in the *Daily Californian*, the student newspaper at the University of California,

Berkeley, offers $10,000 for eggs; one in the *Harvard Crimson* offers $35,000 to "one truly exceptional woman who is attractive, athletic, under the age of 29" and $50,000 to an "extraordinary egg donor." An ad from a San Diego company called A Perfect Match seeks women who are "attractive," under the age of twenty-nine, and have SAT scores over 1300.

As education costs rise, students are becoming increasingly enticed by these ads and the stories of other women their age making thousands of dollars off their fertility. The most famous is Julia Derek, a senior at George Mason University who saw an ad in the *Washington Post* from a couple offering to pay for a young woman's eggs. Derek went through twelve cycles, made $50,000, financed her postgraduate degree, and then went on to write a book called *Confessions of a Serial Egg Donor*.

Shore's main job is to build a profile of the donor from every angle, including personality, intellectual capabilities, motivation, level of responsibility, and health background. Her questions cover the donor's education history and GPA, and her family's professional background. She asks the donor to describe her personality traits—is she talkative, shy, confident, caring?

Many potential donors do not make the cut. Women who smoke, use illicit drugs, or consume excessive amounts of alcohol are immediately rejected. But psychological disorders are a gray area, Shore explains. Most doctors will not accept a donor if she has been diagnosed with schizophrenia or severe manic depression.

"It depends on the severity," she says. "A mild history of anxiety or depression usually does not preclude them from becoming donors. We ask how many generations back it goes, and whether they've had an episode recently. It all goes into the report, and it's up to the doctor to make the decision."

After this meeting, I talk with Brigid more, and she goes into a little more detail and explains that if the woman has a history of depression and is on medication for it, the agency might reject her. I immediately think about all the brilliant and depressed artists that might not be born because of these decisions. Where as a society do we draw the line between eradicating debilitating diseases and cleansing the population of the less clear-cut social and genetic imperfections that give some definition to all of our lives?

When I pose this question to Brigid, she tells me that they usually turn to a genetic counselor to make the call. For example, if a donor shows a strong family history of a certain kind of cancer, it may raise a red flag indicating a pattern that could repeat itself.

"If she has a grandfather who had a stroke, clearly that's not a big deal," she says. "But if the paternal grandfather, two paternal uncles, and her dad all had a stroke, that would sound like something that runs in the dad's family."

Brigid puts me in touch with Megan McCoy to learn more about how recipients consider the details of a donor's genetic background. "It hasn't gotten to the point where we're testing for the breast cancer gene," says Megan McCoy, a genetic counselor in Los Angeles. "People are more concerned with birth defects that would affect a baby than they are about adult-onset disorders. But the gene testing is available, so it could get to that point."

As I think about the choice I would make as a potential mother by donor egg, I see a slippery ethical slope. I want a healthy child, and so I think I would definitely want eggs that were screened for birth defects that would affect my baby. That poses no moral problems for me—I see it as equivalent to getting an amniocentesis or chorionic villus sampling test during pregnancy. But what if I could also screen for cancer genes, or choose to have a particularly creative or tall child? No parent wants their child to suffer as a baby or as an adult, but how much should we try to control the future? How far should we go in using science to create more perfect children, and how much should we leave up to nature and chance?

~

After talking to Dr. Shore, I'm eager to talk to an actual donor. Brigid refers me to Natalie McMenany, who is twenty-three and has gone through three cycles. Natalie tells me that she is half-Lebanese, with olive skin, silky dark hair, and bright blue eyes. She lives in Dallas, Texas, with her husband, and works as an administrative assistant in an investment bank. She is attending college part-time to get a degree in psychology.

We speak on the phone one evening, a few hours after her eggs have been retrieved.

"My retrieval went really well," she says in a nonchalant tone. "They said that I have something like thirty eggs. Usually the meds wear off within a few hours and I just sort of sleep it off. There's obviously a little bit of cramping, sometimes some spotting, but its really workable, nothing too serious."

I ask her if she feels any attachment to her eggs.

"It's not really my child," she says. "I guess technically it is biologically, but I'm doing it for someone else. It's not like in ten or fifteen years I'm going to be trying to track down this child."

I'm not sure I would feel this way. I thought of Nancy Vitali, the psychiatrist who decided to freeze embryos, who told me that she feels the urge to go check in on them. After freezing my eggs, I too find myself thinking about them sometimes. I know that if I had donated eggs to help someone else create a life, I would wonder every day about the child I had helped to create. I think I would find it hard to resist the urge to find him or her.

A few days later, I talk with another donor, Jennifer Green, a twenty-eight-year-old mother of two. She tells me that she never thinks about her other biological offspring.

"I'm just giving away my genetic material," she says.

Jennifer is 5'7", with dark blond hair and hazel eyes—and worked as a fashion model in the past. She speculates that her attitude about her eggs might be due to the fact that she is a mother already. Also, she works as a research assistant in the University of Missouri's department of veterinarian science, studying ovarian failure in mice as part of a project directed at creating new fertility drugs.

"I'm not carrying the baby," she says. "They are. They are doing the work."

Jennifer tells me that she would be open to meeting the recipients of her eggs in the future, but she's not sure she would encourage a relationship beyond answering questions about her family history.

"I'm going to cross that bridge if I come to it, because you never really know how the recipient couple is going to handle it—whether or not they're going to tell their child they come from a donor egg."

Both Natalie and Jennifer are serial donors. Natalie has donated three times; she earned $4,000 for the first cycle, $5,000 for the second, and $7,000 for the third. Jennifer has already completed three cycles since the fall of this year, for which she's made close to $20,000. Both women are saving the money for a down payment on a new home. And both women say they were attracted to donating their eggs for altruistic reasons—they like the idea of this biological economy, a new sisterhood between younger and older women.

"I kept thinking, 'What if my husband and I had problems getting pregnant?' I know that I would have felt really blessed if someone out there had been willing to help me," says Jennifer. "We have a finite number of eggs, and I'm not using them, so I'm happy to help someone else."

In the winter of 2007, Mary Fusillo, a registered nurse who is executive director of The Donor Solution, a donor egg agency, conducted an independent survey of thirty-eight egg donation centers in order to find out what motivated egg donors. She found that for 68 percent it was the desire to "help someone have a family" and for 29 percent it was financial compensation. The average amount earned was $5,482. When she asked the women what they planned to do with the money, 46 percent said they were going to use it to pay off credit cards and pay tuition, and 36 percent said they planned to put the money toward building a savings account. She found that 11 percent intended to spend the money on travel and luxury items; the number one luxury item these women planned to buy was a designer handbag.

~

On a bright sunny day in early fall, Karen Lehman*, a warm, bouncy real estate agent of fifty-three, watches from afar as her two blond-haired, blued-eyed five-year-old twins, Tammie* and Taylor*, chase their friends—blond-haired, blue-eyed twin girls—around the large grass amphitheater of the Dallas Arboretum.

"I've never seen the kids so siblinglike," she says to her girl-friend Kelly Grier*, the forty-seven-year-old mother of the twin girls. Both women are single mothers by choice.

Since the more extreme beginnings of motherhood are on my mind, I've decided to fly to Texas for the weekend to stay with Karen in order to better understand what it's like to become a mother of twins at forty-eight, on one's own, and against the backdrop of one of the most politically and socially conservative parts of the country. She and Kelly, her best friend, have gathered with three other single mothers for the yearly gathering of the Dallas chapter of Single Mothers by Choice. The group also includes Alice Gray*, a divorced fifty-three-year-old executive at Canon who adopted her daughter from China, and Andrea English*, a divorced schoolteacher from a tiny suburb north of Dallas who had twins through donor insemination at the age of forty.

An outgoing, opinionated, and highly assertive former party girl, Karen moved to a suburb of Dallas, when she decided to start trying to get pregnant.

"In L.A., I drove a Corvette and had a condo in Santa Monica," she says. "My friends thought I was crazy when I moved here." But her new town, she explains, is a child-friendly place, and it's near where her sister lives.

These days, she lives in ranch-style house on a perfectly straight street. The houses all look exactly the same, and each one has a perfectly manicured lawn. Were it not for the Range Rover SUVs and Ford Taurus station wagons sitting in the driveways, the neighborhood would seem like a caricature of a 1950s subdivision.

Karen is about as atypical as you can get for this intensely evangelical Christian, Republican corner of America. Karen considers herself a social liberal and doesn't believe in organized

religion. Her father, a Methodist minister, considers her an un-
wed mother.

Karen is one of two single mothers at her children's school,
and she is by far the oldest parent.

Sitting on the lawn as her children play, Karen tells me
that she spent all of her thirties engaged to a man who was ten
years younger, wavering about whether or not to marry him.

"Love alone wasn't a good enough reason to get married,"
she says. "There is a lot more to marriage than just love. You
have to be compatible. He wanted me to cook and clean.
That's not me. I was a morning person and he was an evening
person. He couldn't fix things. I didn't respect him."

"But you can't have everything," I say.

"No," she says. "I didn't want that."

After a few years of counseling, Karen concluded that she
was just happier alone.

"I'm not a lonely person," she says.

Just shy of her fortieth birthday, Karen started thinking seriously about becoming a single mother.

"On my fortieth, I threw a big party in L.A. and then moved
to Texas a few weeks later and began interviewing fertility doctors," she tells me.

Karen used money from an insurance settlement that resulted from earthquake damage to her condo for the down payment on her home outside of Dallas and starting the next phase
of her life. But she quickly discovered that Texas was not L.A.

"The first doctor I went to in this area asked if I was gay. He
told me he wouldn't help a lesbian," she says, rolling her eyes.

She told him that she wasn't—she just wasn't married. He
said that he had to go home to talk to his wife about whether
or not he could help her. A few days later, he called and said

he would help because he believed she would be a better mom than most married people he knew.

Karen bought donor sperm from Xytex Corporation. Her donor was a 6'5" German-Irish music teacher with light blond hair. She was inseminated just shy of her forty-first birthday. But she didn't get pregnant. She tried again a few months later, got pregnant, but then miscarried. Over the next two years, she tried six more intrauterine inseminations and she didn't get pregnant, until her doctor finally suggested that she move on to IVF. She then went through two IVF cycles and got pregnant on the second. But she miscarried again. Her doctor then told her that she might want to consider donor eggs or adopting.

Karen became profoundly depressed from the failed cycles and gave up trying. But around her forty-sixth birthday, she got reinspired to try again when a friend she made at her fertility clinic asked her if she wanted to split a batch of donor eggs. Though Karen would be forfeiting any sort of genetic relationship with her children if she used both a donor egg and donor sperm, adoption was always out of the question for her. She wanted to be pregnant, and she wanted to be able to choose the genetic background of her children.

Within a few months, she was trying to get pregnant again with the eggs of a blond, twenty-year-old Norwegian-German donor that her friend found through the Egg Donation Center of Dallas. She was from northern Illinois and studying to be a schoolteacher. At the end of her profile she wrote, "I'll have a great sense of pleasure giving you the gift of life, so that you can give the gift of love."

Karen flew her donor, along with her boyfriend, to Dallas. Both lived with her during the retrieval process. Karen wanted to monitor the donor's shots and her overall health.

"We became friends," Karen tells me. "I took care of her like a big sister through the process," she says. "I told her, 'If you have sex in this time frame and get pregnant, I will kill you because I paid a lot of money for you to be here.'"

In early spring, Karen's doctor implanted two embryos—made from the music teacher's sperm and the future school-teacher's eggs—in Karen's uterus. Three weeks later she found out that she was pregnant with twins—and when she had her amnio and CVS a few weeks after that, she learned that she was going to have a son and daughter. It was a few months after her forty-seventh birthday.

Taylor and Tammie were born at five months via C-section. The twins and Karen spent a month in the neonatal unit. Karen's medical bills came to nearly $500,000, though most of the amount was covered by insurance.

The morning after the single-mother gathering at the Dallas Arboretum, I show up at Karen's house to talk further about her choice. We sit in her kitchen over coffee. Tammie, her daughter, sits on the floor next to her, playing with a teddy bear that she made at a birthday party the night before. Every few minutes she leans over and pushes her brother, Taylor, who is watching a video I took on my trip to India of a tiger drinking from a river.

"I'm just surviving," says Karen. "I didn't have my kids for me. I had them for my family. At school, they had to draw a picture of their family. It was me, Uncle Jim, Aunt Carol, Grandma and Grandpa, my brother in L.A., and the nanny. They think they have the biggest family of anyone."

I ask her what made her go through all those years of the stress on her body, paying all those medical expenses, and whether she feels it was worth it.

"I was frustrated that I wasn't getting what I wanted. I'm used to getting what I want," she says in a tense tone. "After a while it became a challenge. And people kept bringing me opportunities. I'm a believer that when opportunities present themselves, I shouldn't ignore them."

She pauses me for a minute. And then whispers to me:

"You know, I love my kids," she says. "But after all of that I now realize that I would have been OK child-free."

I've never imagined that I, myself, could go this far down the road of infertility treatment, but suddenly I understand where Karen is coming from. I, too, don't like not getting what I want.

"But how old do you think is too old?" I ask.

"I think I'm pushing it," she says. "I'm having fun, but it's tough. They drive me nuts. I don't have a lot of tolerance. That's the whole thing about being older. Things don't roll off your back as easily."

But still, she tells me, she thinks it would have been harder if she had become a mother twenty years earlier.

"I would have been less prepared for it."

She admits, though, that she gets sad when she thinks that her parents, who are in their eighties, probably won't get to see Tammie and Taylor graduate from high school. But this is part of the reason why she's happy she has twins.

"They have each other, and my brother just adopted, so they have a cousin, but they won't have the same life I had, getting to be fifty-three and still having your parents living."

I ask Karen for her advice. "So do you think I should just go for it on my own? What would you do if you were my age?"

Karen shakes her head, "Don't do it. You're not like me—you don't want to be alone. You need to concentrate your efforts on finding the relationship. I think modern technology will make sure you end up with a baby."

Tammie, who has lost interest in the teddy bear, joins her brother to watch the video.

"Honey, don't you want to use your watercolors?" asks Karen, handing her daughter some paper and a tin of paints. "Her donor was artistic," Karen explains to me.

A few minutes later, when I look down at Tammie's painting, I see that she has painted a picture of an orange tiger next to a stick figure of a girl wearing a purple triangle dress.

"Is that you?" I ask.

Tammie looks up at me.

"No, that's you."

# Epilogue: Summer

When I was born, one of my mom's friends, the poet Lucille Clifton, wrote a poem to welcome me into the world. Ever since I can remember, the poem hung on my childhood bathroom wall, and I would read it from time to time while brushing my teeth. One section has remained embedded in my memory:

> *To Rachel*
> *you will notice some*
> *edges*
> *often you will catch yourself*
> *before falling     or not*
> *this happens*
> *and circles*
> *you may go around for days*
> *going around*
> *it is not perfect     still*
> *welcome to what we have*

I begin the summer still wondering about my future as a mother. I am also thinking about my drive to have it all in a world of imperfect edges.

My friend Mollie is pregnant and planning her (second) wedding, she and her fiancée are building a house for their new family, and she continues to work as a writer and editor.

"It's overwhelming," she told me on the phone the other day.

I accused her of false modesty.

"No!" She said. "It's really hard. You'll see."

Of course it's really hard—but it's what I want, what I've always wanted, and what I think every woman deserves: a fulfilling career, an equal partnership, and the opportunity to have children if that's what she chooses.

What has become clear to me is that not every woman will take the same path to get there; some will take longer than others. All of the choices I've investigated are means of achieving the same goal on different schedules. And while many of these options—advanced reproductive technology, single motherhood, adoption, instant families—may seem unnatural to some, the truth is that I've met a lot more happy older mothers than unhappy ones.

And what seems unnatural to us now is likely to seem downright retrograde in ten years, or when our daughters start to have children. Technology is moving much faster than the habits of human thought. In 2007, I attended a seminar at the American Society for Reproductive Medicine's annual meeting. Elaine Gordon, a clinical psychologist who specializes in counseling couples and individuals in need of advanced reproductive technology, offered a view of what the near future might hold: "In the future, kids could have five parents: sperm donors, egg donors, gestational carriers, and rearing and social parents. Doctors, attorneys, and mental health professionals are all picking and choosing each and every genetic component in order to build a superbaby. You'll be able to select for sex, hair color, confidence index, optimism or pessimism, athleticism or a literary bent. This could be the ultimate shopping experience. You might even one day find a book on Amazon.com called *How to Create a Superbaby*.

Although her speech was more hyperbole than reality, this future may be closer than we think. While women and couples have a broad and often confusing range of choices now, re-searchers are currently working on a whole new set of technolo-gies. For instance, it may soon be possible to insert the DNA of an older woman's egg into the mechanism of a younger woman's egg, thus allowing the former's genetic material to be passed on well after she is capable of having a baby naturally. And scien-tists are looking into the possibility of generating new eggs from stem cells.

These new technologies are exciting, and they may well move women much further toward liberation from infertility and the tyranny of the biological clock. But they will also raise complicated ethical issues. The more we learn about the hu-man genome—and therefore the closer we come to identifying genes for everything from eye color to creativity—the more able we will be to manipulate and arrange parts and pieces of individuals into new configurations. Designing a baby could soon be as easy (and probably nearly as expensive) as designing a house to specification. We'll be able to pick the height and temperament of our children the way we pick the right color marble for our kitchen counters. In her book *The Baby Busi-ness: How Money, Science, and Politics Drive the Commerce of*

*Conception*, Debora L. Spar, an economist at Harvard Business School, writes: "As reproductive technologies push the envelope of possibilities, they will create children—and mistakes—that demand restitution. They will blur the edges of what is now formally forbidden—cloning, for example, and fetal research—and what is allowed. In the end, of course, the market will win. We will continue to buy, sell, and modify our children, generating substantial profits in the process. But this market will not reign forever unfettered. Instead, the pulling and hauling of politics will create—must create—a regulatory framework in which the business of babies can proceed."

The story of reproductive technology is just beginning. At the 2008 ASRM conference in San Francisco, Dr. Alan D. Copperman, director of the division of reproductive endocrinology at Mount Sinai Medical Center—the doctor who spoke at the Extend Fertility event I attended a few years earlier—announced that he was spearheading the launch of the first national registry of frozen eggs. The registry is designed to study the potential of frozen eggs and the development of children born from frozen eggs. At the same conference, two new studies closely related to my personal research were released. One showed continued improvements in implantation and pregnancy rates from frozen eggs. The other, a health status report on 156 babies born from frozen eggs, showed that 99 percent were genetically healthy.

For now, however, my story is coming to a close. Part of me wishes that I could offer a fairy-tale ending. I'm discouraged that I have yet to achieve the goal I've fantasized about—the crescendo of walking down the aisle toward my perfect love, with a tiny bump in my belly. But at the beginning of the summer of 2008, I am still single.

Yet I've completed my first book—and this is an accomplishment in its own right. And in the course of researching and writing, I have learned that there are many different kinds of fairy-tale endings—and beginnings. This discovery has profoundly changed me.

I no longer see myself as having fallen behind. Throughout this journey, I've seen so many friends, who I thought had passed me in a race, end up divorced with two kids—or worse, stuck in bad marriages. I have realized that I have not gotten to where I am because I have failed to do something right along the way. I am here because of the choices I've made, and I'm proud of those choices: I have not settled for a relationship that is less than what I want and need; I have remained true to myself and to my values; I have worked, and will continue to work, on myself so that I will be ready for a more perfect love.

I talked on the phone recently with my friend Katie's aunt, the woman who suggested at an engagement party that I set a deadline for single motherhood. Our conversation reminded me to keep enjoying my independent life. When the subject of marriage and family came up, she said, "Maybe you just haven't been really ready." She might be right. I know it is a privilege to be able to make these choices, one hard fought by other women over decades and centuries. To be able to say, "No, this isn't right," or, "I want to wait," or, "Yes, finally, it is you that I need, and this, now, is exactly what I want."

In July, I decide to move out of the city for a while, to a little house I've rented with a couple of friends; it's on the bay in the East Hampton Springs. Living and writing at the beach, I try to reconnect with the lesson I learned when I was traveling in India: to let go of control and have faith that someone else's hands will catch me on the other side.

In mid-July, at my brother's thirtieth birthday party, I meet a man five years younger than me, an entrepreneur with sexy blue eyes. After dating for a few weeks, he comes to spend a few days at my house at the beach. We frolic in the waves, we drink wine and watch the sunset, and he kisses me, and for a moment, I think, *this is my ending.*

In the weeks that follow, I receive many bits of news from friends and people I've met through my journey. I get an e-mail from Christy Jones, the founder of Extend Fertility, who is now thirty-nine years old, announcing the birth of her baby girl. She did not use her frozen eggs, but she is thinking about using them for her second child. A week after that, Mollie gets married for the second time, at dawn on the beach in Martha's Vineyard, this time in a green dress, eight months pregnant.

Soon after, my friend Jane, the woman who married Adam when she was eight months pregnant, announces the birth of her second daughter, Mabel, born at six pounds, eleven ounces at 12:50 p.m. It's a few months before Jane's forty-third birthday. I write to her and ask how she feels.

"I wish I hadn't been so miserable when I was alone," she says. "I had no faith, and I should have had faith."

Then, on a very humid day in late August, I hear from an acquaintance that Jacob is engaged. He first met his fiancée at a dinner party we attended together before I went to India, and he began to pursue her then. Although I am absolutely gutted by the news, I'm glad to know the truth finally. I realize that my girlfriend was right about Jacob's tight-lipped smile— behind it was indeed a capacity for emotional duplicity.

"It's not like he's riding off into the sunset and you're left be-hind," my father says when I report the news. "Real life doesn't work that way. Leave that to the fairy tales." He tells me that

I'm lucky not to have committed my life to a man from whom I have such different views about the emotional honesty, often painful and messy, that keeps intimacy and marriage swimming forward in the long run.

My father is, of course, right. Jacob's insta-choice may have gotten him to the altar before me, but it's not a race for first place. It's the happily-ever-after I'm interested in. After we broke up, I kept wondering if we could have made it work, but now I understand that I would not have been happy with him in the end. And when it comes to love, no one is competing for the same pool of happiness; that he may have found his has no bearing on how or when I find mine.

I choose to take the high road and write Jacob a note wishing him and his fiancée the best.

And then I decide I'm going to have the best rest of the summer I possibly can. A girlfriend and I learn to sail, and I begin reading *War and Peace*. I learn new lessons from both. In sailing, I learn that you have to stay your course but also be flexible so you can respond to the quick changes of the wind. From Tolstoy, I learn a vital lesson about happiness. "There is nothing in the world to be dreaded," he writes. "Just as there is no condition in which man can be happy and entirely free, so there is no condition in which he needs to be unhappy and not free."

As the leaves begin to turn, so does my summer romance. He admits to me that he is not ready to be in a serious relationship so soon after a breakup with a woman with whom he spent six years. I'm disappointed, but I accept that the timing is just wrong. So much of love and relationships, I have learned, is about timing. So around Halloween, a few weeks before my thirty-ninth birthday, I make a vital decision. Next summer, if I'm not in the right relationship, I'm going to start trying to get pregnant through intrauterine insemination. I'm ready to begin the next phase. My eggs are frozen, and if one day I can no longer conceive naturally, maybe I'll use them with my love to make a baby to whom we are both biologically related. I'm not giving up on finding the best love for me and doing the work to create a healthy relationship—even if that means integrating my child into it. Personally, I'm just ready to take the step I first talked about with Dr. Schiffman: to separate love and procreation. I'm ready to be a mother. I'll be forty next November, and in thinking about that milestone, I determine that I would be more unhappy turning forty without a baby than without a partner.

None of this is to say that I've given up looking for a relationship with a man who will be a good father; I still think a child really deserves a father. But I've realized that it's OK if I don't do everything in the right order to create the perfect situation. I'm confident now that if I start out as a mother on my own that I will give my child a good life and enough love until I find an intimate relationship that works for our life, and we all form that more perfect family. And until then, I know a lot of men who will give my baby a role model.

I'm not planning to be rigid. If, in the next year, fate and timing do collide and I do fall in love with someone who wants the same things as I do, I will no doubt trim the sails for him. But whenever that happens—and I know it will happen someday—I won't expect it to be perfect, any more than I expect becoming a single mother to be perfect. Whichever path I take, I know there will be some happy days, some angry days, some boring days, and some sorrowful days. My more perfect love will accept my imperfections, and I will accept his, and the two of us will be strong enough to stay the course through the storms as well as clear blue skies.

So much can happen in a year, and all the others that follow. For now, I've taken charge of the things that I can control, and accepted that there is a great deal more that I cannot. I don't feel bitter. I feel independent and scared, vulnerable and strong. Most of all, I feel ready to welcome whatever this strange, jagged-edged, beautiful, imperfect, and deliriously exciting new world brings my way.

# Acknowledgments

Lydia Wills is not just Ms. Super Agent Extraordinaire but also an amazingly honest, loyal, and real friend who holds a big and influential place in my brain and conscience—not to mention that she's a brilliant decorator who knows exactly when to pull me out of my head and make me see that I need a new rug.

The day that Lara Heimert, my editor, showed up at our first marketing meeting dressed like the cover of this book, with an orange flower in her hair, I realized that her humor and emotional sense of the world are as much a part of her hyperintelligence as her intellect. Her editing gave me confidence and taught me to be a better and more honest writer.

Pamela Paul gave me the idea for this book six years ago over drinks in the West Village. Abby Ellin listened to everything, almost every day, and in Panama, India, and Argentina. My writers group—named Matilda, after the cat at the Algonquin Hotel, including Alissa Quart, Debbie Siegel, and Maia Schalvitz—read, edited, talked endlessly, and kept me on track and on time with their warmth, wit, and savvy advice. My parents—Natalie Robins and Christopher Lehmann-Haupt—showed me that a craft is still passed down from generation to generation. They taught me, supported me, and loved me. My brother, Noah Lehmann-Haupt, kept me rational, and my entire extended family gave me love and confidence: Mildred Vogel, my grandmother; Carl Lehmann-Haupt; Celestine Lehmann-Haupt; Roxanna Lehmann-Haupt, Lou Bruno; Sandy Lehmann-Haupt; and John Lehmann-Haupt.

I'm grateful to my friends and colleagues, near and far, for their loyalty, love, and support in my life and in my writing of this book: Mollie Doyle, Nicole Maurer, Warren St. John, Ted Rose, Josh Shenk, Laura Rich, Molly Jong-Fast, Amanda Bernard, Elizabeth Brekhus, Velleda Ceccoli, Jennifer Kriz, Rebekah Meola, Mary Jane Horton, Will Bourne, Larry Smith, Rachel Elson, Art Lenahan, Ahn Ly, Jennifer Krauss, Lauren Barack, Michael Learmonth, Cullen Curtiss, Kim Cutter, Lynn Nesbit, Priscilla Gillman, Louanne Brizendine, Caroline Waxler, Bill Brazell, Laurel Touby, Elizabeth Sheinkman, Regina Joseph, Patricia Garcia-Gomez, Daniela Vitali, Amy Linn, Jean Tang, Allison Gilbert, Lauren Kern, Emily Nussbaum, Adam Moss, Kim Meisner, Rob Stein, Sara Reistad-Long, and, of course, all the Bowlers—you know who you are. I also thank the entire staff at NYU Fertility Center, and above all, Dr. Nicole Noyes, for their sensitive advice and care.

# Notes

## INTRODUCTION

6    **all of this new status and power** Sylvia Ann Hewlett, *Creating a Life: What Every Woman Needs to Know About Having a Baby and Career* (New York: Hyperion, 2003), 32.

7    **the sisters were doing it to themselves** Nancy Gibbs, "Making Time for a Baby," *Time*, April 15, 2002.

7    **these days the independence that seems so fabulous** Vanessa Grigoriadis, "Baby Panic," *New York*, May 13, 2002, http://ny mag.com/nymetro/urban/family/features/6030/. "The city's single women knew we could do everything men could, even in our Jimmy Choos. But while we were busy with business, bars and Barney's, did we miss out on motherhood? For the *Sex and the City* generation, it looks like the rules of the game have changed."

7    **"marriage crunch"** Daniel McGinn, "Rethinking Marriage after 40: Twenty Years Since the Infamous 'Terrorist' Line, States of the Union Aren't What We Predicted They'd Be," *Newsweek*, September 2006.

8    **the American Society for Reproductive Medicine reports** *Age and Fertility: A Guide for Patients* (Birmingham: American Society for Reproductive Medicine, 2003), http://www.asrm.org/Patients/ patientbooklets/agefertility.pdf. See chart on page 6.

8    **a 2004 study** Henri Leridon, "Can Assisted Reproduction Technology Compensate for the Natural Decline in Fertility with Age? A Model Assessment," *Human Reproduction* 19, no. 7 (June 2004): 1,548–1,553.

9    **after thirty-five** Liza Mundy, *Everything Conceivable: How Assisted Reproduction Is Changing Men, Women, and the World* (New York: Alfred A. Knopf, 2007), 39.

9    **2006 study of the Israeli military database** Abraham Reichenberg et al., "Advancing Paternal Age and Autism," *Archives of General Psychiatry* 63 (2006): 1026–1032.

10   **costing both a middle-class husband and wife or a single parent over $10,000 a year** Mark Lino, "Expenditures on Children by Families: U.S. Department of Agriculture Estimates and Alternative Estimators," *Journal of Legal Economics* 11, no. 2 (2008).

10   **the age of first-time motherhood and fatherhood is rising** *Births: Final Data for 2005*, National Center for Health Statistics, Centers for Disease Control, Tables C, 1, 10, 32.

CHAPTER I

20   **having all of these choices generally doesn't make us any happier** Barry Schwartz, *The Paradox of Choice: Why More Is Less* (New York: HarperCollins, 2004), 3.

21   **Match.com claims as many as 15 million members** Interview with Allison Clark, public relations representative for Match.com, October 8, 2007.

23   **study of single women in their twenties** Kim DaCosta, *Marriage and Motherhood: A New Perspective on Commitment, Sacrifice, and Self-Development*, unpublished master's thesis, University of California, Berkeley, 1995.

28   **in 1964, the average age of first marriage for a woman was twenty** "Current Population Survey," Current Population Reports, Series P20–553; "America's Families and Living Arrangements: 2003."

29   **"love" has overtaken marriage** Interview with Stephanie Coontz, professor of history and family studies at Evergreen State Univer-

sity and author of *Marriage, a History: From Obedience to Intimacy, or How Love Conquered Marriage* (New York: Viking Press, 2005), September 2006.

33 **the real predictive value of FSH** Interview with Daniel Stein, November 15, 2005.

35 **premature ovarian failure** Interview with John Zhang, New Hope Fertility Center, November 20, 2005.

35 **the problem with measuring just FSH** Interview with Bill Ledger, University of Sheffield, November 15, 2005.

38 **this companionate, egalitarian ideal raises the bar** Pepper Schwartz, *Love Between Equals: How Peer Marriage Really Works* (New York: The Free Press, 1994), 6.


CHAPTER 2

46 **approximately two hundred babies have been born worldwide from previously frozen eggs** Jason Barrit et al., "Report of Four Donor-Recipient Ooctye Cryopreservation Cycles Resulting in High Pregnancy and Implantation Rates," *Fertility and Sterility* 87, no. 1 (January 2007): 189.

47 **Reproductive Medicine Associates of New York had completed a research study** "Extend Fertility and Reproductive Medicine Associates of New York Report Encouraging New Egg Freezing Results," Extend Fertility press release, November 15, 2005, http://www .extendfertility.com/downloads/documents/EF_RMA_results.pdf.

47 **taking together the clinical results** Eleanora Porcu and Stefano Venturoli, "Progress with Oocyte Cryopreservation," *Current Opinion in Obstetrics and Gynecology* 18, no. 3 (2006): 5.

51 **the birth rate for embryos created from thawed eggs hovers around 4 percent** *Clinic Summary Report 2006*, Society for Advanced Reproductive Technology, https://www.sartcorsonline .com/rptCSR_PublicMultYear.aspx?ClinicPKID=0.

53 **2002 story in the *Wall Street Journal*** Amy Dockser Marcus, "Fertility Clinic Set to Open First Commercial Egg Bank— Controversial Facility Will Target Women Waiting for Mr. Right," *Wall Street Journal*, April 17, 2002.

53      **5 million single, childless women in their 30s** Erika Brown,
        "The Big Chill," *Forbes.com*, September 20, 2004, http://www
        .forbes.com/business/forbes/2004/0920/294.html.

53      **it may not stop single thirtysomethings from lining up** Clau-
        dia Kalb, "Fertility and the Freezer," *Newsweek*, August 2, 2004,
        http://www.newsweek.com/id/54729.

54      **almost every company that makes the tools for in vitro fertil-
        ization** Interview with Jorn Lyshoel, September 10, 2006.

56      **U.S. clinics live and die by their success rates** Interview with
        Barry Behr, Stanford University, September 11, 2006.

60      **2002 case in Texas** "Court Won't Hear Battle over Embryos,"
        *New York Times*, August 26, 2007.

62      **occurrence of cancers and genetic abnormalities in "frosties"**
        "What's Wrong with Assisted Reproductive Technologies?"
        press release, Institute of Science in Society, March 11, 2003,
        http://www.i-sis.org.uk/wwwART.php.


CHAPTER 3

69      **number of households headed by single women** *America's Fam-
        ilies and Living Arrangements 2007*, U.S. Census Bureau, http://
        www.census.gov/population/www/socdemo/hh-fam/cps2007.html.

78      **in her monthly SMC newsletter, Jane always addresses the
        "daddy issue"** Jane Mattes, "The Daddy Question: Excerpts
        from *Single Mothers by Choice: A Guidebook for Single Women
        Who Are Considering or Have Chosen Motherhood*," Single Moth-
        ers by Choice newsletter 105 (Summer 2008).

79      **the Sperm Bank of California published the first study on the
        children of donors** Raymond W. Chan, Barbara Raboy, and
        Charlotte J. Patterson, "Psychosocial Adjustment among Chil-
        dren Conceived via Donor Insemination by Lesbian and Het-
        erosexual Mothers," *Child Development* 69, no. 2 (April 1998):
        443–457.

83      **Iowa is 80 percent white** *America's Families and Living Arrange-
        ments 2007*, U.S. Census Bureau, http://www.census.gov/
        population/www/socdemo/hh-fam/cps2007.html.

86     **California Cryobank, one of the largest sperm banks in the United States** Interview with Marlo Jacob, marketing director of the California Cryobank, March 12, 2007.

86     **in 1954 a court in Illinois** David Plotz, *The Genius Factory: The Curious History of the Nobel Prize Sperm Bank* (New York: Random House, 2005), 167.

86     **a man could clandestinely make some extra cash** Interview with an anonymous sperm donor, March 12, 2007.

87     **Repository for Germinal Choice made worldwide headlines** David Plotz, *The Genius Factory: The Curious History of the Nobel Prize Sperm Bank* (New York: Random House, 2005), 34.

87     **hundreds of sperm and egg banks across the country** Amy Harmon, "Are You My Sperm Donor? Few Clinics Will Say," *New York Times*, January 20, 2006.

87     **it's tempting to think that with enough knowledge** David Plotz, *The Genius Factory: The Curious History of the Nobel Prize Sperm Bank* (New York: Random House, 2005), 181.


CHAPTER 4

103    **many women choose single motherhood after a "catalytic" event** Rosanna Hertz, *Single by Chance, Mothers by Choice: How Women Are Choosing Parenthood without Marriage and Creating the New American Family* (New York: Oxford University Press, 2006), 29.

114    **it allows people to make clear-cut choices** Interview with Dr. Albert Anouna, director of the New York Sperm Bank, June 22, 2006.


CHAPTER 5

129    **marital happiness takes a nosedive** Arthur C. Brooks, *Gross National Happiness: Why Happiness Matters for America—And How We Can Get More of It* (New York: Basic Books, 2008), 64.

133    **as a result of increasing economic independence for women** Nicola Branson, *The South African Labor Market 1995–2004: A Cohort Analysis*, SALDRU working paper number 06/07, University of Cape Town, October 2006, 7, www.tips.org.za.

CHAPTER 7

161    **brides are not only not hiding their pregnancies** Mireya Navarro,
       "Here Comes the Mother-to-Be," *New York Times*, March 13,
       2005.

165    **early bliss makes people stick it out longer** Kaja Perina, "The
       Success of a Marriage," *Psychology Today* (May/June 2003):
       http://www.psychologytoday.com/articles/pto-20030703
       –000001.html.

165    **living together for a long period of time before getting married**
       Catherine L. Cohan and Stacey Kleinbaum, "Toward a Greater
       Understanding of the Cohabitation Effect: Premarital Cohabi-
       tation and Marital Communication," *Journal of Marriage and
       Family* 64 (2002): 180–192.


CHAPTER 8

176    **I don't know how I got to be so old** Wendy Paris, "In the Grip
       of Nature's Own Form of Birth Control," *New York Times*, No-
       vember 26, 2006.

180    **at age thirty-five, about 66 percent of women will conceive
       within in a year** Henri Leridon, "Can Assisted Reproduction
       Technology Compensate for the Natural Decline in Fertility
       with Age? A Model Assessment," *Human Reproduction* 19, no. 7
       (June 2004): 1548–1553.

181    **the personalities of women who intentionally delay childbear-
       ing** Julia C. Berryman and Kate C. Windridge, *Motherhood after
       35: A Report on the Leicester Motherhood Project* (Leicester:
       Leicester University Press, 1995).

182    **children of older parents are significantly better off** Interview
       with Brian Powell, professor of sociology, Indiana University,
       March 11, 2005.

183    **families with mothers who had the most economic indepen-
       dence** Sara McLanahan, "Diverging Destinies: How Children
       Are Faring under the Second Demographic Transition," *Demog-
       raphy* 41, no. 4 (2004): 607–627.

184     **due to the higher miscarriage rates in women over thirty-five**
        Julia C. Berryman and Kate C. Windridge, *Motherhood after 35:
        A Report on the Leicester Motherhood Project* (Leicester: Leicester
        University Press, 1995).

187     **men who became fathers at forty or older** Abraham Reichen-
        berg et al., "Advancing Paternal Age and Autism," *Archives of
        General Psychiatry* 63 (2006): 1026–1032.

187     **offspring born to men in their middle and late forties** E. Sloter
        et al., "Qualitative Effects of Male Age on Sperm Motion," *Hu-
        man Reproduction* 21, no. 11 (2006): 2,868–2,875.

188     **level the playing field between men and women in the premar-
        ital dating game** Roni Rabin, "It Seems the Fertility Clock Ticks
        for Men, Too," *New York Times*, February 27, 2007.

188     **sperm quality declines as men age due to mitosis** Interview with
        Dr. Harry Fisch, New York-Presbyterian Hospital/Columbia Uni-
        versity Medical Center, September 15, 2007.

190     **the absence of any marker on a second trimester scan** Fion-
        nuala M. Breathnach, Ann Fleming, and Fergal D. Malone,
        "Second Trimester Fetal Sonogram," *American Journal of Medical
        Genetics* 145, no. 1 (February 2007): 62–72.

CHAPTER 9

206     **in India 90 percent of marriages are still arranged** Divya
        Mathur, "What's Love Got to Do with It? Parental Involve-
        ments and Spouse Choice in Urban India," University of
        Chicago, dissertation.

CHAPTER 10

223     **searching for an alternative to freezing extra embryos** Inter-
        view with Dr. Rafaela Fabbri, Department of Obstetrics and Gy-
        necology at the University of Bologna, October 12, 2007.

225     **she did not support the commercialization of egg freezing** In-
        terview with Dr. Eleanora Porcu, Department of Obstetrics and
        Gynecology at the University of Bologna, November 19, 2006.

225 **28 percent pregnancy rate from frozen eggs** Interview with Dr. Eleanora Porcu, Department of Obstetrics and Gynecology at the University of Bologna, October 12, 2007.

229 **study of egg freezing** John K. Jain and Richard J. Paulson, "Oocyte Cryopreservation," *Fertility and Sterility* 86, no. 4 (October 2006): 1037–1046.

230 **she has now done seventeen egg freezing cycles** Interview with Dr. Nicole Noyes, November 5, 2007.

CHAPTER 11

247 **fifteen studies on the risk of developing breast cancer after IVF** W. Al Sarakbi, M. Salhab, and Kefah Mokbel, "In Vitro Fertilization and Breast Cancer Risk: A Review," *International Journal of Fertility* 50, no. 5 (2005): 5.

247 **six cases of ovarian cancer** A. Venn et al., "Breast and Ovarian Cancer Incidence after Infertility and In Vitro Fertilization," *Lancet* 14, no. 346 (October 1995): 995–1000.

CHAPTER 12

273 **women and couples in their forties and fifties are turning to adoption** Interview with Adam Pertman, author of *Adoption Nation: How the Adoption Revolution Is Transforming America* (New York: Basic Books, 2000) and executive director of the Evan D. Donaldson Adoption Institute of New York, April 6, 2006.

273 **1,802 attempts (IVF cycles) in 1992** Centers for Disease Control, "The Fertility Clinic Success Rate and Certification Act of 1992," *Federal Register* 64, no. 139 (July 21, 1999): 102.

273 **16,161 in 2005** "2004 Assisted Reproductive Technology (ART) Report: Section 4—ART Cycles Using Donor Eggs," Centers for Disease Control and Prevention, Department of Health and Human Services, 2004, http://www.cdc.gov/art/art2004/section4.htm.

273 **Americans are spending about $38 million to buy eggs** Debora L. Spar, *The Baby Business: How Money, Science, and Politics*

*Drive the Commerce of Conception* (Boston: Harvard Business School Press, 2006), 3 (Table 1–1).

273 **number of paid donors is unknown** "2005 Assisted Reproductive Technology (ART) Report: Section 4—ART Cycles Using Donor Eggs," Centers for Disease Control and Prevention, Department of Health and Human Services, 2005, http://www.cdc.gov/art/art2005/section4.htm.

281 **the Donor Egg Bank is beginning to offer the option of buying an egg directly from the bank** Interview with Brigid Dowd, director of the Donor Egg Bank, Los Angeles, April 2, 2008.

282 **52 percent live-birth rate from embryos created from fresh donor eggs** "2005 Assisted Reproductive Technology (ART) Report: Section 4—ART Cycles Using Donor Eggs," Centers for Disease Control and Prevention, Department of Health and Human Services, 2005, http://www.cdc.gov/art/art2005/section4.htm.

284 **Julia Derek, a senior at George Mason University** Julia Derek, *Confessions of a Serial Egg Donor* (New York: Adrenaline Books, 2004).

288 **independent survey of thirty-eight egg donation centers** M. M. Fusillo and A. Shear, "Motivations, Compensation and Anonymity in Oocyte Donors from 38 A.R.T. Centers in the United States," *Fertility and Sterility* 88 (September 2007): S10.

EPILOGUE

296 **in the future, kids could have five parents** Elaine Gordon, "From Cells to Superbabies," presentation at the American Society for Reproductive Medicine annual meeting, Washington, D.C., September 16, 2007.

298 **as reproductive technologies push the envelope of possibilities** Debora L. Spar, *The Baby Business: How Money, Science, and Politics Drive the Commerce of Conception* (Boston: Harvard Business School Press, 2006), xix.

298 **continued improvements in implantation and pregnancy rates from frozen eggs** Jason Barritt et al., "Report of Four Donor-Recipient Oocyte Cryopreservation Cycles Resulting in High

Pregnancy and Implantation Rates," *Fertility and Sterility* 87, no. 1 (January 2007): 189.

298 **health status report on 156 babies born from frozen eggs** M. Tur-Kaspa, M. Gal, and A. Horwitz, "Genetics and Health of Children Born from Cryopreserved Oocytes," *Fertility and Sterility* 88 (September 2007): S14.

301 **there is nothing in the world to be dreaded** Leo Tolstoy, *War and Peace* (New York: New American Library, 1968), 1266.

# Index